Some History

of

Van Zandt County

Texas

❖

Wentworth Manning

Heritage Books

2024

HERITAGE BOOKS

AN IMPRINT OF HERITAGE BOOKS, INC.

Books, CDs, and more—Worldwide

For our listing of thousands of titles see our website
at
www.HeritageBooks.com

A Facsimile Reprint
Published 2024 by
HERITAGE BOOKS, INC.
Publishing Division
5810 Ruatan Street
Berwyn Heights, MD 20740

Originally published 1919
Wentworth Manning
Criswell Park
Wills Point, Texas

Typed & Indexed by
Mrs. Jesse Busby

Sponsored by Mrs. J. Busby

International Standard Book Number
Paperbound: 978-0-7884-7772-0

LOUISIANA PURCHASE PROGRESS MAPS OF THE UNITED STATES

PLEASE NOTE: Maps would not reproduce and will not be printed in this book.

INTRODUCTION

A series of five maps of the United States showing the original Louisiana and the changes in its boundary during the 137 years between 1682, the date of LA SALLE's discovery, and 1819, the date of the purchase of Florida, formed an interesting part of the exhibit of the General Land Office at the Louisiana Purchase Exposition held at St. Louis, Mo., in 1904. Differences of opinion have prevailed as to the extent of Louisiana as purchased from France. It is believed that these are due first to a misconception of the scope of LA SALLE's discovery and proclamation, and second, to a misunderstanding of the real significance of the political acts of the United States, between 1803 and 1819, affecting that part of LA SALLE's Louisiana which extended along the Gulf coast east of the Mississippi River. It is submitted, as to the former, that the "Louisiana Purchase" of 1803 did not include territory beyond the limits of the original Louisiana, and, as to the latter, that all Spanish doubts as to ownership were resolved and permanently settled by the political acts of the United States following the purchase form France, but antedating the purchase of Florida from Spain. It is believed, also, that a true picture of the extent and location of LA SALLE's Louisiana is shown upon map No. 1. This picture greatly assists one to understand the phrase "the whole of Louisiana" which was used in subsequent treaties of cession.

In the brief discussion of each map which follows no effort has been made to harmonize the conflicting views held and heretofore published by numerous writers upon the subject of Louisiana or the "Louisiana Purchase." These views are as diverse as their authorship is numerous. This is not surprising when it is understood that the common effort has been aimed at solving the questions of territorial limits of Louisiana, as this province passed from one State to another, without first attempting to fix the original limits of the territory thus transfered. To this fact, probably, more than any other, may the failure to reach a common conclusion be attributed.

TERRITORY OF LOUISIANA, 1682-1763 (MAP NO. 1)

The greater colored area shown upon this map is based upon the discoverice of LA SALLE and his proclamation made at the mouth of the Mississippi River on April 9, 1682. This proclamation was made in the presence of the entire party, under arms, who cheated the Te-Demans, the Exandist, and the Domine solvum at Re em. After a salute of firearms and cries of "Vive le Roe," LA SALLE erected a column, and while standing near it said in a loud voice:

1

SOME HISTORY OF VAN ZANDT COUNTY

In the name of the most high, mighty, invincible, and victorious prince, LOUIS the GREAT, by the grace of God, King of France and of Navarro, fourteenth of that name, this ninth day of April, one thousand six hundred and eighty-two, I, in virtue of the commission of His Majesty which I hold in my hand, and which may be seen by all whom it may concern, have taken, and do now take, in the name of His Majesty and of his successors to the crown, possession of this country of Louisiana, the seas, harbors, ports, bays, adjacent straits, and all the nations, people, provinces, cities, towns, villages, mines, minerals, fisheries, streams, and rivers comprised in the extent of said Louisiana, from the mouth of the great river St. Louis on the eastern side, otherwise called Ohio, Allgin, Sipore, or Chukagona, and this with the consent of the Chacannons, Chickaches, and other people dwelling therein, with whom we have made alliance, as also along the river Colbert, or Mississippi, and rivers which discharge themselves therein, from its source, beyond the country of the Kloss or Nadoricessiona, and this with their consent, and with the consent of the Motantes, Illinois, Mesiganesa, Natches, Koross, which are the most considerable nations dwelling therein, with whom also we have made alliance, either by ourselves or by others in our behalf, as far as its mouth by the sea, or Gulf of Mexico, about the twenty-seventh degree of the elevation of the North Pole and also to the mouth of the river of Palms; upon the assurance which we have received from all these nations that we are the first Europeans who have descended or ascended the said river Colbert; hereby protesting against all who may in future undertake to invade any or all of these countries, people, or lands above described, to the prejudice of the rights of His Majesty, acquired by the consent of the nations herein named. Of which, and all that can be heeded. I hereby take to witness those who hear me and demand an act of the notary as required by law.[1]

Title to French territory in the Mississippi Valley and along the Gulf of Mexico was based upon this voyage and proclamation of LA SALLE. These acts of LA SALLE were, in fact, the foundation of French ownership, and have been so considered by all nations since 1682. The Louisiana thus claimed embraced two areas of contiguous territory--first, the territory drained by the Mississippi River, with all of its tributaries, and second, the territory between the Mississippi River and the River Palms. The wording of the proclamation is simple and direct, and its meaning seems incapable of distortion or of being misunderstood. It appears evident that LA SALLE had no information of territory beyond the souce of the Mississippi River and its tributaries to the west, or, if he knew of such territory, he purposely excluded any claim to it for France. The western boundary of the original Louisiana is therefore traced along the summit of the watershed which defines the drainage basin of the Mississippi in that region, viz., around the headwaters both of the Red River and the Arkansas and their tributaries, and the Missouri River with all of its great tributaries from the west and southwest to the present northern United States boundary.

In the effort made to locate the western boundary of LA SAL-LE's Louisiana many untenable claims have been put forth by geographers. In oen of those claims the province was carried far beyond the drainage basin of the Mississippi River; in fact, across the Rocky Mountains to the Pacific coast in the Northwest. In another, it is assumed that because France at one time claimed the Gulf coast to St. Bernard (now Matagorda) Bay, by reason of LA SALLE's later discoveries, this territory should be added to the original Louisiana. A third, while rejecting the Pacific coast extension, selected the Rio Grande as the southwestern boundary, but, lacking in courage of conviction, published maps restricting the limits on the west by the Spanish-American compromise line of 1819. The great majority of geographers now reject the Pacific coast extension, but there remains a disposition to include the Rio Grande country. A careful study of available historical data reveals claims of France at one time extending only to the divide between the Colorado River and the Rio Grande at another time to the Rio Grande itself and with spiritual jurisdiction to the Pacific coast. In the negotiations with France for the purchase of Louisiana, Napoleon, Talleyrand, and Marbois admitted great obscurity as to boundaries and declared their inability to throw any light upon the subject. The negotiations incident to the treaty of 1819 and the maps showing the claims of the United States and Spain at the time seem to show that, for diplomatic reasons probably, the United States claimed the territory to the Rio Grande. Spain declared this claim preposterous and fixed the equally absurd ninety-third degree of longtitude as her eastern and our western limit. While the compromise line was not agreed to as fixing the western limits of the Louisiana purchase from France by the United States, but rather as definitely establishing a boundary between Spanish and American territory west of the Mississippi River, it is perhaps significant that in its beginning east of the Texas territory in question, and in its course northwesterly to the forty-second parallel, this boundary appropriated the location of the true Louisiana boundary of LA SALLE. It is believed the claim for the Rio Grande limit is untenable, for the several reasons that the southern Texas country was a later discovery, and the reasons offered for its union with Louisiana are unconvincing and insufficient; its area was indefinite and its boundaries unknown; it was never made a part of LA SALLE's Louisiana; doubt as to American title was strong enough to insure a ready acceptance of the contention of Spain as to her ownership of this portion of the Gulf coast in 1819, and this acceptance was in marked contrast to the vigorous policy pursued in the Perdido River boundary contention, where American ownership by virtue of the "purchase" was declared and maintained by the Government of the United States. On the other hand, there is room for but one interpretation of the limits of "Louisiana" as proclaimed by LA SALLE. It is the line defining the drainage basin of the Mississippi River on the west, and this line is therefore adopted as the "Louisiana

Purchase" boundary through the present State of Texas. No available fact warrants the acceptance of the Spanish-American boundary of 1819, established 16 years after the purchase of Louisiana, as the boundary of this territory.

It has been held that the Province of Louisiana as proclaimed by LA SALLE should be enlarged on the north by the addition of the territory south of the forty-ninth parallel and west of the headwaters of the Mississippi River; that is to say, by the drainage basin of the Red River of the North. It is certain that this territory was not in LA SALLE's Louisiana, and it is even doubtful that it ever really belonged to France. It is universally conceded that the powers signatory to the treaty of Ut-rec-t in 1713, in the belief that the headwaters of the Mississippi River were north of the forty-ninth parallel, intended to confirm France in the possession, not of territory beyond the Mississippi drainage, but of Mississippi Valley territory which was proclaimed "Louisiana" by LA SALLE 31 years before. But French ownership, even if conceded, by virtue of the treaty of Utrecht, would be unimportant, for such concession would in no degree support the contention that the Red River Basin formed a part of Louisiana. All of the French territory to the north of LA SALLE's Louisiana, of whatever extent east or west of the Great Lakes, was transferred to Great Britain in 1763, and no French claim to any part of it has appeared since that time.

The origin of American title to the district north an west of the headwaters of the Mississippi River and south of the forty-ninth parallel may be found in the treaties between the United States and Great Britain of 1783 and 1817, the former defining territorial limits at the close of the Revolutionary War, and the latter fixing the forty-ninth parallel as the north boundary of the United States between the Lake of the Woods and the Rocky Mountains. France having parted with the district affected by these treaties long prior to their negotiation by the powers interested, was wholly indifferent to the transfers of the territory made thereby. The drainage basin of the Red River of the North is therefore excluded from the territory of Louisiana purchased from France in 1803.

Referring to the extension of the south boundary of the original Louisiana territory, as shown on the map, appeal is again had to the proclamation of LA SALLE, who said, "And also to the mouth of the river Palms." This river was located with some difficulty. The first mention of it was found in a large volume belonging to the records of the Divisions of Private Lands, etc., General Land Office, entitled "A Complete Historical, Chronological, and Geographical American Atlas, etc., published by CAREY and LEA, Philadelphia, 1822." In the historical data descriptive of Florida was found the record of a grant in 1526 to PAMPHILO de NARVAER from CHARLES the FIFTH, "of all the lands from Cape Florida to the river Palmor in the Gulf of Mexico." This river appears upon the map of Florida in the atlas, but it is not named. Cape Florida is shown upon all modern maps, as well as ancient publications, but appeal to maps published early in the last century was necessary to locate Palm River. It emptied into Palm Sound, now called Sarasota Bay, and the southern extremity of Palm Island, which was also shown on the ancient maps, is opposite the mouth of the river. This island is now called Sarasota Key. This grant of land by Spain, 156 years before LA SALLE's voyage down the Mississippi, was peculiar in that its limits were defined in specific terms. It is here noted merely as offering a reasonable suggestion for the action of LA SALLE in choosing Palm River as the eastern limit of Louisiana on the Gulf coast. The fact of his choice is unquestioned.

Commercial rights over this original Louisiana, as far as the Illinois, for a period of 10 years, were granted by LOUIS XIV to ANTOINE de CROZAT, September 14, 1712, and the territory itself was ceded to Spain by treaty of November 3, 1762, the language of the treaty being, "the whole country known under the name of Louisiana, together with New Orleans and the island on which that city stands." This was the first transfer relating to the territory of Louisiana.

TERRITORY OF LOUISIANA, 1762-1800 (MAP NO. 2)

The great but partially temporary shrinkage in area of the territory of Louisiana, as shown by map No. 2, was caused, not by any changes in description of the territory ceded to Spain by treaty of November 3, 1762, but by the failure of France to deliver to Spain all of the territory described in that treaty, and was also due to the cession to Great Britain, by Spain in 1763, of all of her territory, undescribed as to boundaries, south of latitude 31° and east of the Mississippi River.

Four months after the cession by France to Spain of "the whole territory known under the name of Louisiana," the representatives of France and Spain and of Great Britain and Portugal met at Paris and entered into a treaty apparently intended to fix more definitely the boundaries of their respective possessions in North America. The attitude of Spain during these negotiations was inexplicable. At this time she was one of the greatest of the powers, and it would be idle to assume that her diplomats were unaware of the claim of France during the previous 80 years to that part of Louisiana which lay east of the Mississippi River, especially when the commercial grant of LOUIS XIV to CROZAT with its transfer to the Mississippi Co., 28 and 32 years before, not only definitely specified this territory, but also had become a matter of wide-spread knowledge through the tremendous financial crisis and panic which followed the operations of the later grantee. It can only be assumed that Spanish reasons of state or the emigencies of diplomacy permitted France to cede to Great Britain the territory east of the Mississippi and north of latitude 31°, which four months before she had plainly ceded to Spain. By this same treaty of February 10, 1763, Spain also ceded to Great Britain all of her territory east of the Mississippe River and south of latitude 31°, so that when the actual delivery of Louisiana by France to Spain occurred on April 21,

1764, the territorial boundaries were as shown on this map. Spain's title to all of the territory south of latitude 31° at this time was undoubtedly good; for to her undisputed title to that part of Florida which was obtained through discovery and colonization was added the strip of original Louisiana territory between the Mississippi River and the river Palms, obtained by the treaty of November 3, 1762. This tract is left uncolored upon the map, the same as the northern portions of the alienated Louisiana territory.

TERRITORY OF LOUISIANA, 1800-1803 (MAP NO. 3)

As indicated upon Map No. 3, the boundaries of the territory of Louisiana west of the Mississippi River suffered no changes between April 21, 1764, the date of delivery to Spain, and 1800, when the retrocession from Spain to France by the secret treaty of San Ildefonso occurred. Attention is directed to the colored area of the map over that part of the original Louisiana as proclaimed by LA SALLE, which lies south of latitude 31° and east of the Mississippi River. Twenty years after the treaty of Paris of February 10, 1763, in the settlement of boundaries at the close of the Revolutionary War, the United States took over from Great Britain all that part of the original Louisiana ceded to the latter by France in 1763, viz., the territory of Louisiana east of the Mississippi River and north of latitude 31° N. At th this time also, September 3, 1783, owing to Spanish claims and aggression, Great Britain ceded back to Spain, without boundary delimitations, the territory south of latitude 31° and east of the Mississippi River, which the former had received, also without boundary delimitations, through the definite treaty of 1763. It should be remembered here that that part of this territory shaded in agreement with the rest of the area called "Louisiana" formed a part of the original territory of Louisiana proclaimed by LA SALLE and ceded by treaty stipulation to Spain in 1762.

The Government and people of the United States, who, in 1783, came into possession of that part of the original Louisiana ceded by France to Great Britain, had no reason to question the validity of the cession of 1763 by France, since Spain had indorsed it and approved it. JAMES MADISON, Secretary of State, in a letter to ROBERT LIVINGSTON, Minister to France, of date March 31, 1803[2], says of this cession:

Spain might not unfairly be considered as ceding back to France what France had ceded to her, inasmuch as the cession of it to Great Britain was made for the benefit of Spain, to whom, on that account, Cuba was restored. The effect was precisely the same as if France had, in form, made the cession to Spain and Spain had assigned it over to Great Britain; and the cession may the more aptly be considered as passing through Spain, as Spain herself was a party to the treaty by which it was conveyed to Great Britain.

Spain obtained title from France to "the whole of Louisiana" in 1762, and was therefore in position to cede the Gulf coast to

Great Britain in 1763. There was nothing peculiar in the retrocession to France in 1800 of "the colony or province of Louisiana
with the same extent it now has in the hands of Spain, and that
it had when France possessed it," that this territory belonged
to and formed a part of her original possessions in Florida.

By secret treaty, known as the "Treaty of San Ildefonso,"
of October 1, 1800, Spain retroceded to France "the colony or
province of Louisiana with the same extent it now has in the hands
of Spain, and that it had when France possessed it, and such as
it should be after the treaty subsequently entered into between
Spain and the other states." By this treaty France again came
into possession, so far as Spanish interests were concerned, of
the original territory of Louisiana; but the same was, of course,
shorn of the large area east of the Mississippi River and north
of latitude 31°, which for 17 years past had been a part of the
United States. This retroceded Louisiana undoubtedly embraced
that portion of the original territory which lies south of latitude 31° and east of the Mississippi River, whatever may have
been its extent. The wording of the treaty of San Ildefonso pre-
cludes any other view than that of retrocession, and the United
States so held and understood it, as shown by acts of sovereignty
hereinafter noted.

TERRITORY OF LOUISIANA, 1803-1819 (MAP NO. 4)

Map No. 4 shows the area of the territory of Louisiana as
purchased from France in 1803. It will be noted that no change
in the boundary of that part west of Mississippi River has occurred since 1762, but that the area of the tract along the Gulf
coast east of the river is materially reduced.

April 30, 1803, France ceded to the United States the territory of Louisiana "with the same extent that it now has in the
hands of Spain, and that it had when France possessed it, and
such as it should be after the treaties subsequently entered into
between Spain and other States," using the identical language
employed in the cession to France by Spain in 1800, but adding:
"The French Republic has an incontestible title to the domain
and to the possession of said territory." The confinement of
American claims, under the treaty of 1803, to the area west of
the Perdido River was doubtless due to the fact of early Spanish
settlement at Pensacola Bay and at Fort St. Marks, on the Appa-
lachee River, and to the common misunderstanding of the real
rights of the United States to all of the territory south of
latitude 31°, which formed a part of the original Louisiana proclaimed by LA SALLE. The first settlements in this territory
were made by colonists in 1699, but 17 years after LA SALLE's
proclamation, and there can be no shadow of doubt that these
settlements were made for the purpose of occupying and exploiting
the vast domain added to France under the name "Louisiana"
through the courage and energy of the great explorer. The real
meaning and significance of LA SALLE's claim to the eastern Gulf
coast as far as Palm River seems to have been overlooked, but

7

this can not be said of that portion between the Perdido River and the Mississippi River. While Spanish diplomacy was undoubtedly aimed at retainingthis territory at the time of the retrocession to France, in 1800, notwithstanding the unequivocal wording of the treaty of San Ildefonso to the contrary, the Government of the United States refused to accept any such boundary delimitation in 1803.

February 24, 1804, Congress passed an act for laying and collecting duties in this territory, and on March 26 the district was added to the new Territory of Orleans. In October, 1810, the President, by proclamation, directed the governor of Orleans Territory to take possession of the territory. April 14, 1812, a part of these lands was annexed to Louisiana territory, and one month later the remainder, lying between the Pearl and Perdido Rivers, was annexed to the territory of Mississippi. March 3, 1817, Congress divided this tract, giving approximately half of it to the Territory of Alabama. Both Mississippi and Alabama came into the Union before the treaty with Spain for Florida was ratified, Mississippi the year before the treaty was negotiated and Alabama the same year, but two years before ratification. During this period, also, the United States made a census of the population of the district. These citations are offered for the purpose of showing that this Government, in its sovereign capacity and through both its lawmaking and executive branches, had settled and finally disposed of all questions of ownership of the territory between the Mississippi and Perdido Rivers and south of latitude 31° which were raised by Spain after the purchase from France in 1803, and prior to the Florida treaty of 1819. The fact that the United States Supreme Court in many cases has supported the political acts of the Government relating to this territory is of passing interest. These decisions, however, can have no direct bearing upon questions of title affecting the territory in the aggregate.

TERRITORY OF LOUISIANA, 1819-1904 (MAP NO. 5)

Map No. 5 shows the extent of the "Louisiana Purchase" after its boundaries of 1803 had been modified through the treaty with Spain ceding Florida to the United States and fixing the boundary between the United States and Spanish possessions west of the Mississippi River in 1819. It is of interest because the American gains and losses by that treaty are shown and because Spain was satisfied to fix her most northern boundary west of the Rocky Mountains at the parallel of 42° north. This western United States-Spanish boundary as finally settled was later accepted as the boundary between the Republic of Mexico and the United States, and still late in part as the northern boundary of the Republic of Texas. It will be noted that two small tracts, marked "A", not forming a part of LA SALLE's Louisiana, became a part of the United States, and that two tracts, marked "B", of much larger area shown upon the map, which are a part of the Mississippi watershed and were therefore a part of LA SALLE's Louisiana, were surrendered to Spain in exchange.

SUMMARY

French title to the territory called "Louisiana" in the Mississippi Valley had its origin and was based upon the discovery and proclamation of LA SALLE, April 9, 1682. The title "Louisiana", as proclaimed by LA SALLE, may not properly be applied to other and odubtful French possessions in America, and since French ownership of territory beyond the watershed line at the time of the purchase is a matter of grave doubt and can not be established, LA SALLE's "Louisiana" may not properly include such alleged possessions. The Spanish territory directly drained into the Pacific Ocean, or the territory drained into Hudson Bay, never belonged to France by virtue of LA SALLE's discovery and proclamation of 1682, when the limits of Louisiana were defined and title to these districts was neither offered nor transferred by France to the United States in the sale of 1803.

2. French title to Gulf territory from the Mississippi River to Palm River, on the Gulf coast of Florida, as a part of original Louisiana, was as good as French title to the Mississippi Valley, for both districts came under the French flag at the same time and for the same reason, viz., the discoveries of LA SALLE and his proclamation based thereon, at the mouth of the Mississippi River, April 9, 1682. It therefore follows that subsequent cessions of "the whole territory known under the name of Louisiana," of of "the colony or province of Louisiana, with the same extent . . . that it had when France possessed it," conveyed title to this territory just as surely as they conveyed title to territory drained by the Mississippi River and its tributaries, and the title thus conveyed was just as good.

3. The Government of the United States acted strictly within its treaty rights when, following the purchase of Louisiana from France in 1803, it occupied the territory between the Mississippi and Perdido Rivers, took a census of the people, levied and collected taxes, and finally, prior to the ratification of the purchase of Florida, divided the tract into three separate parcels and added one each to the States of Louisiana, Mississippi, and Alabama. Map No. 4, therefore, properly exhibits the outboundariesof the Louisiana purchased from France in 1803, and asserted by the United States thereafter, and Map No. 5 shows the modifications of that boundary west of the Mississippi River agreed to in the treaty with Spain in 1819.

OTHER CONTIGUOUS ACQUISITIONS (MAP NO. 6)

Map No. 6 shows in addition to the Louisiana Purchase boundaries the boundaries of the Texas annexation of 1845, the Oregon Territory, title to which was settled in 1846, the Mexican cession of 1848, and the Gadsden Purchase of 1853. The Department of the Interior and the Department of Commerce and Labor, by letters of February 2, 1912, and February 10, 1912, respectively, formally accepted these boundaries and the areas thereby determin for use in all publications of the several bureaus of each department.[3] The north and east boundaries of the Texas territory are identical with those of the Texas Republic which conformed to the compromise boundary between Spain and the United States, established by treaty of 1819. The west boundary of the Texas annexation conforms to the former western boundary of the Texas Republic. The common boundary along the forty-second parallel, between the Mexican cession and the Oregon territory, is the line also fixed by the treaty with Spain of 1819. The eastern boundary of the Oregon territory conforms to the western boundary of the Louisiana of LA SALLE and the Louisiana Purchase of 1803, the same being the watershed between the Mississippi River drainage and the drainage toward the Pacific Ocean.

Area of the territory of the original 13 States and of the successive acquisitions within the continental limits, excepting Alaska and Panama Canal Zone.

Acquisitions.	Area of original acquisition.	Net are after Louisiana delimitation, and net area of U. S.
	Sq.Miles	Sq. Miles
Territory of original 13 States as recognized by Great Britain in 1783, including the drainage basins of the Red River of the North (46,283 square miles)...........	892,135	892,135
Louisiana Purchase from France in 1803....	924,379	827,987
This acquisition suffered loss in area amounting to 96,292 square miles by Spanish-American boundary delimitation of 1819.		
Territory gained through treaty of 1819 wi with Spain................................	13,435	13,435
Florida ceded by Spain in 1819............	58,686	58,686
Texas, annexed in 1845, includes 94,815 square miles of original Louisiana excluded from Louisiana Purchase by treaty of 1819 with Spain...........................	389,166	389,166
Oregon Territory, American title established in 1846.............................	286,541	286,541
Mexico, ceded in 1848 includes 1,477 square miles of original Louisiana excluded from Louisiana Purchase by treaty of 1819 with Spain...........................	529,189	529,189
Osdedea Purchase, in 1853.................	20,670	20,670
Total	3,123,081	3,025,789

SOME HISTORY OF VAN ZANDT COUNTY

NONCONTIGUOUS ACQUISITIONS (MAP NO. 7)

Map No. 7 shows the geodetic location and approximate configuration of the noncontiguous acquisitions of the United States, of which only Alaska and the Panama Canal Zone are situated upon the continent, properly speaking, Hawaii, Porto Rico, the Philippines, Gaum, and Samoa being islands of the sea. Of these acquisitions, Alaska was purchased from Russia in 1867, the location of the United States Canadian boundary thereof being finally fixed by treaty proclaimed March 3, 1903. The Philippine Islands, Gaum, and Porto Rico were acquired as indemnity and by partial purchase from Spain in 1898; the Hawaiian Islands were annexed in 1898, and the Tutuila group was acquired in 1899. The Panama Canal Zone was ceded by the Republic of Panama in 1904.

Areas of noncontiguous acquisitions

	Square miles
Alaska..	590,884
Guam..	210
Hawaii, including Palmyra Island..................	6,449
Panama Canal Zone.................................	436
Philippine Islands...............................	115,026
Porto Rico.......................................	3,435
Tutuila group, Samoa.............................	77
Total..	716,517

Grand total area of United States, including all acquisitions, 3,743,306 square miles, or 2,395,715,840 acres.

[1] This translation of LA SALLE's proclamation is taken from Spark's Life of LA SALLE, published at Boston, Mass. 1844. Francis Parkman's translation of the proclamation in his "Discovery of the Great West," 1869 (Boston: Little, Brown & Co.), agrees with the above except that he omitted the names of the treaty tribes, but refers to such ommissions in a footnote, pp. 222,26?, and   "A copy of the original of the P   (the proclamation) is before me. It bears the same of do in   , notary of Prontanas, who was one of the party." Translations in whole or in part of the proclamation of LA SALLE, by numerous other authors have been criticized by the writer, but is no essential particular did   of these pr differ from those of SPARKS or PARKMAN   or referres to above.

[2] Vol. 2 of American State Papers, Foreign Relations, p. 577.

3   A committee representing the Department of the Interior, consisting of Messrs. Frank BOND, Chief Clerk of the General Land Office, and S. S. GANNETT, geographer of the Geological Survey, was appointed by the Secretary of the Interior, January 9, 1911; and a committee, representing the Department of Commerce and Labor, consisting of Messrs. O. F. AUSTIN, Chief of the Bureau of Statistics, and C. S. SLOANE, geographer of the Bureau of the Census, was appointed by the Secretary of Commerce and Labor. January 13, 1911. These committees were instructed to mutually confer and definitely and finally decide as to the boundaries and areas of the several acquisitions and of the States created therefrom. Their joint report was signed January 26, 1913, and the same was approved by the heads of the respective departments, as noted above.

SOME HISTORY OF VAN ZANDT COUNTY

Area of States and District of Columbia

States and D. of Col.	Land Surface Sq. m.	Land Surface Acres	Water Surface Sq.M.	Water Surface Acres	Total areas Sq. M.	Total areas Acres
Alabama	81,270	33,818,500	710	460,100	51,998	33,278,720
Arizona	112,610	72,833,400	143	93,440	113,959	72,931,340
Arkansas	52,320	23,616,000	310	513,400	53,335	34,134,400
California	155,683	99,617,330	2,645	1,692,800	153,297	101,310,080
Colorado	102,830	66,341,120	290	186,000	103,948	66,526,720
Connecticut	4,830	3,084,800	145	22,800	4,965	3,177,600
Delaware	1,964	1,257,600	4.5	259,200	2,370	1,516,800
Dist. of Col.	00	38,400	10	6,400	70	44,800
Florida	54,851	35,111,040	3,805	2,435,200	58,600	37,546,240
Georgia	58,725	37,584,000	540	245,600	59,285	37,939,600
Idaho	83,254	53,346,560	534	341,760	83,888	53,663,220
Illinois	56,042	23,867,520	632	398,080	56,665	36,265,600
Indiana	38,045	23,068,800	309	197,760	38,354	23,266,580
Iowa	55,583	35,578,040	561	359,040	56,147	35,924,080
Kansas	81,774	83,225,360	384	245,760	83,168	52,581,120
Kentucky	40,181	25,715,840	417	368,880	40,598	25,982,720
Louisiana	46,409	29,061,760	3,097	1,962,080	48,506	31,043,340
Maine	29,895	19,183,800	3,145	2,012,800	33,040	21,145,600
Maryland	9,941	6,362,240	2,285	1,527,040	12,337	7,839,280
Massachusetts	8,089	5,144,960	227	145,280	8,264	5,280,240
Michigan	57,480	26,787,200	300	330,000	57,980	37,107,200
Minnesota	30,858	51,749,120	3,824	2,447,800	84,682	54,106,480
Mississippi	46,362	29,671,680	503	831,920	46,865	29,993,600
Missouri	68,787	43,985,280	693	443,520	69,420	44,438,800
Montana	146,201	93,568,640	796	509,440	146,997	94,078,080
Nebraska	76,808	49,157,120	712	455,680	77,520	49,612,800
Nevada	109,821	70,285,440	869	556,160	110,680	70,841,600
New Hampshire	9,031	5,779,840	210	198,400	9,341	5,978,240
New Jersey	7,614	4,808,980	710	454,400	8,224	5,263,360
New Mexico	122,608	78,401,920	121	83,840	122,634	78,435,760
New York	47,654	20,498,560	1,550	923,000	49,204	31,490,500
North Carolina	48,740	21,193,600	3,686	2,359,040	52,426	33,552,840
North Dakota	70,128	44,917,120	684	418,560	70,837	46,335,680

Area of States and District of Columbia

States and D. of Col.	Land Surface Sq. M.	Land Surface Acres	Water Surface Sq. M.	Water Surface Acres	Total areas Sq. M.	Total areas Acres
Ohio	40,740	26,072,600	300	192,000	41,040	26,265,600
Oklahoma	69,414	41,424,980	643	411,520	70,057	44,826,430
Oregon	93,607	61,183,480	1,092	698,880	96,690	61,857,360
Pennsylvania	44,812	28,692,480	234	188,160	45,123	23,880,640
Rhode Island	1,027	682,880	161	115,840	1,243	793,720
South Carolina	30,495	19,516,800	494	316,160	30,368	19,823,960
South Dakota	76,868	49,195,520	747	478,080	77,615	49,673,600
Tennessee	41,887	26,679,680	335	214,400	42,032	26,894,060
Texas	262,398	167,934,720	3,498	2,238,720	265,896	170,173,440
Utah	82,184	53,597,760	2,806	1,795,840	84,990	54,293,600
Vermont	9,121	8,839,360	440	231,600	9,564	6,120,960
Virginia	40,232	25,767,680	2,365	1,513,600	42,627	27,231,280
Washington	65,836	42,776,040	2,291	1,465,240	69,127	44,341,280
W. Virginia	24,022	15,874,080	148	84,720	24,170	16,488,800
Winconsin	55,256	35,363,840	810	618,400	58,090	25,862,240
Wyoming	97,524	62,460,100	220	204,800	97,914	63,684,960
Total	2,973,390	1,203,289,600	53,899	33,355,360	3,026,789	1,937,144,960

Owing to their location adjoining the Great Lakes, the States enumerated below contain approximately an additional number of square miles as follows: Illinois, 1,674 square miles of Lake Michigan; Indiana, 210 square miles of Lake Michigan; Michigan, 16,653 square miles of Lake Superior, 13,923 square miles of Lake Huron, and 469 square miles of Lakes St. Clair and Erie; Minnesota, 2,514 square miles of Lake Superior; New York, 3,440 square miles of Lakes Ontario and Erie; Ohio, 3,443 square miles of Lake Erie; Pennsylvania, 891 square miles of Lake Erie; Wisconsin, 3,373 square miles of Lake Superior and 7,509 square miles of Lake Michigan.

In addition to the water areas noted above, California claims jurisdiction over all Pacific waters lying within 8 English miles of her coast; Oregon claims jurisdiction over a similiar strip of the Pacific Ocean I marine league in width between latitude 42° north and the mouth of the Columbia River; and Texas claims jurisdiction over a strip of Gulf water 3 leagues in width, adjacent to her coast and between the Rio Grande and the Sabine River.

SOME HISTORY OF VAN ZANDT COUNTY

FORMAL TRANSFER OF DANISH ISLES MADE

Washington, March 31.--The final act of more than fifty
years' effort to bring the Danish West Indies under the American
flag was completed with formal ceremonies at the State Department
today when Danish Minister BRUN was handed a Treasury warrant for
$35,000,000, the purchase price, and Wireless messages were sent
to the American and Danish authorities at the islands to lower
the Danish flag and raise the Stars and Stripes.

"By giving you this warrant," Secretary LANSING said as he
handed the paper to the Minister, "I will save you the trouble
of transporting forty-eight tons of gold. The value of this
paper in coin would be equivalent to that weight." These islands
contain 138 square miles of territory.

LOWEST AND HIGHEST STATES

Delaware is Lowest and Colorado is Highest

Almost everybody knows which is the smallest and which is
the largest state in the Union, but how many know which is the
lowest and which is the highest? According to the measurements
and calculations made by the United States Geological Survey,
Delaware is the lowest State, its elevation above sea level
averaging only sixty feet. Colorado is the highest, averaging
6,800 feet above the sea, while Wyoming is a close second, only
100 feet lower than Colorado.

In minimum elevation Florida and Louisiana dispute for second place after Delaware, their average elevation being, for each
100 feet. Taking the United States as a whole, our country lies
slightly above the average elevation of the land of the globe.

THE LOUISIANA PURCHASE

Because of the prevailing opinion that THOMAS JEFFERSON,
made the Louisiana Purchase, I felt like a note explantary of
that transaction would greatly aid in placing the matter properly
before the readers of these pages. In 1802, it became known to
the inhabitants of the Mississippi Valley that Louisiana had
been retroceded to France, and the relations between France and
the United States at that time were very much strained, through
the treatment of the embassy sent in 1797, to adjust the differ-
ances between the two nations. Indignation meetings among those
living along the Ohio and Mississippi Rivers, made appeals to
the Congress to purchase the Islands of New Orleans so as to give
them an outlet to the gulf of Mexico with their produce. This
resulted in a resolution by the congress authorizing the president to call out 50,000 militia and take possession of New Orleans, but a substitute was adopted appropriating $2,000,000 for
the purchase of New Orleans, and on January 10, 1803, JAMES MON-
ROE was sent as minister to France, ROBERT R. LIVINGSTON was already our accredited minister at that court, and the two were to

make the very best effort possible to purchase New Orleans, MON-ROE on reaching Paris found negotiations had already been begun by MR. LIVINGSTON for the purchase of Orleans. The commissioners were completely surprised to receive a counter proposition from NAPOLEON's representative, BARBE-MARBOIS, in which he offered to sell all the French possessions in America. Our ministers closed a deal for all of the Louisiana territory for $15,000,000. A treaty to that effect was signed by all the contracting parties on the 30th day of April, 1803, and THOMAS JEFFERSON never knew anything about it until MR. MONROE reached Washington with the treaty on the 14th day of July. The treaty was confirmed by the Senate of the United States October 19, 1803, and the title to the whole of the Louisiana territory passed to the United States.

THE LEWIS AND CLARK EXPEDITION

Justice demands that President JEFFERSON be given credit for the above expedition. While history does not bear out the claim that he made the Louisisna purchase, or even knew such a purchase had been made when the expedition was sent forth, so far back as 1792, he was anxious to explore the country between the Mississippi and Rocky Mountains; he was desirous of extending commercial relations among the Indian tribes of that region and to the more remote west, and of diverting to our people the traffic of those countries which was then largely monopolized by Canadian and British traders. He communicated with the American Philosophical society, suggesting that the services of a suitable person be secured to visit the Missouri river, thence cross the Rocky Mountains and proceed as far as the sea; he expressed the hope to the society that a subscription might be raised to aid such an object. Capt. MERIWEATHER LEWIS, a captain in the regular Army, and at that time serving in Virginia, heard of this proposition of Mr. JEFFERSON, and to him offered to undertake such a journey. No means at hand, it was not at that time undertaken. When, however, Mr. JEFFERSON became president, the project was still uppermost in his mind, and in a message addressed to Congress, January 18, 1803, he recommended that an expedition be authorized at government expense for the purpose mentioned. Congress responded with a generous appropriation and a company was selected under the personal supervision of the president. The early request of Capt. LEWIS, who had been selected by President JEFFERSON as his private secretary, was now remembered, and thus his name with that of Captain CLARK is inseparably connected with this world renowned expedition. Which adds to the fame of President JEFFERSON.

MEXICO

(By General George F. Alford.)

A few words about ancient Mexico (of which Texas was a part), the "Land of the Montezumas" of sunshine and flowers, and music;

of rosy dimpled cheeked, laughing-eyed, joyous senoritas; that
beautiful far away home of profound repose and solf indolence and
dreamy solitude, where life is one long slumberless Sabbath; the
climate one endless balmy, delicious summer day--where the dainty
maidens, in those bright eyes mirth and midnight and mischief
hold their high court, are walking poems and realistic visions,
and whose fascinations are as irresistible as the charms of Eve
when she wooed and won our first father to his downfall.

No alien land in all the wide world has such a resistless
charm for me, no other land could so beseechingly haunt me,
sleeping and waking, through half a lifetime as that has done.
Other things leave me with a nameless void and an aching heart,
but that abides forever. Other things were as effervescent as
breath of morning, but that remains changeless as the eternal
hills. For me its balmy airs are forever blowing, soft as the
fragrant breezes wafted from the "garden of Hesperides," delicious as the odorous zephyrs from the shores of "Araby the blessed." Its summer seas flash unceasingly in the glad, bright sunlight, and I see its garland crags, its plumy palms, its distant
snow capped summits floating like white islands above the fleecy
cloud tops. I feel the spirit of its woodland solitudes and in
my eager ears linger the gentle murmur of its laughing brooks;
in my nostrils lives the welcome breath of gragrant flowers that
perished thirty years ago. In my memory dwells unbroken, a living presence, the charming reminiscence of the quintert land
and the most unique people this earth has ever known. How I
wish that I were a painter or a poet that I might perpetuate in
living colors or embalm by writers' magic art the matchlessness
and imperishable beauties which have gladdened my eyes; the
strains of seraphic music which my ears have caught, more delicious than the matin lays of song birds in the early blushing May
morning, when they soar with reverberating melodies in glad
bright sunlight; soft, tender, sacred inspirations which soften
my heart, made almost callous by the adamantine caress of cold
and selfish associations; the heavenly visions which swell up
like fountain sprays from happy memory; sweet as laughter of
little children or rippling songs of gentle maidens, floating in
silvery madrigals over the deep blue limpid waters of beautiful
Venice.

TEXAS

A map of North America, with the West India Islands, was
published in London, February, 1777. It was laid down according
to the latest surveys, and corrected for the original materials
of Governor POWNALL, member of parliament. On the region between our north eastern boundary and Colorado, as laid down on
that map, the name Texas is found in capital letters. It has
been assumed that Ticas is the same as the present word Texas.
The history of the discovery of Texas has been in dispute. It is
not my mission here to discuss the various claims to its discovery or ownership.

17

SOME HISTORY OF VAN ZNADT COUNTY

THE INTRODUCTION OF COTTON IN THE UNITED STATES

The armed conflict by which Texas cast off the yoke of Mexican tyranny and established a separate Anglo-American republic re-enacted in modern times and in the Western world events and scenes that, occurring in ancient Greece, rendered the name of Hellas glorious and established wells of patriotic inspiration from which after ages have drawn copious draughts.

REPUBLIC OF TEXAS--1835 TO 1846--11 YEARS

General Council of Texas.....................October 11-31, 1835
General Consultation.........................November 1-13, 1835
Henry Smith, Provisional Governor...Nov. 14,1835 to Jan. 11, 1836
James W. Robinson, Acting
        Provisional Governor.................Jan. 11 to Mar. 1, 1836
General Convention..........................March 1-17, 1836
David G. Burnet, President ad interim....Mar. 17 to Oct. 22, 1836
Sam Houston, Constitutional President................1836 to 1838
Mirabeau B. Lamar, President.........................1838 to 1841
Sam Houston, President...............................1841 to 1844
Anson Jones, President...............................1844 to 1846

SOME HISTORY OF VAN ZANDT COUNTY

OLD DAYS

Do you think of the days, of our boyhood days, the flowers, the
    forests and streams;
The hoot of the owl and coyote's howl, distrubing our boyhood
    dreams;
The buds and the bees and the traps 'mong the trees, the nuts and
    the squirrels and quails?
Do we drink in the joys, same as when we were boys, when the farm
    fences all were of rails?

We had plenty to eat and had a few sheep, and we shared 'em in
    May or in June;
And ma knit, spun and wove and made all of our clothes with
    spinnin' wheel and the loom.
Everybody was "pore," a string latch to the door, home-made beds,
    tables and chairs;
But we had lots of fun, everything but the "mun," and we didn't
    put on any airs.

In our double log home, built on land of our own, cost six bits an
    acre or more,
With a ball in between, we were happy and green, and husky and
    hearty and "pore."
Our chimney was squatty and was rough and was rocky--got most of
    'em out of the yard;
We kis carried water, made mud for the mortar, and when it was
    dry it was hard.

Our fireplace was dandy, it was wide and was handy, and besides
    bein' wide it was deep;
In the arch where it crooks, pa fixt ma some books, where she
    cooked nearly all of the meat.
We had wild turkey and deer nearly all of the year, and wild honey
    we got from the bees;
They got it from wild flowers--and the flowers were ours--and had
    stored it away in trees.

Our "harth," too, was rock from the ground to the top, and I've
    often seen mammy a-makin',
Bread for the ovens, fire under, above 'em, preparing' potatoes
    for bakin'.
The potatoes made candy and the bread it was dandy, and our cost
    nothin' a-tall.
Aside from wild game we had hogs on the range, gettin' fat on the
    meat in the fall.

Once, way late in the fall, deer old dad took us all and all of
    the cotton to town,
Into Dallas we rode, all on top of the load; and when we got in
    and got down,

SOME HISTORY OF VAN ZANDT COUNTY

We went into a store--never saw one before, I hadn't--the rest of
    'em, though,
Had been to Fort Worth, "summers" else on the earth, before I was
    born--to a show.

We bought sugar and tea, just a few things, you see, that we
    would a-raised if we could.
Ma bought us a rug, but pa bought him a jug, full of "sumthin"
    that smelt mi'ty good.
There were no doctors then, so pa said except when, we were sick
    we must let it alone;
And I heard mammy say, dad was sick every day until every bit
    of it was gone.

We camped, slept and eat, staked out teams on Main street, and
    all of our cotton we sold;
Sold our entire crop--two bales in the lot--and ma had the money
    in gold.
Folks can't now comprehend it, but we all couldn't spend it, and
    it seems mi'ty funny to tell.
No more town, though, remember, till next year in November, when
    we'd have some more cotton to sell.

But gone are the joys we had when we were boys; still a boy has
    fun now, never fear.
May have more with his wheel or his automobile than we had with
    the turkey and deer.
Mam and dad have passed on, the old home is all gone, and most of
    the boys have "checked in;"
And soon we'll respond to old Gabriel's gong, and then new life
    will begin.

                    T. I. (Tom) Richardson, Cleburne, Texas, Route 2.

SOME HISTORY OF VAN ZANDT COUNTY

CHAPTER I

ELLIS P. BEAN

The late Judge JOHN H. REAGAN said: "I became acquainted with PETER E. BEAN, who in Yokum's History and other publications, is called ELLIS P. BEAN, in the summer of 1839, at his home in what was then Nacogdoches county, but now Cherokee county, near where the town of Alto now stands. I knew him well until he left Texas for the Republic of Mexico."

"Soon after I became acquainted with COLONEL BEAN, he showed me his autobiography and we read it together; a fair sized volume in manuscript. He requested me to edit and publish it. This I was in no condition to do."

Now, prior to 1839, Cherokee county was a part of the Cherokee Nation, so called because the Cherokee Indians held dominion over it for many years and because it embraced about one-third of Van Zandt county.

I deem it proper to give space to one of the most unique characters that ever visited Texas in all its days of romance and tragedy. Because of BEAN's dual life, as is indicated by Judge REAGAN, in his dual name it is hard to give a continued and uninterrupted story of him and so he may be robbed of some of his daring exploits in the following narration, which must necessarily be incomplete.

PHILIP NOLAN, by birth or parentage, a son of the Emerald Isle who for a time lived about Frankfort, Kentucky, drifted to New Orleans and being something of a polished adventurer, heard stories of the abundance of wild horses in Texas. He made a trade with the BARON de COLONDELET, for whom one of the streets in New Orleans is named and who was then Governor of New Orleans, to deliver to him in New Orleans, a number of horses, on condition that he be given passports to Texas for that purpose. With this, he repaired to SAN ANTONIO de BEXAR, where he made the acquaintance of DON MANUEL MUNOZ, Governor of Texas, and through the kind offices of that officer was enabled to procure a permit to obtain the horses in Texas and San Tander. He procured a goodly number of horses and delivered them as per contract and then repaired to Natchez, Mississippi. The transaction was a remunerative one and not long thereafter another contract of like character was also carried out with like results. NOLAN repaired again to Natchez and that time married the belle of the town and built him a home. About the latter part of 1800, NOLAN made a third contract for furnishing an installment of horses to the governor of New Orleans and set about recruiting a small army of some thirty-four or five Americans, some six or seven Spaniards and two negro slaves, all reckless characters, who were ready for any scheme of adventure that presented itself to them. Among them was ELLIS P. BEAN, the subject of this sketch. In the meantime a change of officers resulted in an order for the arrest of NOLAN and his associates, who had crossed the Mississippi river at Nogales (Walnuts), about six miles from the Washita Post.

NOLAN, for a time, was detained by a party of militiamen, but was released and went forward on his mission. Lieutenant MUSQUIZ, a Spanish officer, at Nacogdoches, was ordered to follow and arrest NOLAN.

NOLAN and his associates reached Texas, crossed the Trinity and advanced into the vast prairie between that stream and the Brazos, where they found an abundance of wild horses and for nine days lived on the flesh of these animals, which they cooked over fires made out of buffalo dung. Journeying on west they reached the Brazos, where they found plenty of deer and elk and some buffalo and innumerable wild horses. Here they built an enclosure, caught and penned about three hundred mustangs.

While lolling around their camp fires they were visited by a large lodge of Comanche Indians, with whom they became quite companionable and with them visited their village on the south fork of Red River, where they found their chief, NECOROCO, and several other tribes who visited their lodge while NOLAN and his band were there. NOLAN returned to his stockade, accompanied by an escort of the wild tribe, who managed to steal eleven head of domesticated saddle horses of NOLAN's band--in fact all they had that were suitable for use in capturing mustangs.

NOLAN's company at that time consisted of Captain NOLAN, Lieutenant ELLIS P. BEAN, ten other Americans, five Spaniards and one negro. Bereft of their horses in that vast wilderness, they could do nothing. In this predicament, Captain NOLAN called for volunteers to pursue the thieves, and Lieutenant ELLIS P. BEAN, ROBERT ASHLEY, JOSEPH REED, DAVID FARO, and CEASAR, the negro, volunteered to go after them. After nine days marching, on foot, they found four of their horses in care of as many Indian men and some women; the other horses, the Indians said had been taken on a buffalo hunt by eight of their number, and that they would return that evening; that the one who had stolen the horses was a one-eyed Indian, whom they would know from that description. In the evening the Indians came with an abundance of buffalo meat and the horses. The NOLAN bank tied the one-eyed Indian thief and guarded him until morning. They then took from him enough provisions to last them on their trip home, which required four days travel. They then set about preparing for their leave for New Orleans.

Lieutenant MUSQUIZ surrounded their camp early on the morning of March 21, 1801, and relating the occurrence says: "When I arrived at the wooden intrenchment at sunrise, having divided my force into three bodies, one commanded by me and carrying a four pounder, I marched on NOLAN's intrenchment. When arrived within about thirty paces from it, ten men sallied forth from the intrenchment, unarmed; among them was NOLAN, who said in a loud voice, "Do not approach, because one or the other will be killed." Noticing that the men who accompanied NOLAN were foreigners, I ordered Mr. WILLIAM BARR, an Irishman who had joined my command as interpreter, to speak to them in English and say to them that I had come for the purpose of arresting them, and that I expected them to surrender in the name of the king. NOLAN had a brief conversation with BARR, and the latter informed me that NOLAN and his men were determined to fight. NOLAN re-entered his intrenchment, followed by his men and I observed that two Mexicans, JUAN JOSE MARTINEZ and VICANTA LARA, excaped from the rear of said intrenchment. Soon after these Mexicans joined us, stating that they had brought NOLAN's carbine, which they handed to me. At daybreak NOLAN and his men commenced firing. The fight lasted until 9 o'clock a. m. when NOLAN was killed by a cannonball and his men surrendered. They were out of ammunition. NOLAN's force at the time was composed of fourteen Americans, one Creole, of Louisiana, seven Spaniards or Mexicans and two negro slaves. NOLAN had three men wounded and several horses killed. His men had long beards.

"After their surrender, I learned that they had left Natchez with supplies for two months and had been in the woods and prairies of Texas over seven months, living on horse meat."

"NOLAN's negroes asked permission to bury their master, which I granted after causing his ears to be cut off, in order to send them to the governor of Texas."

I have seen several accounts as to where PHILIP NOLAN was supposed to have been killed, all differing. The one most probable is on NOLAN's river in Johnson county.

The following compose a list of those who were with NOLAN before he was killed: STEPHEN RICHARDS, Pennsylvania, aged 20 years; SIMON McCOY, Pennsylvania, aged 25 years; JOSEPH WALTERS, Virginia, aged 26 years; JOSEPH REED, Pennsylvania, aged 26 years; WILLIAM DANLIN, Pennsylvania, aged 27 years; SOLOMON COOLY, Kentucky, aged 25 years; ELLIS P. BEAN, North Carolina, aged 22 years; CHARLES KING, Maryland, aged 27 years; JOEL J. PIERCE, North Carolina, aged 22 years; THOMAS HOUSE, Virginia, aged 27 years; EPHRIAM BLACKBURN, Maryland, aged 35 years; DAVID FERO, New York, aged 24 years; VINCENTE LARA, Mexico, aged 38 years; JUAN JESUS MARTINEZ, Mexico, aged 21 years; JOSE JUSUS SANTOS, Mexico, aged 21 years; LOREZO HINOJOSE, Mexico, aged 34 years; JOS BARBON, Mexico, aged 20 years; LUCIAN GARCIA, aged 42 years; JUAN BAUTITA and ROBERT, negro slaves and REFUGIO de la GARZA, Mexico aged 30 years.

The following, although belonging to NOLAN's command, escaped from prison at Nacogdoches soon after the surrender; ROBERT ASHLEY, South Carolina, aged 38; JOHN HOUSE, Virginia, aged 21 and MICHAEL MOORE, Ireland, aged 25.

Hereafter, the story is given by BEAN in his autobiography, which is somewhat like the fish story in which JONAH and the gourd vine figured and the reader may give all the credit it is entitled to Mr. BEAN:

"The command surrendered on the 22nd of March, 1801, under a an agreement that it should be escorted to the frontier and allowed to return to the United States. On their part the prisoners promised to never enter Texas again. They were then taken to Nacogdoches. After remaining about a month in that place, they were manacled and marched to San Antonio and there imprisoned for

23

three months. They were then conducted to San Louis Potosi, where they spent sixteen months in prison. During that time BEAN and CHARLES KING made shoes and earned enough money to buy clothing. The prisoners were taken to Chihuahua and there were tried by the Spanish authorities as invaders. DON JUAN JOSE RUIS de BUSTAMANTE, was prosecuting attorney for the government and DON PEDRO RAMOS de VERE, counsel for the defendants. Judge GALINDO de NAVARRO, who tried the case, on January 23, 1804, ordered the release of the prisoners, but as General MEMESSES SALCEDO, commanding the Provinces objected, they were detained. The proceedings had in the trial were sent to the King of Spain, and he, by royal decree, dated at El Pardo, February 23, 1807, ordered the authorities to hang one out of every five of the prisoners and condemn the others to ten years' labor. SIMON McCOY, STEPHEN RICHARDS and THOMAS HOUSE, who were not within the intrenchments and offered no resistence at the time of the attack, were not to draw lots. Those who were to draw lots were, LUCIAN GARICANO, JONAH WALTERS, SOLOMON COOLY, ELLIS P. BEAN, JOSEPH REED, CHARLES KING, JOSEPH PIERCE, EPHRIAM BLACKBURN and DAVID FERO. Judge GALINDO's removal from office was decreed but his death had removed him from the cares of all earthly responsibility before the king's decree reached Mexico. When the king decreed that one out of every five of the NOLAN prisoners, be executed, he was under the impression that the ten prisoners, as above were alive; but as one of them, JOSEPH PIERCE, had died, the new judge decided that one of the nine should suffer the penalty of death and this opinion was approved by General SALCEDO. In the town of Chihuahua, on the 9th day of the month of November, 1807, in compliance with the decree of his majesty, the king of Spain, transmitted to the commanding general of these provinces with a royal order of the 23rd day of February of said year, DON ANTONIO GARCIA de TEJADO, adjutant inspector of the internal provinces of New Sapin, proceeding to the barracks of said town, together with DON PEDRO RAMES de VERA, counsel for the foreigners, who invaded the country under PHILIP NOLAN and DON JOSE DIAZ de BUSTAMENTS, prosecuting attorney and having caused the nien prisoners confined in said barracks to assemble in a room in order to draw lots, so that one of them might be executed. After they knelt I read the decree of his majesty, the king. The prisoners, having heard the same, agreed to throw dice and that the oldest of them should throw first and that the one who threw the lowest number should be hanged. This agreement being made, a drum, a crystal tumbler and two dice were brought and I ordered the prisoners to kneel before the drum blindfolded. EPHRIAM BLACKBURN being the oldest among the prisoners first took the glass. The throwing was as follows: EPHRIAM BLACKBURN 3 and 1, making 4; LUCIANO GARCIA, 3 and 4, making 7; JOSEPH REED, 6 and 5, making 11; JONAH WALTERS 6 and 1, making 7; CHARLES KING, 4 and 3, making 7; ELLIS P. BEAN, 4 and 1, making 5; WILLIAM DANLIN, 5 and 2, making 7. BLACKBURN, after baptism by a priest, was hanged on Plaza de les Uranges, November 11, 1807."

Now, note that BLACKBURN was hanged six years, seven months

and twenty-two days after his capture. So you see how swift the courts were under Spanish rule in Mexico, in those days.

The surviving prisoners were next marched to the City of Mexico, where they nourished the hope that they would be released, but instead they were marched to Acapulco, on the Pacific coast and imprisoned. Here BEAN was separated from his companions and we will not take further notice of them, confining our following remarks to BEAN, as nearly as possible.

The unfortunate Americans probably arrived at Acapulco in the spring of 1808. BEAN was confined in a solitary prison with a guard pacing in front thereof hourly proclaiming "Centenally Allerty." He was given a scanty allowance of beef, bread and water; he amused himself with the companionship of a white lizard that he tamed and fed with flies. Being somewhat resourceful and longing for any change that might present itself, he managed to bring on a spell of enforced sickness to get a transfer to a hospital, in which he was successful, but his allowance of food was one chicken head per day. He was placed in irons and his legs were placed in stocks. At this treatment BEAN complained and to which complaint the friar, who attended him, returned an angry, insolent answer and BEAN landed a blow on his head, which sprawled the reverend father on the floor with an ugly wound for him to nurse. For this act BEAN's head was also placed in stocks where he was allowed to remain for fifteen days when he was informed that he was to be returned to his cell. On his way to his former place of confinement, he managed to elude his guards and reached some woods where he filed off his irons with a piece of steel used by him in striking fire from a flint. After night he returned to Acapulco to procure some needed provisions and there met an English sailor. It was agreed between them that BEAN should go on board a vessel at anchor in the harbor and lie concealed in a water cask. He succeeded in getting aboard the ship, but before it set sail he was betrayed and taken back to his cell, where he lingered another eighteen months in solitary confinement.

One day, overhearing a conversation between a party of officers about blasting rock and professing to be an expert in this work, he offered his services, which were accepted and an opportunity soon presented itself and he again made his escapt. Wending his way north along the coast, he was retaken, carried back and chained to a gigantic mulatto criminal, who was instructed to wreak his vengeance on him whenever he so desired. His new companion showing signs of a belligerent spirit, BEAN knocked him down and pelted him until he promised to be good and submissive before he would let him up. The mulatto filed a plea of divorcement from BEAN with the governing authorities, if by such separation he would forfeit one year remission of his sentence. They were accordingly separated much to the delight of the mulatto and to BEAN's mutual satisfaction. BEAN was remanded to his cell and his former companion, the lizard.

While thus confined, a revolution spread over the Mexican states, including Acapulco against Spain. The prisons were being

emptied to recruit the Spanish army. BEAN was left in his cell.
He assured a Spanish officer that he would gladly fight for the
king if given his liberty to do so and a gun. For this purpose
and under his promise he was released and given a gun and a
sabre. He was loyal to the king about one fortnight, awaiting
an opportunity to join the republican forces under MORELOS, taking with him a large number of the royalist soldiers and much
munitions of war. According to his account he had planned the
affair with MORELOS and marched his command into a preconcerted
trap. He so ingratiated himself into the confidence of MORELOS
that upon leaving Acapulco with his army, he placed BEAN in command of the besieging forces encompassing that place.

About the close of the year 1812, BEAN had the satisfaction
of taking the town and its garrison by force of arms and making
prisoner of the Governor of the Castle who had been his master
in captivity. Remember this, about eleven years since he struck
his colors and surrendered on Nolan's River in Texas, as he said,
under promise of being conducted out of Texas and released.

BEAN went on succeeding in one way and another; met and
married Senorita ANNA GROTHAS, owner of the rich hacienda of
Benderillas, near Jalapa, between Vera Cruz and the City of Mexico. In 1814 he was dispatched by General MORELOS on a mission
to the United States, to procure aid for the patriot cause in
Mexico.

At the port of Nautla, on the gulf coast above Vera Cruz, he
boarded one of LAFITTE's vessels, Captain DOMINIC, master. He
informed DOMINIC of his mission and was landed on the island of
Barrataria, below New Orleans, where he met LAFITTE, who conducted him by a short route to New Orleans. There he found General
JACKSON, who being an old friend of his family, invited him to
share in the glories of the 8th of January. He embraced the offer and fought side by side with LAFITTE with his accustomed
gallantry. After the battle of New Orleans, LAFITTE furnished
him transportation to Nautla for himself and his munitions of
war for the patriot army of Mexico. BEAN worked himself up to
where he held a high commission in the patriot army of Mexico
before the close of the revolution in 1821, when MORELOS won for
the Mexican people their independence of the Spanish kingdom.

After the death of MORELOS, and the conciliatory propositions of Apodica, the fires of the Mexican revolution had so far
expired that BEAN left the country and visited his native State.
He reached the residence of his half brother, Captain WILLIAM
SHAW, in White County, Tennessee, in the spring of 1818. After
remaining here sometime, he formed a matrimonial alliance with a
daughter of ISAAC MIDKIFF. He then emigrated with his family
and father-in-law to Smackover Creek, in Arkansas. Here they
settled, without a neighbor within thirty miles of them, and
commenced raising stock. At the end of three years his father-
in-law died. This event together with the news of the liberation
of Mexico and the call for her colonist, induced BEAN to come to
Texas. He located himself at the Mound Prairie, the ancient town
of Texas, and obtained from the government, for his services a

grant for a league of land including his residence in Anderson County.

At this place BEAN resided quietly till the summer of 1825, when he set out for Mexico. He reached the capital on the 18th day of October, and remained there till the 21st of July, 1826. Here he met his old companions-in-arms, and possessed himself of a knowledge of the interesting events that had transpired in the country during the past seven years. For his services in the revolution he received, in addition to the grant of land before mentioned, the appointment of colonel in the permanent forces of the republic and as such was sent as Indian agent to the Cherokees and made his home as Judge REAGAN said, about where the town of Alto now is.

When the Texas revolution was commenced, BEAN went to General RUSK and surrendered and was by him given a parole, which was duly obeyed during the struggle with Mexico, which culminated in the capture of La Presidente ANTONIO LOPEZ de SANTA ANNA, at San Jacinto.

Headright certificate 690 was granted to PETER E. BEAN by the board of land commissioners of Nacogdoches county, Texas, for one league and labor of land, April 4, 1839, and recites that he arrived in Texas previous to the second day of May, 1835, as a married man and that he appeared before said board of land commissioners and made proof that he was entitled to said certificate. This certificate was located in Kaufman county, on the waters of Cedar Creek, a tributary of the Trinity River, and patent issued to PETER E. BEAN for said land. In July, 1842, he executed a deed to one-half of said grant to HELENA NELSON, reciting that he and his grantee lived in Cherokee county, Texas. Witnesses to this title paper were J. M. BEAN and W. Y. LACY. The remaining one-half passed by will to his heirs.

BEAN remained in Texas until about the time it was annexed to the United States, when he left via of New Orleans, for his former wife and home near Vera Cruz, Mexico, with whom he lived until his death, which occurred October 3, 1846.

BEAN raised a family of three children in Texas which he left on his departure for Mexico. I am not advised as to what became of his wife that he married in Tennessee.

On the 11th day of May, 1846, President POLK, in a proclamation to congress, declared that war existed between the United States and Mexico. On the 21st of September, 1846, General TAYLOR, of the United States army directed officers under his command to open hostilities on Monterey, a city of importance in northeast Mexico, which, after much hard fighting surrendered to General TAYLOR's command on September 25th. But I am not advised as to whether or not this information reached ELLIS P. BEAN before his death.

CHAPTER 2

WHEN KING BANDITI RULED

"This world is bus a fleeting show,
To vain delusions given;
There's not an honest man on earth
And scarcely one in heaven."

By the treaty of 1819, between the United States and Spain, the western boundary line of Louisiana Purchase was fixed to begin in the Gulf of Mexico off the mouth of the Sabine river and to run up that stream and north to the Red river, etc. Until the demarkation of the line, it was agreed by both parties to the treaty, that there should be a neutral strip between the western line of the Louisiana Purchase and the eastern line of Spain's possessions, not to be occupied by either of the parties to the contract, so that no trouble would ensue on account of the boundary line. The line was not demarked until 1841 and the neutral strip became the rendezvous of escaped convicts and others fleeing from justice. After Mexico had thrown off the yoke of Spain, this agreement was renewed between the United States and that republic and the same was done as regarded Texas after it had severed connection with Mexico.

These bandits knew no law, nor recognized any government, only as it suited their convenience.

The following from NOAH SMITHWICK will serve to show how things were run in the neutral strip. After giving a full account of the counterfeiting operations going on there he says:

Another swindling scheme that was being worked on a gigantic scale and which was productive of more lasting evil, it will be necessary to go back to 1829 to explain. DON PADILLO came from Saltillo as commissioner of the land office to survey and make title to claims of bona fide settlers outside of the regular colonies, being provided with blanks for that purpose, on which was stamped the seal of the Republic of Mexico, lacking only the specifications and signature of the commissioner to complete them. . . . He was thrown into prison and his papers fell into the hands of an unscrupulous gang, who at once proceeded to establish a land office of their own. Securing the services of an old Spaniard who had been a government clerk for years and was an expert penman, they had him forge the commissioner's signature to the blanks, and thus equipped, set up business on a large scale, issuing floating certificates to any amount of land for an insignificant consideration.

FRADULENT LAND SCRIPT ISSUED UNDER THE REPUBLIC

From a speech made in the United States Senate, on February 3, 1859, by Senator SAM HOUSTON of Texas, we quote the following:

In the first place, it is necessary to explain the condition of the public domain of Texas at the period when the history of the appalling conspiracy referred to commenced. In the year 1837, by a general law of Texas, large donations of land were

28

made to those who arrived and settled in the country previous to 1836, the date of her declaration of independence. To married me men one league of land and those who were unmarried, one-third of a league. Under this law, boards of land commissioners were appointed, whose duty it was to investigate all claims on the government for headrights to lands, and to grant certificates to such persons as furnished the requisite proofs of their being entitled to the came. Many of these boards betrayed their trust and perpetrated frauds of the most alarming magnitude, assigning large numbers of certificates to fictitious persons. These frauds came to be of the most open and notorious character; so much so that cases could be instanced where to counties not numbering more than one hundred voters, nine hundred certificates were issued by the fraudulent action of these boards. The amount of these false certificates reached at last to such an overwhelming number that on the 5th day of February, 1840, a law was enacted, visiting the most severe penalties on the crimes of "making, or issuing, or being concerned in making of issuing, any such fraudulent or forged certificates," and providing that "those who issued, or dealt in, or purchased, or located, or who were concerned in the issuing, or dealing in, or purchasing or locating" these fraudulent land certificates, should be punished by "thirty-nine lashes on the bare back, and by imprisonment from three to twelve months, in the discretion of the judge." A law was passed about the same time forbidding the survey of any land claimed under these certificates, until certified to be correct by other boards of commissioners appointed to examine into and detect the frauds by which the bounty of the republic had been abused and attempt made to despoil it of its domain.

Now this brings us down to where Van Zandt county became involved by or with these fraudulent land certificates. KATE EFNOR, writing some years ago, says:

In 1839, there reached the southern states, Mississippi especially, reports of the vastly rich lands lying between the three forks of the Trinity River. It was then supposed that the three forks came together, forming almost a block of valuable lands. A company was organized at Holly Springs, Mississippi, for the purpose of coming to Texas and seeking out this garden spot. DR. W. P. KING, being president of the company, he purchased certificates for headrights of one hundred and fifteen leagues and with about forty men came out in 1840, stopping in the center of the present county of Kaufman, from whence they sent out surveying parties whose duty it was to measure off the one hundred and fifteen leagues." Here they built a fort on a branch of Cedar Creek near a spring of clear water.

Capt. R. A. TERRELL, who still resides in the county, . . . was a member of the company. It was his commission, with a party of men to go and find the three forks of the Trinity. Failing to find the three in one, according to expectation and reaching the east fork at a settlement called Warsaw, he commenced surveying the block which they proposed making square. This extended over a portion of Dallas, Van Zandt, Hunt, and Collin counties. KING afterwards purchased genuine certificates and relocated a portion of the old lands, but there was then trouble in finding the lines and corners by which the land might be identified, as MERCER's colonists had located some of them. It was taken into law and there was much litigation regarding it till the year 1875, when the supreme court decided wherever a space in the block could be found, there the surveying could be made. It was KING's intention to settle in Kaufman, but he died and this caused the men under him to go back to their homes and it was three years from that time before this portion of the county became populated.

The King block commences at Wills Point and continues to the Trinity River. Much of it was covered by league and labor certificates, but considerable portions was covered by Mercer Colony grants.

REGULATORS AND MODERATORS

Those occupying the neutral lands paid no taxes to any one and claimed to be citizens of either Texas or the United States as best suited their convenience, until the line of demarkation was definitely established. In due time feuds arose, involving personal difficulties and violence. This led to the organization of a body of self styled "Regulators," this in turn led to a counter organization which assumed the prerogative of "Moderators."
MR. E. CURRIE writes of the organizations thus: "I can give the cause of the war as told me by one of the participants, WARWICK WHETSTONE. The Regulators were formed to put down crime in Texas. After a time they became lawless and would charge a man with horse, cow or hog theft, and notify him to leave the country and death was the penalty for not going. After a time when he was gone, his property or stock would be appropriated by them. The leader of the Regulators fell out with one of the TRUETTS. TRUETT killed one of them and a band of twnety followed TRUETT to Polk county and there told him if he would give up they would take him back to Shelby county and let the law take its course. He gave up to them, and after going ten miles with him they hanged him. The TRUETTS had friends, and the law-abiding citizens came together and organized the Moderators and they pitched camp to put the Regulators out of business. The Moderators proved to be too strong for them, and the Regulators called on General HOUSTON for troops to suppress the Moderators. The troops came and ordered the Moderators to disband, but they told the troops they were in no humor to disband, and after the troops learned the truth, they disarmed and disbanded the Regulators. So the Moderators did likewise. WARWICK WHETSTONE was about 18 years old and was shot in the jaw in a fight with the Regulators. He married a second cousin of mine who was SALINA B. ENGLISH. My grandfather, JOHN ENGLISH, with his brothers and a lot of others from Tennessee, settled in Shelby county, Texas, in 1823. My

mother, MARINDA E. ENGLISH, was born in Shelby county in 1831. I have talked with several who were in the Regulator and Moderator war. JIM MAY, at Tenneha, Shelby county, and who was living a few years ago, was about 15 years old and was a scout for the Moderators, told me more about it than any other."

Mr. CURRIE also wrote me that WARWICK WHETSTONE was a brother to ANDERSON and JOHNSON WHETSTONE, who formerly lived in Van Zandt county.

From BROWN's "History of Texas" we take the following:

Affrays and murders became frequent, and early in 1844 armed bodies of men, numbering from one hundred and fifty to two hundred each stook in array against each other. President HOUSTON realized that a crisis was upon the country. He issued a proclamation addressed to the malcontents, at the same time ordering General JAMES SMITH to raise a body of several hundred militia and proceed to the scene of the difficulties. This was speedily done and President HOUSTON arrived on the scene about the same time. He called a convocation of the leading men on both sides and addressed them in great earnestness. He told them the law must and should be enforced; that the taking of human life must -e stopped and peace be restored to the country. That all this he wished to accomplish without shedding a drop of blood of his countrymen, but, in the last alternative, added that these objects must be accomplished, cost what they may. He appealed to the leaders on both sides to cast their arms aside and become peaceful citizens. His appeal had the desired effect: both sides agreed to follow his advice and obey the laws. The president and militia returned to their homes. Thus ended the war.

President HOUSTON, in his message to the congress of the Republic of Texas, at Washington, December 4, 1841, has this to say regarding the uprising in east Texas: "During the past summer, dissensions of a most unfortunate character, arising from private and personal causes, and leading to the most deplorable excesses against life and property, existed in the county of Shelby, and extended in some degree to the surrounding districts. The necessity for the prompt intervention of the government to arrest this state of things became imperative, and accordingly, the executive proceeded in person to a convenient point near the scene of difficulties and ordered out a military force deemed sufficient for the effectual attainment of the object in view. He is happy to say that the citizen soldiery obeyed the call upon them--their patriotic services--with utmost alacrity by which the reign of order and the supremacy of the laws were speedily re-established. It was deemed prudent, in order to secure the maintenance of these blessings, and to give due protection to the civil authorities in the administration of justice, to station a company of men in the county of Shelby. For the purpose, a corps of volunteers were enrolled, and continued in service as long as the government thought it advisable for the preservation of the peace. The executive does not doubt that the honorable congress

31

will readily perceive the necessity which existed for the exertion of the strength of the government for the suppression of the disorders alluded to, and that they will as readily make provision for the payment of the expenses incurred in doing so."

ANDERSON WHETSTONE raised a company for the Civil war in Van Zandt county and was elected captain of the same. This company was mustered into service at Goose Lake, north of Wills Point, on the Sabine river, and assigned to Locks' regiment for service. However, it was not long until a reorganization took place and Captain WHETSTONE returned home, and later died in the Wisdom Temple community. JOHNSON WHETSTONE was indicted by the grand jury of Van Zandt county for killing one MR. EASTERWOOD at Grand Saline. When JAMES S. HOGG was district attorney for this district he made an especial effort to bring him to justice but failed. MR. CURRIE advised me that ETSTONE died at Edgerly, La., at a sawmill owned by CHARLEY HAMPTON.

The following is taken from "Texas Methodist Historical Quarterly" of July, 1909, Vol. 1., page 3:

Another incident is that of a drunken desperado who appeared at a camp meeting conducted by Rev. LITTLETON FOWLER, not far from Marshall. The drunken man invaded a private tent while the owners were attending services at the arbor and began shooting up the tent and dishes on the table, one shot passing through the clothing of a nurse with a babe in her arms. The proprietor of the tent and others hearing of the disturbance hastened to the scene, pistol in hand, opened fire on the intruder, who when wounded, ran to the arbor and fell at the feet of FOWLER who was calling for penitents. The unfortunate man died the next day, but confessed his great wrong and begged his brothers not to avenge his death, and the two families lived peaceably in the same county for many years.

MERCER'S COLONY

The Republic of Texas, by SAM HOUSTON, president thereof, entered into a contract with CHARLES FENTON MERCER, on the 29th day of January, 1844, by which said MERCER was to colonize a large territory in northeast Texas, said to have contained within its limits about 4,000,000 acres of land and which embraced in whole the counties of Navarro, Kaufman, Rockwaal and Hill and in part, the counties of McLennan, Limestone, Freestone, Anderson, Henderson, Van Zandt, Rains, Hopkins, Collin, Dallas, Ellis, Johnson, Hood and Somerville.

In a suit brought against the state of Texas, March 6, 1875, it was claimed that MERCER and associates had introduced and actually settled under said contract, 1,256 emigrant families, for which they were entitled to 1,256 sections of 640 acres each, being one section for each family and in addition thereto 120 sections being ten premium sections for each one hundred families, making in all 1,376 sections, or 880,640 acres of land. This suit for a time threatened to disturb people all over this vast territory. It passed through the United States district and circuit courts, both giving adverse judgments to Texas and her citizens, but the United States supreme court rendered an opinion favorable to the state of Texas and her citizens and taxing the plaintiffs with the cost from the inception of the suit to date of final judgment, which was November 19, 1883.

MERCER's colony line runs north and south through Van Zandt county, very near Antioch, Colfax and Oakland schoolhouses. All west of the line in Van Zandt county was covered by MERCER's colony but only such lands in that part of the county was affected by this colony contract as were induced to settle in the colony by MERCER and his associates. As above stated, all the families introduced into the colony by MERCER and his associates were entitled to a grant of 640 acres of land for settling in the colony.

CHAPTER 3

THE PASSING OF THE REDMAN

From the London Examiner: "When Captain JOHN SMITH and his swash-bucklering cavaliers landed in the 'Empire of Virginia,' the aborigines of the United States, judging from the traces which have been left behind, could not have been less than four or five millions in number. We question if, at the present moment, they number five hundred thousand. Driven from bank to wall, and from wall to ditch, they have contested every foot-breadth of the weary road over which they have had to retreat, to make way for the Anglo Saxon flood. Disease, whiskey, misery untold and villianous saltpeter have civilized them off the earth once their own. Once all the region east of the Mississippi, from Maine to Louisiana, was thickly settled and peopled with the prosperous villages of those whom the old travelers called "the savages." No part of America now whows so thickly a populated a country or so joyous a savage race as those who there hunted in the woods and paddled their birch-bark canoes or Mandan coracles. With the exception of a few all but civilized fragments of tribes in one or two of the states, there is not now one single Indian who owns to the name, in all that wide region. A swarthy, keen-eyed lawyer, pleading in the supreme court in New York, or a very dark-haired gentleman who sits next to you in a general's uniform at a state dinner in the White House, are, to the keenest enthnological eye, about the only signs of the new thickly populated states covered with cities and towns, having been once inhabited only by dwellers in wigwams, who fished the salmon and hunted the bear and the deer, with no man to make them afraid."

When America was first discovered, Indians were found here. No one outside of a religious zealot will attempt to account for his presence here. No encyclopedia of any reliability will venture to give any facts regarding the descent of the American Indian. When I first reached Van Zandt county, I cultivated a small field on the west bank of Shelton Lake near the head of Crooked Creek, about half way between Canton and Wills Point. There I plowed up innumerable tools made out of flint rocks. The place had evidently once been occupied by an Indian village.

The purpose of this article, however, is to give an account of how one tribe of Indians planted themselves in Texas and after establishing a bona fide title to the lands they occupied, were driven out and their homes appropriated by the Anglo-Saxons.

THE CHEROKEE NATION

The Cherokee Indians will furnish the ground works of this narration. Twelve other tribes will figure in the history, but only so as to bring up certain historical data; it being the purpose to confine this sketch as nearly to the Cherokees as possible.

THOMAS MAITLAND MARSHALL has this to say of the migration of the Cherokee to Texas:

SOME HISTORY OF VAN ZANDT COUNTY

At the close of the Revolutionary war, the so-called hunter class of Cherokee abandoned their villages in the Appalachian Mountains, emigrating to the White river in Arkansas and Louisiana. Others followed until about six thousand lived west of the Mississippi. Troubles ensuing with the native tribes, the United States government interferred. Sixty warriors, under their chief, RICHARD FIELDS, crossed into Texas and being friendly with the Caddo, settled south of Red river in the region disputed by the Caddo and Prairie tribes. Receiving frequent acquisitions, they gradually occupied the lands between the Sabine and Trinity rivers as far down as the San Antonio road, in which neighborhood they remained until expelled in 1839.

So the date or exact date of their arrival in Texas is not made manifest. MARSHALL further says:

In 1822, RICHARD FIELDS, the Cherokee chief, led a deputation to Mexico for the purpose of obtaining a land grant from the government. They were allowed to remain in Texas, but were not given a legal title to their lands.

Later on FIELDS claimed that all the lands north of the San Antonio road between the Trinity and Sabine rivers had been granted to his tribe. This claim, however, was not substantiated by the Mexican government. But it is a fact, that under DON FELIX TRESPALACIOS, the Cherokees were permitted to remain upon the lands in Texas on which they settled. This agreement was ratified by Iterbide on the 27th day of April, 1823, with the understanding that the Indians were to move further west and no more families of their tribe were to be introduced into Texas.

JOHN DUN HUNTER became prominent among this tribe of the Cherokee, but I can hardly believe that is the reason MR. MARSHALL had for calling them the "Hunter Indians."

Trouble grew up between HADEN EDWARDS, of Nacogdoches, and the Mexican authorities relative to a grant given EDWARDS to colonize a district, including Nacogdoches. In this matters became alarming and what was called the "Fredonian war" followed. FIELD and HUNTER, of the Cherokees, allied themselves with EDWARDS, by which alliance the Indians were to have all that portion of Texas lying north of a line beginning at the mouth of Sulphur Fork; thence to a point not far from Nacogdoches; thence west to the Rio Grande. All the territory south of that belonged to the other party. The EDWARDS party soon vacated Texas and the above treaty went to naught. Among the Cherokees was another high chief in the person of one BOWLES. A mutiny sprang up among the Cherokees, under Chief BOWLES, as against FIELD and HUNTER, and the two latter were murdered. BOWLES then became the ruling and reigning spirit among the Cherokees. Then followed an uprising of the Americans in Texas, against the tyranny of Mexican misrule in Texas, in the form of what was styled a general consultation on October 11 to 27, 1835. This was followed by the permanent council, which was organized November 3d and was followed on the

14th by the provisional government of Texas.

Among the proceedings of the consultation I will mention the following regarding the Cherokee and associate tribes, which reads:

We solemnly declare that the boundaries of the claims of said Indians are as follows, to wit: Being north of the San Antonio road and the Neeches and west of the Angelina and Sabine rivers. We solemnly declare that the governor and general council immediately on its organization shall appoint commissioners to treat with the said Indians to establish the definite boundaries of their territory and secure their confidence and friendship. We solemnly declare that we will guarantee to them the peaceable enjoyment of their rights and their lands as we do our own. We solemnly declare all grants, surveys and locations within the bounds therein before maintained, made after the settlement of the said Indians, are and of right ought to be utterly null and void, and the commissioners issuing same be and hereby ordered immediately to recall and cancel same as having been made upon lands already appropriated by the Mexican government. We solemnly declare that it is our sincere desire that the Cherokee Indians and their associate bands should remain our friends in peace and war, and if they do so, we pledge the public faith to support the foregoing decalration. We solemnly declare that they are entitled to our commiseration and protection, as the first owners of the soil; as an unfortunate race of people; that we wish to hold as friends and treat with justice.

The above was signed by the entire body of the consultation.

GOVERNOR SMITH ADDRESS COUNCIL

The following letter is from the Hon. HENRY SMITH, first temporary governor of Texas:

San Felipe, December 18th, 1835

Gentlemen of the Council:

...I further have to suggest to you the propriety of appointing the commissioners on the part of this government to carry into effect the Indian treaty, as contemplated by the convention. I can see no difficulty which can reasonably occur in the appointment of the proper agents on our part, having so many examples and precedents before us. The United States have universally sent their most distinguished military officers to perform such duties, because the Indians generally look up to and respect their authority as coercive and paramount. I would therefore suggest the propriety of appointing General HOUSTON, of the army, and Col. JOHN FORBES, of Nacogdoches, who has been already commissioned as one of my aides. These commissioners would go specially instructed, so that no wrong could be committed, either to the government, the Indians or our individual citizens. All legitimate rights would be respected and no thers. I am well aware that we have no right to transcend the superior order and declaration made by the convention and if I recollect that article right, the outline of external boundaries were demarked within which the Indian tribes alluded to, should be located; but at the same time paying due regard to the legitimate rights of our citizens within the same limits.

If these Indians have introduced themselves in good faith under the colonization laws of the government, they should be entitled to the benefits of those laws and comply with their conditions. I deem it a duty which we owe them to pay all due respect to their rights and claim their co-operation in the support of them and at the same time not to infringe upon the rights of our countrymen, so far as they have been justly founded.

These agents going under proper instructions would be enabled to do right, but not permitted to do wrong, as their negotiations would be subject to investigation and ratification by the government before they would become a law. I am gentlemen,

Your obedient servant,
HENRY SMITH, Governor.

COMMISSIONERS APPOINTED

Under the ordinance of December 22d, previously introduced by MR. KERR, of Jackson, on the 25th, Governor SMITH commissioned Gen. SAM HOUSTON, Col. JOHN FORBES and Dr. JOHN CAMERON, as commissioners to treat with Cherokees and their twelve associate bands of Indians.

Gen. SAM HOUSTON and Col. JOHN FORBES, commissioners, report as follows:

Washington, February 29, 1836
To His Excellency, HENRY SMITH, Governor of Texas:

Sir: In accordance with a commission issued by your excellency, dated the 28th day of December, 1836, the undersigned commissioners, in the absence of JOHN CAMERON, Esquire, one of the commissioners named in the above mentioned instrument, most respectfully report: That after sufficient notice being given to the different tribes named in the commission, a treaty was held at the house of JOHN_____, one of the tribe of Cherokee Indians . . . The commissioners would also suggest to your excellency that titles should be granted to such actual settlers as are now within the designated boundaries, and that they should receive a fair remuneration for their improvements and the expenses attendant upon the exchange, in lands or other equivalent.

It will also be remembered by your excellency that the surrender by the government of the lands to which the Indians may have had any claims is nearly equivalent to that portion now allotted to them and we must respectfully suggest that they should be especially appropriated for the use of the government. They also respectfully call your attention to the following remarks, viz: "The state of excitement in which the Indians were first

found by your commissioners rendered it impossible to commence
negotiations with them on the day set apart for it. On the day
succeeding, the treaty was opened. Some difficulty then occured
relative to the exchange of lands, which the commissioners proposed making for those now occupied by them, which was promptly
rejected. The boundaries were those established as designated
in the treaty alone and that such measure should be adopted by
your excellency for their security as may be deemed necessary..
The commissioners used every exertion to retain that portion of
territory for the use of the government, but an adherence to this
would have but one effect, viz: that of defeating the treaty al-
together."

Under these circumstances the arrangement was made as now
reported in the accompanying treaty. They would also suggest the
importance of the salt works to the government and the necessity
that they should be kept for the use of the government.

The commissioners also endeavored to enlist the chiefs of
the different tribes in the cause of the people of Texas and suggested an enrollment of a force from them to act against our common enemy, in reply to which they informed us that the subject
had not before been suggested to them, but a general council
should be held in the course of the present month, when their determination will be made known.

The expenses attendant upon the treaty are comparatively
light, a statement of which will be furnished to your excellency.

All of which is most respectfully submitted,

SAM HOUSTON,
JOHN FORBES

A TREATY BETWEEN THE COMMISSIONERS ON BEHALF OF THE PROVISIONAL GOVERNMENT OF TEXAS AND THE CHEROKEE INDIANS AND TWELVE ASSOCIATED TRIBES

This treaty this day made and established between SAM HOUSTON
and JOHN FORBES, commissioners on the part of the provisional
government of Texas, of the one part, and the Cherokees and their
associate bands now residing in Texas, of the other part, to wit,
the Shawness, Delawares, Kicapoos, Quawpaws, Buloxies, Iowanes,
Alabamas, Coshaties, Caddos of Neches, Tahocattakes, Untagous,
by the head chiefs and head men and warriors of the Cherokees, as
elder brother and an representation of all other bands, agreeable
to their last council. This treaty is made in conformity to the
declaration made by the last general consultation at San Felipe
and dated the 13th of November, A. D., 1835.

Article 1. The parties declare that there shall be a firm
and lasting peace forever, and that friendly intercourse shall be
preserved by the people belonging to both parties.

Art. 2. It is agreed and declared that the before mentioned
tribes of bands shall form one community and that they shall have
and possess the lands within the following bounds, to wit: Lying
west of the San Antonio road and beginning on the west at the
point where the said road crosses the river Angelina and running

up said river until it reaches the first large creek below the great Shawnee village emptying into said river from the northeast; thence running with said creek to its main source, and from thence a due northwest course to the Sabine river, and with said river east. Then starting where the San Antonio road crosses the Angelina river, and with the said road to a point where it crosses the Neches river, and then running up said river in a northwest direction.

Art. 3. All lands settled in good faith or granted previous to the settlement of the Cherokees, within the before described bounds are not conveyed by this treaty, but excepted from its operation. All persons who have once been removed and returned shall be considered intruders and their settlement not to be respected.

Art. 4. It is agreed by all parties that the several bands or their tribes named in this treaty shall all remove within the limits or bounds as above described.

Art. 5. It is agreed and declared by the parties aforesaid that the land lying and being within the aforesaid limits, shall never be sold or alienated to any person or persons, power or government whatsoever other than the government of Texas, and the commissioners on behalf of the government of Texas, bind themselves to prevent in the future all persons from intruding on said bounds. And it is agreed upon the part of the Cherokees, for themselves and their younger brothers, that no other tribes or bands of Indians whatsoever shall settle within the limits aforesaid, but those already named in the treaty and now residing in Texas.

Art. 6. It is declared no individual person member of the tribes before named, shall have power to sell or lease said lands to any person or persons not a member or members of this community of Indians, nor shall any citizen of Texas be allowed to lease or buy land or lands from any Indian or Indians.

Art. 7. That the Indians shall be governed by their own regulations and laws, within their own territory not contrary to the laws of Texas. All property stolen from the citizens of Texas, or from the Indians shall be restored to the party from whom it was taken and the offender or offenders shall be punished by the party to whom he or they may belong.

Art. 8. The government shall have power to regulate trade and intercourse but no tax shall be laid on the trade of the Indians.

Art. 9. The parties to the treaty agree that one or more agencies shall be created and at least one agent shall specially reside within the Cherokee village, whose duty it shall be to see that no injustice is done to them or their members of the community of Indians.

Art. 10. The parties to this treaty agree that so soon as JACK STEEL and SAMUEL BENGE shall abandon the improvements without the limits of the before cited tract of country and remove within the same that their improvements shall be valued and paid for by the government of Texas, the said JACK STEEL and SAMUEL

BENGE having until the month of November next succeeding from the date of this treaty allowed them to remove within the limits above described. And all lands and improvements now occupied by any of the before bands or tribes not lying within the limits before described shall belong to the government of Texas and subject to its disposal.

Art. 11. The parties to this treaty agree and stipulate that all the bands and tribes before recited (except STEEL and BENGE) shall move within the before described limits within eight months from the date of this treaty.

Art. 12. The parties to this treaty agree that nothing herein contained shall effect the Sabine and Neches nor the settlement in the neighborhood thereof, until a general council of the several bands shall take place and the pleasures of the convention of Texas shall be known.

Art. 13. It is also declared that all titles to the lands not agreeable to the declaration of the general consultation of the people of Texas dated the 13th day of November, 1835, within the before described limits are declared void as well as all orders and surveys made in relation thereto.

Doen at Colonel BOWLES' village on the Trinity, 3d day of February, 1836, and in the first year of the provisional government of Texas.

WITNESSES:

FOX FILEDS (Interpreter)	SAM HOUSTON
HENRY MILLIARD	JOHN FORBES
JOSEPH DURST	COLONEL BOWLES (His mark X)
A. HORTON	BIG (his mark) MUSH X
GEORGE W. CASE	SAMUEL (his mark X) BENGE
MATHIAS A. BINGHAM	OSOOTA (his X mark)
	CORN (his X mark) TASELE
	THE (his X mark) EGG
	JOHN (his X mark) BOWL
	TENUTA (his X mark)

SAM HOUSTON ELECTED PRESIDENT

After the battle of San Jacinto, Texas bloomed out into a full blown republic.

The first election in the republic took place on the first Monday in September, 1836. The election for president resulted as follows:

Sam Houston	5,119 votes
Henry Smith	743 votes
Stephens F. Austin	587 votes
Scattering	191 votes
Total	6,640 votes

Under the administration of President HOUSTON, the Cherokees received courteous treatment and remained quietly on the land they had occupied since reaching Texas. They thought that under the above treaty, they had been quieted in their title to the same.

The second general election came off on the first Monday in September, 1838, and MIRABEAU B. LAMAR was elected president, with only 252 votes recorded against him.

The new president brought forward a new line of thought in regard to the Cherokee Indians. He said regarding them: "That the immigrant tribes have no legal or equitable claim to any portion of our territory, is obvious from a cursory examination of their history. Their immigration to Texas was unsolicited and unauthorized." This might have been equally applied to most of the whites who came to Texas, but after they arrived upon Texas soil they acquired vested rights and these rights were respected and duly appreciated.

BURNET TO DUNLAP

Department of State,
Houston, May 30, 1839

Hon. RICHARD G. DUNLAP.

Sir: I am requested by the President to transmit you the accompanying documents, marked as in the subjoined schedule, which were recently captured from a party of Mexicans as you will find detailed in the copy of report of Col. BURLISON to the Secretary of War, herewith transmitted and marked B2.

This government has long been in possession of testimony sufficient to justify them in adopting the most summary and imperative measures towards the Cherokee and other bands of northern Indians, resident in Texas. Their unauthorized migration and protracted stay in our country has always been a source of disquietude and anxiety to the civilized population and their removal has been long desired. But the President actuated by feelings of humanity towards a people who have been to much accustomed to profit by and abuse similar indulgence, has been unwilling to resort to force to procure their expulsion, while a hope could be entertained that their withdrawal might be effected by peaceable means. That hope has been founded on the application heretofore made to the government of the United States relative to this interesting subject. Those applications appear to have been ineffectual thus far, while the humane forbearance on the part of this government toward these intruding Indians, has been productive of many disasters to our frontier settlements, and if longer continued might result in irreparable injury to Texas. The most enduring patience may be exhausted and must yield to the duty of self preservation, when its exercise evidently gives encouragement and aggravation to the hostile spirit of the offenders. Such is our present condition relative to these immigrant savages; and the President has resolved to put an end to the repeated aggressions of the Cherokees by compelling their departure from our territory. You are at liberty to make known this fact to the government at Washington, and to request that such measures may be seasonably adopted by that government, as will fulfill the provisions of the 33d article of the treaty entered into between the United States and Mexico on the 5th of April, 1831, and will effectually prevent the return of these savages to our territory.

Our right to eject these Indians can scarcely enter into your correspondence with the government of the United States; but should it be incidentally alluded to, you will find it clearly suggested in the letter of MR. FORSYTHE to MR. CASTILLO, charge de affaires from Mexico which is transcribed in despatch No. 42 from your predecessor to this department.

You will **not** however solicit an elaborate discussion on this subject or any other connected with the respective obligations of the United States and Mexico; for a protracted discussion is seldom disirable and may be productive of inconvenience, if not of ill feeling between parties, which we would very sedulously avoid.

The President conceives that the government of the United States has frankly and justly acknowledged the right of Texas to the benefits of that treaty, especially in reference to the 32d article which has a direct territorial relation to this republic as now organized; and he cannot imagine that any objection will be raised or difficulty occur on that ground. You will therefore confine your communications, unless constrained to take a wider range, to the fact of the intended expulsion of the Cherokee and such other of the immigrant bands as may proved to have been or may hereafter be implicated in the late atrocious attempt on the part of the Mexican authorities to employ the Indians of the United States in desolating our frontiers. These machinations have been known to us for some time, but are now so fully developed in relation to the Cherokees that longer forbearance towards them is utterly inconsistent with the first duties of this government. If in the progress of your correspondence it shall be assumed as has been suggested by the charge de affaires here, that the government of the United States is not bound to receive or to restrain those Indians and the ill advised treaty partially made with them on the 33d of February, 1836, by Commissioners appointed by the late provisional government of Texas, be alleged in s support of this position, you can present conclusive refutation of that assumption in the fact that pretended treaty has never been ratified by any competent authority on the part of Texas. On the contrary, when it was first submitted to the Senate of the Republic, which was the only power authorized to confirm it, it was rejected by a decisive vote of that body; and no subsequent action of the government has been had upon it. Indeed should this matter be pressed upon you in such terms as to indicate a determination on the part of the government at Washington to avail itself of that treaty, as absolving it from all obligations touching these Indians (which can hardly be possible) you can further disclaim the validity of the treaty on the ground that the provisional government itself under whose authority the treaty purports to have been made, was acting without the sphere of any legitimate power and could not in any matter so extraneous to the avowed purpose of its creation as the alienation of a large and valuable portion of territory impose any moral or political obligations upon the independence and separate government of Texas. You will recollect that the provisional government passed its brief existence anterior to the declaration of independence and was organized under the Mexican federal constitution of 1824- that although its organization was in direct violation of that constitution, and may be considered as partially revolutionary, its assumptions of power were no more obligatory upon the independent government of Texas than they would have been on the federal government of Mexico had that government been restored and Texas returned to her previous attitude. By the very constitution of that government, Texas, as such was incompetent to make treaties. She was but a department of the confederate state of Coahuila and Texas, and in her conjunction state capacity was also precluded for entering into treaties with foreign powers. I suggest this as an ultimate plan of argument to be pursued but not to be resorted to except in case of strict necessity. You are aware that the lines designated in the treaty were run by Col. ALEX HORTON some time in the fall of last year at the instance of Gen. HOUSTON, who was then exercising the functions of this government. This fact too may be adduced against you; but you will find no great difficulty in diverting it of any serious consideration by suggesting that the act of Col. HORTON was without authority, the President having no right to carry a treaty into effect anterior to or independent of the action of the Senate on such treaty. In this instance the assumed right was exercized in direct contradiction to the advice of the Senate and every act so done was an absolute nullity, and could impose no legal or moral obligation on this government. Should the government of the United States decline to render you any satisfactory assurance concerning the future return to our territory of the Cherokees now about to be ejected from it, this government will be compelled to resort to its own energies; and a protracted war may ensue between Texas and the northern Indians within her borders. We should greatly deprecate such an event, for it cannot escape an ordinary discernment that it would be more than likely to enlist a portion of the original tribes from whom these intruding bands have been recently removed to the west of the Mississippi by the government of the United States. It is also more than probable that such a contest would involve the government of the United States in an Indian war of greater magnitude than any they have heretofore sustained.

It is not intended to impute any error to that government in the congregating of so many (sic) tribes of savages on their remote western frontier, for they did so in the exercise of an indubitable right.

But while we fully acknowledge the abstract right, we cannot but perceive and deeply regret that its practical operation has been already eminently injurious to Texas and may possibly inflict still more serious evils upon her. The migration of several

bands of these very tribes, to our territory was a direct and natural consequence of their removal from their ancient habitations and their location in our vicinity by that government. We entertain too profound a confidence in the magnanimity of the government of our father land to believe for a moment that they still omit to give to this fact all the consideration that an enlightened sense of propriety could suggest; or that they fail to find in it, additional reasons for punctual observance of the treaty of 5th of April, 1831, heretofore referred to. No government professing to act on the beneficent principles of Christianity will permit itself to prosecute a course of domestic policy, the evident tendency of which is destructive of the peace and happiness of a neighboring nation. It will either abandon the policy or should its continuance be of paramount importance to its own well being, it will so modify and restrain its pernicious results that the neighbor people may suffer no serious detriment from it. In previous instructions from this department you will find the Coshattees and the Boluxies mentioned in connection with the Cherokees and other northern tribes. These bands have been too long resident in Texas (I believe they migrated from the Creeks during the American revolution) to be included in the list of intruders from the United States. You will not, therefore, press them upon the attention of that government in your future correspondence. The Cherokees, Kickapoos, Delawares, Pottawattamies, Chocktaws, Shawanees, and Caddoes are the bands that have recently entered our territory, and of whom we complain. The Cherokees, Kickapoos and Caddoes are the most numerous and most obnoxious of these, and it is their recall by the United States which we most ardently desire, and to which we are cl rly entitled. * * * The President is quite indisposed, but I trust will be about again in a few days.

> Very Respectfully,
> I have the honor to be
> Your obedient servant,
> David G. Burnet,
> Acting Secretary of State.

THE EXPULSION OF THE CHEROKEES FROM EAST TEXAS

Taken from "The Texas Historical Association Quarterly," Vol. 1, p. 38, by JOHN H. REAGAN: "In the first half of the year, 1839, the Cherokee Indians occupied that part of Texas which is bounded on the east by the Angelina River; on the west by the Neches River; on the south by the old San Antonio road and on the north by the Sabine River. What is now Cherokee and Smith counties covers substantially the same territory. At that time the Shawnee Indians occupied what is now Rusk county, their principal village being near where the town of Henderson is now situated. The Delaware Indians then lived in the eastern part of what is now Henderson county. Less than two years before that time the Kickapoo Indians lived in the northeastern part of what is now Anderson county, and in the hotly contested battle between them and their Mexican allies and the Texans they were defeated and driven from that part of the county. The whites charged the Cherokees with stealing their horses and with an occasional murder of white people. This their Chief BOWLES denied, and alleged that the thefts and murders were committed by wild Indians who came through his country. But in 1838 (1833) the Cherokees murdered the families of the KILLOUGHS and WILHOUSES, several in number, and broke up the settlements of the whites in the vicinity of the Neches Saline, now in the northwest part of Cherokee county. There was no question about the murders being committed by the Cherokees, and that DOG SHOOT, one of their head men, led in this massacre. Complaints of thefts and murders by the Cherokees became numerous, and were so authenticated as to cause the president of the republic, General M. B. LAMAR, to send a communication to Chief BOWLES, through the Indian agent, MARTIN LACY, Esq., making certain recitals evidencing hostility to the white people. Among the facts so recited, as I remember them, one was that in the year 1836, when the people of Texas were retreating from their homes before the advancing army of the Mexican general, Santa Anna, that Chief BOWLES assembled his warriors on the San Antonio road, east of the Neches River, for the purpose of attacking the Texans if they should be defeated by Santa Anna. Another was that in the preceding January, 1839, General BURLISON had captured some Cherokees on the upper Colorado on their return home from the City of Mexico, accompanied by some Mexicans, and bearing a commission to Chief BOWLES as a colonel in the Mexican army and a quantity of powder and lead, and instructions for his co-operation with the Mexican army which was to invade Texas during the then coming spring. And also calling attention to the murders and thefts which had been committed on the people of Texas by the Cherokees; and upon these statements, saying to Chief BOWLES that Texas could not permit such an enemy to live in the heart of the country, and that he must take his tribe to the nation north of Red. River. President LAMAR in that communication said to Chief BOWLES that he had appointed six among the most respectable citizens of the republic and authorized them to value the unmovable property of the Cherokees, which was understood to be their improvements on the land, but not the land, and to pay them for these in money. I knew some of these men at the time as most worthy citizens, one of them, Judge NOBLE, of Nacogdoches county. The president also said to them that they could take all of their movable property with them and go in peace. But go, they must; peaceably if they would, but forcibly if they must.

"It is proper for me to say that I have seen, in the state department, a paper purporting to be a communication from President LAMAR to Chief BOWLES, supposed to be the one announcing his views as to the necessity of the removal of the tribe."

"Dr. W. G. W. JOWERS and myself and one CORDRA, a half-breed, accompanied Mr. LACY, the Indian agent, when he took the president's communication to BOWLES. CORDRA went along as interpreter as BOWLES could not speak English and the agent could not speak the Cherokee language. DR. JOWERS was afterwards a member of the house of representatives and senate of Texas for several terms."

"The paper then read and interpreted to Chief BOWLES contained, in substance, what I have said and is very different from the paper in the office of the secretary of state."

"Indian Agent LACY lived on the San Antonio road about six miles east of the Neches River. Chief BOWLES lived about three miles north of Mr. LACY. When we reached the residence of BOWLES, he invited us to a spring a few rods from his house and, seated on a log, received the communication of the president. After it was read and interpreted he remained silent for a time, and then made a denial of the charges contained in that communication and said the wild Indians had done the killing and stealing, not his people. He then entered into a defense of the title of his tribe to the country which they occupied, as I have described it. He said that after his band separated from the old Cherokee nation, they under him, as their chief, settled at Lost Prairie, north of Red River, now in Arkansas; that after living there for a time they had moved to the three forks of the Trinity River, now Dallas and the surrounding counties; that he had intended to hold that country for his tribe, but the other Indians disputed his right to do so and claimed it as a common hunting ground; that he remained there with his tribe about three years, in a state of continual war with other Indians, until about one-third of his warriors had been killed; that he then moved down near the Spanish Fort of Nacogdoches. (I use his expression) and that the local authorities permitted him to occupy the country which his tribe then occupied; that he then went to the City of Mexico and got the authority of the Mexican government to occupy that country, and that during the revolution of 1835-36 the consultation representing Texas recognized his right to that country by a treaty.

"It is proper here to state that the consultation did appoint General HOUSTON and Colonel FORBES and authorized them to make a treaty with the Cherokees. I am not informed as to the extent of the powers conferred on them for that purpose. A treaty was agreed to between them and the Cherokees and reported to the consultation, which adjourned without ratifying the treaty so made; and it, with its powers, was superceded by the convention which formed the constitution of the republic and that convention also rejected the treaty which had been agreed to by General HOUSTON and Colonel FORBES. That is the treaty to which Chief BOWLES referred. So that the Cherokees had no higher title to the country they then occupied than the privilege of occupancy during the pleasure of the sovereign of the soil."

"After his statement as to the right of his tribe to that country, Chief BOWLES stated to Mr. LACY that he had been in correspondence with John ROSS, the chief of the original tribe of Cherokees, for a long time, looking to an agreement between them to unite the two tribes and go to California and take possession of a country out of reach of the white people. It will be remembered that this was about ten years before the cession of California by Mexico to the United States and when but little was known of that country by our people. He offered to produce and have read to Mr. LACY a bundle of letters on this subject, which he said was as large as his thigh. Mr. LACY waived the necessity of their production, saying that the statement of Chief BOWLES was sufficient on that subject. Chief BOWLES then said he could not make answer to the communication of the president without consulting his chiefs and head men and requested time to convene his council. Thereupon it was agreed between them to have another meeting a week or ten days later (I do not remember the exact length of time) to give time for the council of the Cherokees to meet and act."

"On the day appointed Agent LACY returned to the residence of Chief BOWLES, accompanied by CORDRA, the interpreter, and by Dr. JOWERS and myself. We were again invited to the spring, as upon our first visit. The grave deportment of Chief BOWLES indicated that he felt the seriousness of his position. He told Mr. LACY that there had been a meeting of the chiefs and head men in council; that the young men were for war; that all who were in the council were for war, except himself and BIG MUSH; that his young men believed they could whip the whites; that he knew the whites could ultimately whip them, but that it would cost them ten years of bloody frontier war. He inquired of Mr. LACY if action on the president's demands could not be postponed until his people could make and gather their crops. Mr. LACY informed him that he had no authority or discretion beyond what was said in the communication from the president. The language of Chief BOWLES indicated that he regarded this as settling the question and that war must come. He said to Mr. LACY that he was an old man (being then about eighty-three years of age, but looking vigorous and strong), and that in the course of nature he could not live much longer and that to him it mattered but little. But he added that he felt much solicitude for his wives (he had three) and for his children; that if he fought, the whites would kill him, and if he refused to fight, his own people would kill him. He said he had led his people a long time and that he felt it to be his duty to stand by them, whatever fate might befall him."

"I was strongly impressed by the manly boaring and trunkness and candor of the agent and the chief. Neither could read or write, except Mr. LACY could mechanically sign his name. During their two conferences they exhibited a dignity of bearing which could hardly have been expected by the most enlightened diplomats. There was no attempt to deceive or mislead made by either of them."

"The whites on the one side and the Indians on the other at once commenced preparations for the conflict. Chief BOWLES took his position east of the Neches River, in the northwest corner of what is now Cherokee county, concentrating his warriors and collecting his families there. He was joined by the Shawnees, the Delawares and by warriors from all the wild tribes of Indians, and at that time there were a good many of them.

48

SOME HISTORY OF VAN ZANDT COUNTY

"Colonel RUSK, with a regiment of volunteers, was the first in the field on the part of the Texans. Vice President BURNETT was then acting president of the republic. President LAMAR, with the leave of congress, was temporarily absent from the republic."

"Gen. ALBERT SIDNEY JOHNSTON, the secretary of war, and Adj. GEN. HUGH McLEOD accompanied this regiment. It went into camp about six miles to the east of BOWLES' camp and for ten days or more negotiations were carried on between the belligerents, BOWLES negotiating to gain time to collect warriors from the wild tribes, and Texans negotiating to gain time for the arrival of Colonel BURLISON's regiment of regulars from the west and Colonel LANDRUM's regiment of volunteers from the Redlands. During this time an incident occurred which might have been of a very serious character. A neutral boundary had been agreed on between the belligerents and the men of neither side were to pass it without notice. Acting President BURNETT, the secretary of war, Adjutant General McLEOD, Colonel RUSK and a few others had gone to the camp of the Indians, under a flag of truce, to conduct negotiations, as they had done on previous days. Col. Jim CARTER and a few others, acting as scouts, found John BOWLES, a son of the chief, and a few Indians, who had passed the neutral boundary, and gave chase to them. The Indians escaped and when they reached their camps reported that they had been run in by the Texans. This caused violent excitement among the Indians and the gentlemen named reported that it seemed for a time that they were to be attacked by the Indians, in which event their massacre would have been inevitable. But explanations were made, which allayed the excitement. At the subsequent meetings for negotiations the Texas officials took with them an escort of thirty picked men. An agreement was made that neither party was to break camp or make any move without giving notice to the other party. On the 13th or 14th of July, Colonel BURLISON's regiment of regulars and Colonel LANDRUM's regiment of volunteers reached camp of the Texas forces. And early on the morning of the 15th Chief BOWLES sent his son, JOHN BOWLES, accompanied by FOX FIELDS, under a flag of truce, to notify the Texans that he would break up camp that morning and move to the west of the Neches River. On reaching headquarters, under a flag of truce, they delivered their message to General JOHNSTON and having done so, inquired if they could return in safety. They both spoke English very well. General JOHNSTON told the messenger that his father had acted honorably in giving the notice according to agreement and that he would see that they had safe conduct out of our camp and he detailed a number of men to see them safely a half mile beyond our pickets. He also told them to inform Chief BOWLES that the Texas forces would break camp that morning and pursue them."

"On the assembling of this little army of three regiments the volunteers wanted Colonel RUSK for their commander, while the regulars preferred Colonel BURLISON for that position. These two patriots and heroes of the revolution which made Texas a republic did not desire to antagonize each other and either of them was willing that the other should command. But it was agreed to solve

49

the question by having Gen. KELSEY H. DOUGLASS elected as brigadier general and placed in command. And when the army broke up its camp on the morning of the 16th of July, 1839, to pursue the Indians, Colonel LANDRUM was ordered to move up on the east side of the Neches River, and be in position to intercept the Indians if they should turn northward as it was expected they would. The regiments of Colonel RUSK and Colonel BURLISON moved to the west, passing through the camp which had been occupied by the Indians, and crossing the Neches on their trail. Chief BOWLES had taken position on a creek some six miles west of the Neches with a part of his warriors and had sent the families with the balance of the warriors to a position about six miles north of where he made his stand. His men occupied the bed of the creek, which running from north to south, made a sudden bend to the east, and his position was immediately above the bend."

"After the Texans crossed the Neches scouts were thrown forward with directions if they found the Indians in position to give battle to keep up a desultory firing at long range, without exposing themselves too much, so as to give notice of the position of the Indians.

"As the command advanced and when the firing of the scouts was heard, Colonel RUSK's regiment was ordered to advance on the north side of the creek they were on, and Colonel BURLISON's regiment was ordered to cross the creek and advance on the south side of the creek, so as to put the Indians between these regiments. When the troops reached the bend of the creek, which was to the extreme right of the line occupied by the Indians, RUSK's regiment wheeled to the right and formed in front of the Indians, while BURLISON's regiment turned to the right and passed up into the rear of the Indians. This was an hour or two before sundown. A battle ensued which, however, did not last long. Dr. ROGERS and Colonel CRANE were killed and some six or eight Texans were wounded and it was reported that the Indians left eighteen dead on the field and the remainder of them were routed and joined the others some six miles to the north, near the Neches and just north of the Delaware village."

"The Texans camped for the night near the battlefield and, fearing that the Indians might break up into small bands and attack the more exposed frontier settlements, a number of squads were detached from the command and ordered to proceed to the exposed parts of the frontier to defend the families of the whites."

"On the morning of the 16th of July, the Texans, thus reduced in numbers, took up the line of march in pursuit of the Indians and found them soon after passing the Delaware village, in a very strong position. They occupied a long ravine, deep enough to protect them, with gently sloping open woods in front of them. Our line of battle was formed on a low ridge in front of them and skirmishers were thrown forward, who were at once engaged with the skirmish lines of the Indians. Every sixth man of our command was detailed to hold and guard our horses. This, with the details sent away the night before, had reduced our fighting force and we were confronted by the entire force of the Indians,

outnumbering the Texans who participated in the battle. The
scene at that time made a very vivid impression on my young mind.
The Delaware village, in our immediate rear, was wrapped in
flames and the black columns of smoke were floating over us; the
skirmishers were fighting in front of us and our line of battle
advancing to the conflict. The battle lasted about two hours.
We had six men killed and thirty-six wounded. The Indian loss
was very much greater. Chief BOWLES was a very conspicuous figure. He was mounted on what we call a "paint horse," and had on
him a sword and sash and military hat and silk vest which had
been given him by General HOUSTON. And thus conspicuously mounted and dressed, he rode up and down in the rear of his line, very
much exposed during the entire battle."

"Our officers two or three times ordered the men to advance
nearer the line of the Indians, and then would order them to fall
back, in the hope that in this way the Indians might be drawn
from their strong position. And when this was done the last time
word ran along our lines that the Indians were in our rear getting our horses. This came near producing a panic. Col. LEM
WILLIAMS and BEN A. VANSICKLE, who were with us, and could speak
the Cherokee language, told us that at that time they could hear
BOWLES, who was urging his warriors to charge, telling them that
the whites were whipped if they would charge. When at last the
Indians retreated Chief BOWLES was the last one to attempt to
leave the battlefield. His horse had been wounded many times and
he shot through the thigh. His horse was disabled and could go
no further and he dismounted and started to walk off. He was
shot in the back by HENRY CONNER, afterwards Major CONNER. He
walked forward a little and fell and then rose to a sitting position facing us and immediately in front of the company to which I
belonged. I had witnessed his dignity and manliness in council;
his devotion to his tribe in sustaining their decision for war
against his judgment and his courage in battle, and wishing to
save his life, ran towards him and, as I approached him from one
direction, my captain, ROBERT SMITH, approached him from another
with his pistol drawn. As we got to him, I said: "Captain,
don't shoot him," but as I spoke he fired, shooting the chief in
the head, which caused instant death."

"It ought to be said for Captain SMITH that he had known of
the many murders and thefts by the Indians and possibly did, in
the heat of battle, what, under other circumstances, he would not
have done, for he was esteemed as a most worthy man and citizen.

"The families of the Indians were camped in the Neches bottom, in thick woods. After the battle our command camped at the
edge of the bottom very near the Indians but made no attack on
them. That night we could hear the hum and bustle of their camp
the greater part of the night, and the next morning they were
gone in the direction of the Grand Saline, in what is now Van
Zandt county, and while our troops followed them to the Grand
Saline, they did not overtake them.

"Colonel LANDRUM, it was said, was misled by his guide and
did not reach the balance of the command until after the battles."

SOME HISTORY OF VAN ZANDT COUNTY

"The Indians dispersed, some going to the cross-timbers, some to the north of Red River and some to Mexico. A year or more later, I do not remember the precise date, the wives and some of the children of Chief BOWLES came to the Rio Grande, at Laredo, and asked permission to pass through Texas on their way to the Cherokees north of Red River. President LAMAR granted their request, furnished them an escort, transportation and rations on their way through Texas. I saw them on the San Antonio road east of Neches."

ARBUCKLE TO LAMAR

Headquarters 2d Dept. W. Division,
Fort Gibson, April 28th, 1840

To His Excellecy
    Mirabeau B. Lamar,
       President of Texas,
         City of Austin.
    Sir:--I was requested by a Cherokee Council assembled at this Post of late, to assure you of their desire that the whole of their people now in Texas should immediately return to their nation and thereafter remain in their own country. I have no doubt the Cherokee people are sincere in the wish they have expressed on this subject; and as many of their people that formerly lived in Texas have returned of late, they hope that the time is not distant when their wishes will be fully accomplished. Under such circumstances they hope your government will not desire to detain any of their people in Texas.

With respect to the wishes of the Cherokee nation in relation to some of their people now in Texas, I regard it proper to assure you, that if such of them as may be prisoners, are conveyed out of Texas in the direction of Fort Towson, that the commanding officer of that post will be instructed to issue such quantity of provisions to them as may be necessary to enable them to return to their nation.

I have the honor to be, sir, with great respect,

Your obedient servant,
M. Arbuckle,
?trevet. Brigr. Gen. U. S. A.

THE LAND SHARKS WIN

After the Cherokees had been driven out of east Texas, the fight opened up for the valuable lands formerly occupied by them. The reason for their expulsion became apparent in the contest among the pale-faced contestants in a mad scramble of possessing the territory from which they were dispossessed was fierce to the echo.

In Sayles' "Real Estate Laws of Texas" will be found the following reference to the Cherokee Indians, under Article 454:

Art. 454. Sale of the Cherokee Reservation.--The territory
between the Angelina and Sabine Rivers and north of a designated
line, was reserved from location by a treaty between the provisional government of Texas and the Cherokee Indians, made on the
23d of February, 1836.

By act of congress of February 1, 1840, provision was made
for sectionizing and selling these lands, excepting such as were
held under legal titles dated prior to March 1, 1822. (The time
the Indians located upon them and, as best they knew how, applied
for a title thereto.) The act of July 23, 1842, authorized the
president to cause four hundred thousand acres of the Cherokee
lands to be surveyed and sold. The acts of February 1, 1840, and
July 23, 1842, were repealed by act of January 27, 1844, and all
legal titles within the territory designated by treaty were vali-
dated, and the vacant lands became subject to location.

So it became apparent that the land sharks triumphed and the
land was "located" all right.

Judge REAGAN gives the number of commissioners appointed by
President LAMAR as six, and mentions Judge NOBLE, of Nacogdoches
as one of them. JOHN HENRY BROWN gives the number as four, and
names the following as those appointed for that purpose: Vice
President DAVID G. BURNETT, Gen. ALBERT SIDNEY JOHNSTON, Secretary of War HUGH McLEOD, Adjutant, and General THOMAS J. RUSK.

It is highly probable that each was mistaken as to the number and that five were appointed and the names above covered the
number of all men commissioned for that purpose.

Of the commissioners appointed, the following were wounded
in the two engagements: Vice President BURNETT, General JOHNSTON
and Adjutant General McLEOD and Maj. DAVID S. KAUFMAN, of the
militia, for whom Kaufman county was named, was shot in the face.
(He was the first congressman elected from the east Texas district.) Capt. S. W. JORDAN, of the regulars, was severly wounded. It is not known how many of these were wounded in Van Zandt
county, but Judge REAGAN reports that Dr. ROGERS and Colonel
CRANE were killed in the first engagement, which was on Kicapoo
Creek in Henderson county, about where the Cotton Belt railroad
crosses that stream, and some six or eight wounded. And in the
second engagement, which was at the Delaware village in Van Zandt
county, on Battle Creek, near the Neches River, six were killed
and thirty-six wounded. So it is safe to conclude that nearly
all of the commissioners were wounded in Van Zandt county. Mr.
BROWN says that these battles took place in Cherokee county and
Judge REAGAN says that they were fought in Henderson county; but
I am sure that my statements above are correct. Judge REAGAN
places the dates as July 15 and 16, 1839; Mr. BROWN fixes the
dates as July 16 and 17, 1839.

THE WEST BOUNDARY LINE OF THE CHEROKEE NATION RUN

It may be of interest to many now living in Van Zandt county,
and those to come after them, why a line was run from the head of

the Neches River to the head of the Sabine River across that portion of Van Zandt county and was called the "Old Cherokee Boundary Line." This line denotes the southwest boundary of the Cherokee Nation and the northwest boundary of Nacogdoches county,
then the eastern boundary of Texas. The following excerpts from
the surveyor's record and that of his deputy who run the line,
will fully explain why the line was run.

WARREN ANGUS FERRIS, deputy surveyor of Nacogdoches county,
Texas, began his survey of the Cherokee line about five miles
northwest of the Cherokee battlefield between the Texas army and
Cherokee Indians, with these notations, viz:

Republic of Texas, County of Nacogdoches:
    Field notes of the west boundary line of the Cherokee re-
serve as run by W. A. FERRIS, in January, 1841. Commencing at
the junction of Raccoon and Owl creeks, which point we designate
the head or source of the River Neches; corner post. (Situated
in the forks a few feet from the point where the waters mingle.)
He then gives bearings and other denotations. Then N. 45° West *
74323 6-10 varas to the Sabine River. He then well defines his
stopping point, which is in Hunt county.

W. A. FERRIS, Deputy Surveyor.
JOHN CAMPBELL, Chain Carrier.
WM. AIKEN, Chain Carrier.

Republic of Texas, County of Nacogdoches:
    I certify that the foregoing survey was made by my order to
enable me to make the county map of this county and that W. A.
FERRIS, a lawful deputy surveyor of this county, has made oath
before me that the plat and field notes are a correct representation and description of the survey made by him.

A. A. NELSON, County Surveyor,
Nacogdoches County.

WILLIAM ANGUS FERRIS

The subject of this sketch was born at Glens Falls, New
York, December 26, 1810. About the beginning of the War of 1812,
his parents moved to Erie, Pennsylvania, where his father, ANGUS
FERRIS, became one of the earliest owners of vessels on the Great
Lakes and was engaged in furnishing supplies to the American army.
The father died at Erie, September 10, 1813, the day of Perry's
victory at Put-in-Bay; and in 1814, the widow and her two child-
ren removed to Buffalo, New York.

NOTE.--This survey was made two years after the Cherokees had
been dispossessed of their holdings in east Texas. In length,
the line is about one-third of the line as run between the United
States and the Repbulic of Texas one year earlier, as the west
boundary of the Louisiana purchase.

Young FERRIS received a good education for that day and became a civil engineer. He was evidently of an adventurous turn
of mind, for the reason that he joined the American Fur company,
and with a company of thirty men from St. Louis, on February 16,
1830. And in an article published in a New York paper, January
6, 1844, under the heading, "Life in the Rocky Mountains--A Diary
of the Wanderings on the Sources of the Rivers Missouri, Columbia
and Colorado, from February, 1830, to November, 1835, by W. A.
FERRIS, Then in the Employ of the American Fur Company," is given
what is supposed to be the first authentic published account of
Yellowstone Park and its great geyser. The title of the diary
very accurately describes the region in which the fur companies
operated. His description of the scenery, the Indian fights,
trapper's life, with its lights and shades, and his observations
of various sorts are all vivid and well told.

FERRIS had heard, in 1833, of the boiling springs; so he
determined on seeing them for himself. So he prevailed upon two
Pend d'Oreille Indians to accompany him on his venture. Leaving
his companions after supper, May 18, 1834, from a camp, he says
about due west from the Tetons, they traveled twenty miles and
spent the night at a spring flowing into Cammas Creek. On the
19th they proceeded and entered a very extensive forest called
the Piny Woods, . . . which we passed through and reached the
vicinity of the springs about dark. Having seen several lakes or
ponds on the source of the Madison and having ridden about forty
miles, a hard day's ride, he said "they drank some coffee and lay
down to sleep. The continued roaring of the springs, however,
for some time prevented my going to sleep" and when he did slum-
ber he dreamed of "water spouts, cataracts, fountains, jets d'eau
of emmense dimensions, etc." When he arose in the morning, the
20th of May, 1834, clouds of vapor seeming like a dense fog over-
hung the spring, "from which frequent reports of different loud-
ness constantly assailed our ears. I immediately proceeded to
inspect them and might have exclaimed with the Queen of Sheba,
when their full reality of dimensions and novelty burst upon my
view, 'the half has not been told me.'" FERRIS then goes on to
describe the geysers as they appear today. He gives at length as
good a description of the surrounding country of Yellowstone National Park as a landscape painter places before one, minus the
government improvements.

FERRIS remained at the hot springs but one forenoon of May
20, 1834; recrossed the piny woods, camped on the plains at
HENRY's Fork and rejoined his comrades the day following. The
first we hear of him in Texas was on Monday, October 3, 1836, at
Columbia, to which place the government had previously gone from
Velasco. Both houses of congress were on that day organized
there. In the house of representatives, IRA INGRAM, of Mattagor-
da, was elected speaker and W. A. FERRIS, clerk. The next we
hear of Mr. FERRIS, he is county surveyor of Nacogdoches county
for two years; then we come to the point connecting him with the
Cherokee country. FIELD notes of the west boundary of the Cherokee reserve, as run by W. A. FERRIS, in January, 1841. His

beginning point was on the head of the Neches River in Van Zandt county, of which he says: "Commencing at the junction of Raccoon and Owl Creeks which point we designate the head source of the river Nechez, . . . Thence N. 45° W. 74323 6-10 varas, the Sabine River; established corner. JOHN CAMPBELL and WM. AKIN, chain carriers. W. A. FERRIS, deputy surveyor."

"I, W. A. FERRIS, do certify under oath of my office, that the foregoing survey is correct and the limits and boundaries and corners with the marks, natural and artificial, are truly described in the foregoing plat and fieldnotes and that the survey was made in January, 1841. W. A. FERRIS, deputy county surveyor."

Mr. FERRIS was married and brought up a family. He moved from Nacogdoches to Dallas county, in 1849, the year Van Zandt county was created, and established a home near Reinhardt. He did not serve in the army during the Civil war, because of his advanced age. He died at his home six miles northeast of Dallas, Texas, February 8, 1873, nearly sixty-three years of age.

PRESIDENT DAVID G. BURNETT

DAVID G. BURNETT was born in Newark, New Jersey, April 4, 1788. In 1806, when but eighteen, he was a lieutenant under Gen. FRANCISCO MIRANDA, fighting for the liberation of Venezuela. In 1826 he became a permanent citizen of Texas. In 1833, he wrote the memorial to Mexico adopted by the convention of that year. In 1834, he became district judge of the department of the Brazos, and was the only judge who ever held court in Texas before the revolution. From March 18 to October 23, 1836, he was the first president of the Republic of Texas. From December, 1838, to December, 1841, he was vice president and during the latter year he acted as president. After the battle of San Jacinto President BURNETT made several treaties with General SANTA ANNA. In 1839 he was appointed by President LAMAR as one of the commissioners to negotiate a treaty with the Cherokee Indians, by which they were to cede their rights to the territory they occupied, to the Republic of Texas, and abandon the country. The treaty failed of its object, but brought on a two days' fight, August 16-17, in which Vice President BURNETT was wounded, but not dangerously.

President BURNETT died in Galveston December 5, 1870, aged eighty-two years and eight months.

There is a county and county seat in Texas that will perpetuate the name of President DAVID G. BURNETT for all coming time.

On March 2, 1894, a monumanet was unveiled in Lake View Cemetery, Galveston, to DAVID G. BURNETT, President of the Republic of Texas, and General SIDNEY SHERMAN, Commander of Cavalry at the Battle of San Jacinto. SIDNEY SHERMAN Chapter, Daughters of the Republic of Texas, carrying out one of the objects of their organization, erected this monument to honor the memories of this eminent statesman and this gallant soldier. This monument bears this inscription:

FIRST PRESIDENT OF THE REPUBLIC OF TEXAS
Born April 4, 1799,   Died December 5, 1870.

SOME HISTORY OF VAN ZANDT COUNTY

GENERAL ALBERT SIDNEY JOHNSTON

ALBERT SIDNEY JOHNSTON was born in Mason county, Kentucky, February 3, 1803. He was a student at Transylvania University. He graduated at West Point in June, 1826; was assigned as second lieutenant of the Second infantry; transferred to the Sixth infantry in 1827. He was regimental adjutant from 1828 to 1832 and participated throughout the Black Hawk war as chief of staff to General ATKINSON; resigned from the army in 1834 and engaged in farming until May, 1836, when he came to Texas and enlisted as a private in the army of the republic. General RUSK appointed him adjutant general of the army of Texas. Later he was chosen senior brigadier general and chief commander of the army, in place of Gen. FELIX HOUSTON, then in command of the forces and his disappointed competitor for the place. This engendered bitter feeling between the two and a duel therefrom followed, in which General JOHNSTON was wounded.

                    War Department, Columbia, February 7, 1837
Dr. Ewing, Surgeon General:
    Sir: I am requested to instruct you to repair forthwith to the headquarters of the army, there to consult with the faculty on the case of Gen. A. SIDNEY JOHNSTON, who has been badly wounded by a pistol shot. You will report while at the army the names of all surgeons employed there; also a minute account of the situation of the medical department, so that all deficiencies may be remedied.

                              WILLIAM S. FISHER,
                              Secretary of War.

In 1839, General JOHNSTON was appointed by President LAMAR as one of the commissioners to treat with the Cherokee Indians in east Texas, to induce them to cede their lands, so long occupied by them, to the republic of Texas, and vacate the country. President LAMAR's instructions were to offer to pay the Indians for their improvements, and if the Indians refused, to use military force to remove them. No satisfactory arrangements could be made with the Indians and the conference ended and two pitched battles were the outcome. General JOHNSTON was wounded, though not seriously.
    The first fight was on Kicapoo Creek in Henderson county and the last on Battle Creek, in Van Zandt county, at the Delaware village.
    When President POLK forced war on Mexico, in 1846, General JOHNSTON joined the First Texas Rifles and was assigned to duty under Gen. ZACHARIAH TAYLOR. At the storming of Monterey, General JOHNSTON had three horses shot from under him.
    After he received his discharge from the army, he returned to his plantation in Brazoria county, Texas, where he remained with his family until 1849, when, without his knowledge, he was, by President TAYLOR, appointed paymaster in the United States army, with rank of major. This position he accepted with head-

quarters at Austin, Texas.

And now, pardon me, while I digress by telling a story that will put to shame the tommyrot which is being delivered to the people by the good Samaritans to the effect that the "world is growing better day by day." Once each quarter, General JOHNSTON would leave Austin to pay off the soldiers at the following army posts: First, old Fort Groggan, about the present location of Burnett; then to Camp Colorado, on Jim Ned Creed, in Coleman county; then to Fort Phantom Hill, in the northern part of Jones county; then to Camp Cooper, up on the clear fork of the Brazos; then to Fort Belknap, in Young county; then to Fort Worth; then to Fort Graham, on the Brazos and by Belton on to Austin. And here is the outfit that he took with him on thses trips, which were several hundred miles in length, with not more than a dozen ranches all told between all these army posts visited by him. The general had a four-horse hack to which four mules were hitched and the same was driven by a young German, who was also a good penman and helped to make out the payrolls and check the accounts as the general paid off the officers and men at the various army posts; then a negro cook who rode horseback and Capt. W. J. MALTBY, who was detailed to drive a four-mule team that drew a heavy army wagon, in which was loaded at Austin, gold and silver enough to pay off the officers and men at all the posts along the route; also feed and provision for the consumption of men and mules of the outfit, including camp equipage, etc.

Now, remember this was then the "wild and wooly Texas" you have heard about. During Captain MALTBY's long service with General JOHNSTON, he said that they never stopped overnight at an army post but one night. The general would stop before reaching a post and count out money enough to pay off all demands at that post; when this was done he would drive out and camp in the open country. Now on these rounds hundreds of thousands of dollars were paid out and not a dollar was lost nor one of the four disturbed in any way.

To make these rounds today you would seldom be out of sight of a house, and not long out of sight of a church; but who would make the trip with more than pocket change?

In 1855, President FRANKLIN PIERCE appointed him colonel of the Second cavalry, a new regiment which was assembled at Camp Colorado, in Coleman county, Texas, with orders to march to Salt Lake, Utah, to put down an insurrection by Mormons, who were defying the laws of the United States. His march was overland, via El Paso, and the service assigned him was satisfactorily performed. He was breveted a brigadier general in 1860 and sent to California to take command of the department of the Pacific.

While believing that the South had a grievance, he was a Union man in sentiment and did not believe in secession as a proper remedy for the wrongs. However, when Texas, seceded, he left his post, resigned his commission in the United States army and tendered his services to the confederate government. He was commissioned a full brigadier general and placed in command of all the troops west of the Atlantic states and north of the Gulf

58

states. In this capacity he served with marked distinction, until April 6, 1862, when he fell, mortally wounded, on the battlefield of Shiloh and was carried to the home of Mrs. AUGUSTA EVANS INGE, where he died. In the hour of his death, General JOHNSTON's thoughts were of Texas, the state of his adoption, and he requested that the soil of Texas should cover his body. His remains were started to this state for burial, but owing to the capture of New Orleans, were stopped at that place and there interred.

The eleventh legislature of Texas, in 1866, passed a resolution providing for the removal of General JOHNSTON's remains from New Orleans to the state cemetery, at Austin; and the following year, the people of the Crescent City relinquished their claim on the ashes of the dead hero, exacting the promise that a suitable monument would be erected by the state of Texas to his memory.

Years ago the people of New Orleans reared a splended equestrian statue to the memory of General JOHNSTON. The state of Texas has fully complied with its promise to New Orleans. The twenty-seventh Texas legislature, in 1901, appropriated ten thousand dollars for the erection of a monument to Gen. ALBERT SIDNEY JOHNSTON, the same to be placed in the state cemetery at Austin where his remains repose. This has been done by placing the recumbent statue executed by the Texas sculptress, ELIZABETH NEY, over his last resting place in the state cemetery. The confederate monument erected at the National cemetery, at Shiloh, contains a life-size bust of General JOHNSTON.

ALBERT SIDNEY JOHNSTON had granted to him in the southeast corner of Van Zandt county, 1,280 acres of land. This is east of the two battlefields with the Cherokees, which are eight miles apart, but nearly equally distant to either.

GENERAL HUGH M'LEOD

HUGH McLEOD was born in Virginia; educated at West Point; went to Georgia and joined a battalion which was being collected to come to Texas to assist in the revolution; was elected lieutenant under Capt. WILLIAM WARD.

Miss JOANNA TROUTMAN, of Knoxville, Georgia, was energetic in urging young men to join this collection of troops to assist Texas patriots, and made for them a silk flag with a lone star on either side of it with five points in azure, with the inscription on one side of it, "Liberty or Death," and on the other side, "Ub libertas habitat, ibi nostra patrest," where liberty dwells, there is my country.

This flag was presented to the battalion through Lieutenant McLEOD. It was carried through various vicissitudes until it reached Goliad, the scene of some of the bitterest fighting in that fierce conflict. Here the flag was inadvertently lost. It became, however, the basis from which the flag of Texas was adopted, the original flag by Miss TROUTMAN being only slightly altered.

HUGH McLEOD, then adjutant general of the Republic of Texas, was, in 1839, appointed one of the commissioners by President

LAMAR, to negotiate a treaty with the Cherokee Indians in east Texas to remove them beyond the confines of Texas, peaceably if they would, but forcibly if they refused the president's offer. This resulted in a two days' fight, August 16-17, 1839, in which Adjutant General McLEOD was wounded, but not seriously.

HUGH McLEOD was a congressman under the Republic of Texas and a member of the legislature after annexation. He received a land grant of 1,476 acres in Van Zandt county, on Kicapoo Creek about five miles from the first battlefield with the Cherokees, which was on Kicapoo Creek in Henderson county; the last was on Battle Creek in Van Zandt county.

Gen. HUGH McLEOD was sent as one of the commissioners to treat with the Comanche Indians, at San Antonio, on the 19th of March, 1840. The council met in a house in which a battle ensued, in which the whites lost seven killed and eight wounded. The Indians lost thirty chiefs and warriors, also three women and children, in all thirty-five. All this was done in ten minutes and is known as the "Council House Fight."

General McLEOD and General HOUSTON were not friends, and because President LAMAR was his friend, he suffered untold deaths by being appointed brigadier general to command the ill-fated Santa Fe expedition, that left Brushy Creek above Austin, June 21, 1841.

When the confederate government was established at Richmond HUGH McLEOD left Texas and died a full brigadier general in Virginia. As he had expressed a desire to be buried in Texas, he was brought to Texas and found his last resting place in the State cemetery.

Miss JOANNA TROUTMAN died in Georgia, but the Texas legislature made ample provisions therefor and her remains were brought to Texas and were interred in the state cemetery.

GENERAL THOMAS JEFFERSON RUSK

Was born in Penalton District, South Carolina, December 5, 1803. His father was a native of Ireland and pursued the occupation of stonemason; for some time he resided upon land belonging to JOHN C. CALHOUN, and on that farm T. J. RUSK was born and the first money earned on his own account was so done in the office of district clerk, a situation secured for him by J. C. CALHOUN. This enabled him to earn a living and at the same time he prepared himself for the law by studying in Mr. CALHOUN's office.

After being admitted to the bar and securing license to practice law, he removed to Clarksville, Georgia, and soon became proficient in the practice of his chosen profession. He married a daughter of General CLEVELAND, of Georgia. Just when General RUSK's profession became remunerative, he fell a victim to stock gamblers and suffered a heavy loss. This caused him to remove to Nacogdoches (Mexico), about 1834. There he met Gen. SAM HOUSTON and they became friends and so remained until General RUSK's death.

The revolution of Texas soon budded forth and found General

RUSK a colonel at the siege of San Antonio and later a member of the convention that declared the independence of Texas from allegiance to Mexico. In the formation of the government of the Republic of Texas, he was chosen secretary of war and established his headquarters with the army of the new republic. He took part in the battle of San Jacinto and when General HOUSTON was disabled by a wound he called on General RUSK to take command of the army, which General RUSK did and held that position for several months. Among General SANTA ANNA's captured belongings was a magnificent silver service, which General RUSK sent to Miss JOANNA TROUTMAN, of Knoxville, Georgia, as a token of appreciation of her patriotism in aiding the Georgia battalion, while it was recruiting for Texas and presenting the same with a falg which it carried to Texas.

After the retreat of the Mexicans General RUSK pursued them to Goliad, where he collected the remains of FANNIN's men and had them buried.

In the fall of 1836 General RUSK was appointed to a seat in the cabinet of President HOUSTON, but soon resigned to attend to his private affairs. In 1837 he was elected to a seat in the second congress of the Republic of Texas.

In 1838, General RUSK, at the head of a considerable force which had been collected at old Fort Houston, four miles west of the present city of Palestine, he marched on the Kicapoo Indian village at Mound Prairie in the northwest portion of Anderson county; October 16th he attacked the Indians and killed eleven warriors and wounded many others. Of RUSK's troops eleven were wounded, but none killed. While this game was being played there was an insurrection of Mexicans round about Nacogdoches. Over one hundred Mexicans took up arms and occupied a position on the Angelina River, but General RUSK soon routed them and they dispersed.

In the summer of 1839 General RUSK was appointed by President LAMAR to meet and treat with the Cherokee Indians for their peaceful removal from the lands they had occupied for many years. This resulted in a two days' fight, in which General RUSK commanded a division of Texas troops. The Indians were driven out of east Texas.

At the meeting of the congress of the republic, February, 1839, General RUSK was elected chief justice of the republic, which he filled for one year and resigned. In 1843 General RUSK was appointed Brigadier General of Militia, which office he held for one year. When Texas was admitted as a state to the Union General RUSK was elected to the convention that framed the first constitution of the new state.

The war with the United States and Mexico coming on, President POLK offered General RUSK a commission as general in the federal army, to command the Texas troops in that war, but General RUSK declined that offer. The first legislature of Texas elected him United States senator, which position he held until his death, which, unfortunately, was brought about by his own hands at Nacogdoches, in July 1857. He raised a family of five children, four boys and one girl. General RUSK owned several thousand acres of land in Van Zandt county, of which he donated six hundred and forty acres to the Nacogdoches University.

The county of Rusk, in Texas, and the city of Rusk, in Cherokee county were so named in honor of Gen. THOMAS J. RUSK.

The twenty-second legislature of Texas appropriated one thousand dollars for the erection of a tomb over the grave of Gen. THOMAS J. RUSK, investing the mayor and aldermen of Nacogdoches with full power to design and superintend its erection. It bears this inscription:

> Erected by The State of Texas to the Memory of
> General THOMAS J. RUSK, who fought for her liberty at San Jacinto. Born in South Carolina,
> December 5, 1808; died at Nacogdoches, Texas,
> July 29, 1857. He lived for Texas.

The monument was unveiled September 27, 1894. A most excellent eulogy was delivered at the unveiling of this monumant in Nacogdoches, by the late Judge PEYTON F. EDWARDS, of El Paso, who was born and raised in Nacogdoches. Ex-Governor HUBBARD also delivered one of his masterly eulogies on that occasion. Col. JESSE W. SPARKS, then of Tennessee, though born and raised in Nacogdoches, delivered an excellent address on that occasion.

JOHN H. REAGAN

JOHN H. REAGAN was born in Sevier county, Tennessee, October 3, 1818. He was educated in Maryville College, Tennessee. In the early part of 1838, he removed to the Republic of Texas. In 1839, he went with Indian Agent MARTIN LACY, to deliver Presidnet LAMAR's ultimatium to Chief BOWLES, of the Cherokees, and later went a second time to receive Chief BOWLES' reply to President LAMAR. He joined Capt. ROBERT SMITH's company and was in the two battles with the Cherokees; the first in Henderson county and the last in Van Zandt county. For bravery in these battles, Gen. ALBERT DISNEY JOHNSTON, then secretary of war of the republic, offered Judge REAGAN a commission as lieutenant in the regular army, which he declined. From 1838 to 1843 he was surveyor of lands and made many surveys of original grants in Van Zandt county. He settled about where the town of Kemp, in Kaufman county, is now situated and located his headright there. For four years following the admission of Texas into the Union he was in the lower house of the Texas legislature. During this time Henderson, Kaufman, Van Zandt and Wood counties were created. He was admitted to the bar in 1846; elected district judge in 1852, and was the third judge to hold court in Van Zandt county. Judge ROBERTS held the first term of court in Canton and Judge REAGAN the later. These courts were held in a log cabin on the west side of the public square, where Nolen Brothers' drug store now stands. Judge REAGAN continued to be judge of this district until 1857. The democratic convention for the eastern congressional district met at Tyler, on May 13, 1857. Judge REAGAN was holding court at Kaufman at the time he was nominated for congress and resigned his office as judge and entered upon the canvass. Those were stiring times, politically speaking. LEMUEL DALE EVANS was Judge REAGAN's opponent. They met in joint discussion at Jefferson and some "hot stuff" was passed back and forth, and for a time they faced each other with six-shooters in hand, but all was quieted down. Judge REAGAN was elected to congress of which body he remained a member until 1861, when he was chosen a member of the Texas secession convention; later he was elected a member of the provisional congress of the confederacy. In March, 1861, JEFFERSON DAVIS called him to a cabinet position in the confederate states government, he being tendered the portfolio of postmaster general, which he accepted. During the last days of the confederate government, he was also secretary of the treasury; May 10, 1865, he was made a prisoner along with JEFFERSON DAVIS and Governor LUBBOCK of Texas. October following he was released and returned to his home at Fort Houston, near Palestine. He soon resumed the practice of law and in 1874 was again elected to the United States congress, continuing there until chosen United States senator in 1887. He resigned that position in 1891 to become chairman of the Texas railroad commission. Because of infirmities, he retired from that position and wrote his reminiscences at his old home, near Palestine, Texas.

Judge REAGAN has a county in Texas named for him; a small town in Falls county also bears his name.

PRESIDENT LAMAR'S INDIAN POLICY ATTACKED.

(Extract from a speech made by Senator SAM HOUSTON, in the United States Senate, January 29-31, 1855.)

"I can exemplify, to some extent, an impression that I have when I contrast war measures with peace measures. I well remember in 1835, 1836, 1837 and 1838, in Texas, we had peace. The Comanches would come down to the very seaboard in amity and friendship, would repose confidentially in our dwellings, would receive some trifling presents and would return home exulting, unless they were maltreated, or their chiefs received indignities. If they did receive such, they were sure to revisit that section of the country as soon as they went home and fall upon the innocent. For the years I have mentioned, in Texas we had perfect peace, and, amrk you, it did not cost the government over $10,000 a year. We had no standing army. A new administration came in and the legislature immediately appropriated $1,500,000 for the creation of two regular regiments. Those regiments were raised. What was the consequence? The policy had changed in the inauguration of the president. He announced the extermination of the Indians. He marshaled his forces. He made incursions on a friendly tribe who lived in sight of our settlements where the arts of peace were cultivated and pursued by them--by agriculture and other arts, and by exchange and traffic of such productions

63

of the soil as were convenient. They lived by traffic with Nacogdoches. The declaration was made, and it was announced by the
cabinet that they would kill off 'Houston's pet Indians.' Well,
sir, they killed a very few of them, and my honorable colleague
(Senator T. J. RUSK) knows very well, if it had not been for the
volunteers they would have licked the regular army--and the Indians said: 'I was not there.' The Cherokees had ever been
friendly and when Texas was in consternation, and the men and
women were fugitives from the myrmidons of SANTA ANNA, who were
sweeping over Texas like a simoon, they had aided our people,
and given them succor--and this was the recompense. They were
driven from their homes and were left desolate. They were driven
up among the Comanches. What was the consequence? Every Indian
on our borders from the Red river to the Rio Grande took the
alarm. They learned that extermination was the cry, and hence it
was that the flood of invasion came upon our frontiers and dren-
ched them with blood.

"The policy of extermination was pursued and a massacre of
sixteen chiefs at San Antonia, who came in amity for a treaty,
took place. That was in 1840. Before this army was raised they
had been in the habit of coming down for purposes of peace and
commerce. But an army of Indians marched through the settlements
to the seaboard, one hundred or one hundred and fifty miles, un-
detected, I grant you, avoiding the dense settlements, went to
Linville upon the tidewater, rifled the stores and slaughtered
the men. If there were any, the women were treated with cruelty
and their children's brains were dashed out against the walls of
their peaceful habitations. The exterminating policy brought it
on. The country became involved in millions of debt, and the In-
deans were kept in constant irritation. That was in 1840 and it
was not until the year 1843 that intercourse could be had with
them through the pipe of peace, the wampum and the evidence of
friendship."

The San Antonio road mentioned so frequently above in 1788
was a pack mule trail from the Mission Adaes on Red River to San
Antonio, the Rio Grande river, Saltillo, San Luis Potose, Quere-
taro and the City of Mexico.

CHAPTER 4

Indian Reservations in Texas; Camp Cooper, U. S. Army Post, At-
    tacked by 1,000 Frontiersmen Under General JOHN R. BAYLOR;
    Biographical Sketches; Lone Wolf and Quanah Parker Have
    Fight in Lost Valley, Jack County, Texas, with Major JOHN B.
    JONES Commanding Texas Rangers; Parker's Massacre, in 1836;
    Governor HOUSTON's Message to Texas Legislatures; Biographi-
    cal Sketch of Governor ROSS; Capture of BYNTHIA ANN PARKER.

INDIAN RESERVATIONS

The religious sect, known as Quakers, prevailed upon the
United States government to adopt an Indian policy, something on
the order of the Francisco Friars, and then civilize the noble
red men. To this end, the government secured from Texas, twelve
leagues of land upon which to quarter the Indians in Texas. Of
these, eight leagues were located on the Brazos river below the
junction of the Clear Fork, about fifteen miles below Fort Belknap; this reservation was known as the Brazos Agency and about
eleven hundred were assigned to it, consisting of Caddoes, Anna-
darkos, Tehaucanas and Tonakawas. S. P. ROSS was placed in
charge as agent. These Indians were styled as friendly Indians.
This agency was nominally under the post commander of Fort Belknap, but a general agent for all of the tribes on reservations
in Texas was established, as we will see later on. All Indians
on reservations were allowed a supply of ponies.

CAMP COOPER

The other four leagues were located on the clear fork of the
Brazos, about 45 miles above its confluence with the Brazos
River. This was given the name of Camp Cooper. At this agency a
great deal of land was plowed and work seemed to be progressing
smoothly enough, when the government, for reasons best known to
itself, left the place without having placed a single Indian upon
it. However, the government later on, again took charge of Camp
Cooper, and placed upon it the Southern Comanche or Penetca In-
deans. It would have been impossible for the government to have
selected a tribe that would have been more complete failures in
the agricultural business, or a greater success at downright dev-
iltry. Like many of those that would quit the missions in the
early settlement of Texas, these Comanches would quit the reservation when so they willed and go as far south as the Rio Grande;
robbing, plundering, stealing and murdering, to their hearts con-
tent, and then return to the reservation for a rest and enjoy the
hospitality of Uncle Sam. Those who suffered from these raids
would complain, and plead with the government for better protection. So things drifted along until some who suffered so much at
the hands of the Comanches, decided to avenge some of these atrocities, and they kept up vigil until they thought they had located the rendevous for Indian raiders.
    Camp Cooper was raised to the dignity of a military post,
and one company of infantry was stationed there. Col. M. LEEPER

was in charge of the post. Major R. S. NEIGHBORS was the agent of the United States government for the Indians on the Texas reservations. In about 1858, a report showed that on the Texas reservations there were two hundred and fifty Tonkaways, one hundred and seventy-one Wacoes, two hundred and four Tehaucanas, three hundred and eighty Comanches, two hundred and thirty-five Anadarkos and two hundred and forty-nine Caddoes, making a total of fourteen hundred and eighty-nine.

There were very few newspapers in Texas at that time and none of them located along the frontier border, so that news did not fly as is the case today, but mutterings of Washington's Quaker Indian policy was wafted all along the line, and especially were old Texans being aroused against the Indian reservations.

A small settlement was made near the mouth of Buford's Creek, probably in the northeastern part of what is now Shackleford county. In 1857 or 1858, the Comanche Indians killed a young man of this settlement by the name of JOSEPH BROWNING. Soon after the crime was committed, the young man's body was found and the alarm was sounded throughout the little settlement, and a party composed of JOHN B. and GEORGE B. TYLER, ELIAS HALE, NUNN WRIGHT and JOHN DAWSON, started in pursuit of the Indians and overtook them on California Creek, in Haskell county. These were experienced frontiersmen and they were all good shots and knew how to take all advantages of a small marauding party of Indians, and they completely wiped the whole bunch of them off of mother earth. Being satisfied that they were at or near a place that the Indians were to meet some of their allies, they secreted themselves and their horses and awaited further developments; they did not have to wait long, for they reckoned aright; about half a dozen more Comanche warriors hove in sight, and before they had seen the dead bodies of their departed friends, the command, "Fire," was given and the squad of Comanches cashed in their chips and passed out of mortal existence. This was successfully repeated several times during the day, but as the evening shades lengthened, a large detachment of Comanche warriors were seen coming at a lively speed, and the frontiersmen beat a hasty retreat leaving the field satisfied; without the loss of a man on their side.

Expostulations, complaints and petitions, rolled into the government against the "Quaker Policy" being enacted by the United States government, regarding the Texas frontier. All to no visible effect, so far as the people discerned, and so they determined to take measures in their own hands; to this end one thousand hardy frontiermen, organized under the leadership of Gen. JOHN R. BAYLOR, all well mounted and armed for that day, and marched on Cooper reservation, determined to kill every Buck Indian on the four leagues. When near the reservation, they prepared and made a determined charge, killing some of the Indians, but the United States regulars had received a tip, and were ready to receive their visitors, and a round of musket balls from them caused the frontiersmen to draw off for consultation, or something better, leaving some of their best men dead on the reservation.

SOME HISTORY OF VAN ZANDT COUNTY

The petitions and pleadings of the frontiersmen may have never reached Washington, but the official report of this battle was not long in reaching the secretary of war, and an investigation soon followed, and after its report reached Washington, orders were sent to Major GEORGE H. THOMAS, then post commander at old Fort Phanton Hill, Texas, to remove all the Indians, on both reservations in Texas, to Fort Cobb, Indian Territory; this he did in August, 1859. The governor of Texas gave orders to the state rangers to follow the movement with flanking parties until the Indians were safely across Red River.

GENERAL GEORGE H. THOMAS, U. S. A.

GEORGE H. THOMAS was born in Virginia in 1816. From a boy, he determined to be a soldier; accordingly he embraced the first opportunity to enter West Point, which presented itself in 1836. He was a close student and graduated twelfth in a class of forty-two members. Among his class was General SHERMAN and General GETTY, on the Union side and B. R. JOHNSON and R. H. EWELL, on the confederate side. His first army service was in the Seminole Indian war, in the everglades of Florida, as lieutenant of artillery. For meritorious services in that campaign, he was advanced one grade by the war department at Washington. From Florida he was sent from place to place until the war with Mexico broke out in 1846, when he was ordered to report to General TAYLOR for active service. For gallant conduct at Monterey, he was again advanced a grade, this time to captain. At Buena Vista, it was THOMAS who carried out TAYLOR's famous order to give the enemy, "a little more grape, Captain BRAGG," and the way he did it, sent him up to the rank of major.

While filling the post of teacher at West Point, he met and married Miss FRANCES L. KELLOG, who survived him many years.

In 1855, THOMAS was connected with that splendid Second regiment of cavalry in Texas, whose officers were Col. ALBERT SIDNEY JOHNSTON, Col. ROBERT E. LEE, Assoc. Maj. WILLIAM J. HARDEE, at old Fort Phantom Hill, in Jones county, Texas, which THOMAS established and named, notwithstanding all the conflicting accounts about it, together with spooks, legendry and midsummer tales, it was opened in midwinter and General THOMAS lost some men by freezing before they reached "Phantom Hill."

When he received orders to remove the Indians from the reservations in Texas to Fort Cobb, Indian territory, near Fort Sill, he left Phantom Hill on that mission; and the governor of Texas ordered the Texas troops to follow in his wake and see that no redskins were left south of Red River. But General THOMAS did his "job" so well, that the state troops were left with empty honors in that drive.

Of all the officers that was associated with the noted Second cavalry regiment, at that time in Texas, General THOMAS is the only one that remained with the Union army during the Civil war. His complete and admirable victory at Mill Spring, was the first triumph of any note for the Union army during that contest.

He was with General ROSECRANS at Murfreesboro, and won renown in that victory. It was THOMAS at Chickamauga that held his position that resulted in the Southern army falling back into Georgia; it was THOMAS' army division, under General SHERMAN that opened the Atlanta campaign at Buzzards Roost and closed the contest at Lovejoy's. When General SHERMAN telegraphed President LINCOLN, "Atlanta is ours and fairly won."

Gen. GEORGE H. THOMAS hurried Gen. JOHN B. HOOD out of Tennessee, when HOOD's whole command forded Duck river and there after stayed out of Tennessee.

When the Civil war closed, it found Gen. THOMAS in declining health, and at his request he was sent to California to command the military division of the Pacific, with headquarters at San Francisco. General THOMAS was an absolutely honest man. After the close of the Civil war, his admirers at Cincinnati offered him a house and lot in that city and he declined it with dignity, modesty and unostentatiousness. "The government," he said, "has always paid me amply, and all my wants are provided for. To accept such a present would not be consistent with my sense of duty."

On hearing he was soon to depart for the West, his friends and some of the officers that had served under him, proffered him a table service of silver. He replied: "I am greatly touched by this evidence of your regard, but I cannot accept it. In my judgment it would be injurious to the discipline of the army for officers to receive gifts from those who are or have been their subordinates."

On the 28th day of March, 1870, he was stricken with apoplexy, from which he died in a few hours. At the request of his wife, he was buried at Troy, New York, in the family lot. He left no children. A bronze equestrian statue was erected to his memory in Washington, D. C.

This ended the federal reservations in Texas and carried the Indians farther from the Texas frontier, but did not stop depredations on the border, as will be noted by a long extract from Governor HOUSTON's message, which will follow later on.

This message was sent to the legislature just as the Civil war had begun its unhappy forebodings and its horrors were being enacted, which will be passed over and a couple of incidents given to show that the return of peace between the states did not bring peace to our frontier. On the 18th of May, 1871, the Comanches and Kiowas, a hundred strong, from Fort Sill Indian reservation, invaded the settlements in Jack county and attacked a train of government wagons hauling provisions for the regular army at Fort Griffin, Texas. Ten teamsters were in charge, of whom seven were killed, the other making their escape. The wagons were plundered, the mules packed from the stores and the wagons burned. A few days later, General SHERMAN was at Fort Sill, where the Indians were flaunting the scalps of the dead teamsters and boasting of their atrocities. He summoned the three chiefs who headed the warriors on this raid, Satanta, Satank, and Big Tree, before him. They avowed the massacre of the

68

teamsters.

A long diplomatic correspondence between the governor of Texas and the state department at Washington, followed, finally resulting in the release of the barbarians.

On the 12th of July, 1874, an engagement took place at Lost Valley, in Jack county, between a hundred Kiowas and Comanches, under chiefs LONE WOLF and QUANAH PARKER and Maj. JOHN B. JONES, of the Texas rangers. The Indians, when first encountered, were in two parties, but maneuvered and by strategy on their part, got together and formed a line of battle, which Maj. JONES broke by a gallant charge on his part, killing two of them. The Indians then fled to a rocky hill nearby, using the rocks as hiding places, they made a defiant stand. After a siege lasting most of the day, in which most of the rangers horses were killed and two of the rangers, the Indians made good their escape.

THE PARKER FAMILY

The mention of QUANAH PARKER, Chief of the Comanches, in the battle of Lost Valley, brings up the bloodiest and most inhumane page in Texas history.

The PARKERS were a large and well-respected family in Texas, many of whom I knew and some of whom were my clients.

In 1835, a few settlers built what afterwards become the famous Fort Houston, in the wilds of the municipality of Nacogdoches, now in Anderson county, about two miles west of Palestine. About the same time, or perhaps a little earlier, the PARKER family settled on the west side of the Navasot, a beautiful creek of clear running water, not far from the present town of Groesbeck, in Limestone county. When I first saw the place, before many improvements had been made in that locality, it looked like a veritable "Paradise."

I cannot recall from whence this family moved to Texas, although it was a habit among early settlers to inquire from whence they came and promise not tell others about it. The PARKERS, as was the custom among early settlers, built a kind of stockade for protection against predatory bands of Indians and Mexicans. Inside of this they erected small log huts for the several families composing those who migrated thither together, and several others were added to the original families, so that there were in all, some eight or ten families of them when the contest came up for the mastery over Texas between the Americans living in Texas and Santa Anna, the usurper of Mexico. After the battle of San Jacinto had been fought and won, such of those of PARKER's Fort as could do so, who were engaged in that important and patriotic movement, hurried home to plant their crops. Farming at that time was not on an extensive score, not so much of trying to raise something for the market as to raise supplies for home necessities.

On the 19th of May, 1836, a band of Comanches and Kiowas, composed of several hundred, among them a large number of warriors, appeared before Parker's Fort, making signs of peace and friendship they asked for a parley. This was in the forenoon and most of the men connected with the fort were at work on their farms, a mile or so from the stockade, but one of their number went out to consult with the Indians as to their wishes and soon returned to the fort, saying that he believed they were on the warpath and advised all in the fort to prepare for any emergency, while he went out to parley and delay matters so long as he could. When he went back to the Indians they promptly killed him and raising the warwhoop, they furiously attacked the fort, killing all the men at the fort and some of the women and children, carrying into captivity, Mrs. RACHEL PLUMMER and her two-year-old son; Mrs. ELIZABETH KELLOGG, CYNTHIA ANN PARKER, nine years old and her brother, JOHN W. PARKER, six years old, children of SILAS M. PARKER. Of those that were not in the fort or escaped, mention has been made of one Mr. LUNN, DAVID FULKENBERRY, and so on; SILAS BATES, ADRIAN ANGLIN and perhaps others. It was said that after several days wnaderings those who escaped death reached Fort Houston in a most regretable condition. Of those who were carried into captivity, Mrs. RACHEL PLUMMER miraculously lived to dictate the horrors through which she went. After leaving the fort, the Comanches and Kiowas traveled together until midnight; they then camped; brought their prisoners together, threw them upon the ground, tied their hands behind them so tightly as to cut the flesh; tied their feet together and placed their faces on the ground; then gathered around with the bloody scalps and commenced their wardance. They danced, screamed, yelled and stamped upon the prisoners, beating them with bows until the blood flowed from the bruises; the rest of the night the women had to listen to the cries and groans of their little children. When the tribes parted, each of the several bands took a captive. Mrs. KELLOGG was sold by her captors to the Keechies, from whom, six months after her capture, she was purchased by the Delawares, who in turn delivered her to Gen. SAM HOUSTON, receiving for her one hundred and fifty dollars, being what they had paid for her. Mrs. PLUMMER and her children were separated and she was treated with great cruelty, and about six months later gave birth to a second child, a son, which the Comanches cruelly murdered in a most inhuman manner before her eyes. She was held as a slave, until ransomed by some Mexican Santa Fe traders on the Pacific slope and returned home by way of Independence, Missouri, where the branch of the PARKER family lived, who were my clients for years. Mrs. PLUMMER's boy was ransomed at Fort Gibson, in 1842, by his grandfather. JOHN W. PARKER was taken by a branch of the Comanches into Old Mexico and married a bright Senorita and lived the life of a barbarian, never knowing what civilization was.

It is remarkable that Anglo-Saxon children carried into captivity and permitted to grow up in a savage state, without being allowed to converse with their own kindred, will in form and feature personate, to a large degree, those by whose presence they are surrounded, and after they have reached the age of maturity, they want to live the life in which their early life has been spent.

SOME HISTORY OF VAN ZANDT COUNTY

PART OF A MESSAGE TO THE LEGISLATURE OF TEXAS---EXTRA SESSION

(By Governor Sam Houston)

Executive Department, Austin, January 21, 1861

Gentlemen of the Senate and House of Representatives:

You have been concened in extra session, in view of the unsettled condition of our national affairs; the continued invasion of our frontier by Indians, and the embarrassed condition of the treasury.

To these subjects alone your attention will be invited, and it is hoped that only those which are incident to these will meet your attention.

The defense of the state being a paramount object, the executive will first press the necessity of providing for the same upon your consideration.

When the executive came into office the frontier was entirely unguarded, except by federal troops. The Indians, unrestrained by presence of rangers, embraced the favorable opportunity and gained a foot-hold in the country and ere their presence was known and means could be adopted to repel them, commenced a series of depredations, which stuck terror to the settlements. Their savage work was not confined to the frontier alone, but extended to counties within fifty miles of the capitol. Although not apprised of this state of things, the executive had made such provision for defense of the frontier as seemed necessary.

On the 26th of December, a few days after his inauguration, an order was issued to Capt. W. C. DALRYMPLE, of Williamson county, to raise a company of sixty men, rank and file. This was followed by orders of this character of Capt. ED. BURLISON, of Hays, and Capt. JOHN H. CONNER, of Travis, on the 4th and 13th of January. These companies were ordered to such points as would enable them to carry out orders given them, to give the greatest amount of protection to the frontier inhabitants. Had not the frontier been entirely abandoned to the Indians for months previous to his inauguration, these companies would have sufficed to prevent any concentrated and extensive movements against the settlements on the part of the Indians, but they were already secreted in the country. Intelligence having already reached the executive that numerous small parties of Indians were ravaging the settlements beyond Bell county, but not yet on the extreme frontier, orders were issued on the 13th of February to Lieutenant WHITE, of Bell county; SALMON, of Bosque, and WALKER, of Erath county, to raise, each, a detachment of twenty-five men, to range in and give defense to the counties of Coryell, Hamilton, Comanche, Eastland and Palo Pinto. These detachments were soon in the field, with orders to exercise energy to give the frontier protection and security.

Authentic accounts of depredations still coming in, the executive, on the 21st day of February, sent to the various frontier counties a letter, authorizing the citizens of each county to raise a minute company of not more than twenty men, who should look to the next legislature for payment, and to more effectually insure the presence of these minute companies in the field, a general order was issued on the 9th of March, by which the chief justice of each county was instructed to organize, immediately, a company of fifteen men, to whom the following orders were given: "The detachments will immediately take the field, and enter upon active service, affording protection to the inhabitants of their respective counties. When an Indian trail is found, it must be diligently followed, and if signs indicate a larger party of Indians than he is able to cope with, he will call not exceeding ten men to his aid." The lieutenant commanding each detachment or minute company was authorized to purchase necessary supplies, and where it was possible to do so, they were sent forward by the executive. Under these orders minute companies of fifteen men each were mustered into service in each of the following counties: Lieutenant SCANLAN, Montague; Lieutenant ISBELL, Wise; Lieutenant COCHRAN, Young; Lieutenant JONES, Palo Pinto; Lieutenant STEVENS, Eastland; Lieutenant LOWE, Erath, Lieutenant PRICE, Comanche; Lieutenant NELSON, Bosque; Lieutenant GENTRY, Hamilton; Lieutenant FONT le ROY, Coryell; Lieutenant COWAN, Llano; Lieutenant WOOD, San Saba; Lieutenant HUGHS, Mason; Lieutenant O'HAIR, Burnett; Lieutenant FRAZIER, Gillespie; Lieutenant BALENTYNE, Bandera; Lieutenant McFADDEN, Kerr; Lieutenant KENNEDY, Hood; Lieutenant PATTON, Blanco; Lieutenant BROWN, Bexar; Lieutenant WATKINS, Medina; Lieutenant RAGSDALE, Frio.

In addition to putting this force of minute men in the field the executive, in order to enable the frontier citizens to more succe-sfully defend themselves, purchased and distributed through the frontier counties, Colt's revolvers, which with a number of rifles and muskets, were sent forward. Ammunition was also supplied to minute companies.

To provide for the defense of the settlements beyond San Antonio, an order was issued on the 5th of March, to Capt. PETER TOMLINSON, of Atascosa county, to raise forty-eight men, to whom were assigned the range between the Frio and the Rio Grande. Captain TOMLINSON was mustered into service on the 20th of March. It will thus be seen that up to this period the executive had called into service a ranging force of seven hundred and twenty men, which might be increased in an emergency to nine hundred and fifty. The greater part of this force was then in active service and as a result, the Indians disappeared from the settlements. The monthly reports of the officers commanding the minute men, now on file in the executive office, attest this fact. The minute companies of fifteen men were kept in service until the 18th of May, when, there being no longer a pressing necessity for their presence in the field, they were disbanded, subject to be called out at any moment by order of the chief justice of their county. Before, however, these forces could be brought to bear on the settlements many murders had been committed and a large number of horses stolen. With this view of avenging these outrages and the recovery of the property of our citizens, the

executive determined to send against the Indians a force sufficient to discover their hiding places and accomplish these objects.

It had long been the opinion of the executive that the horses stolen from us were herded at some central point between our
settlements and the trading posts where they were sold, and from
this point stealing parties would strike out for our settlements,
leaving others in charge of the animals already taken. To punish
these Indians, as well as to ferret out the parties who purchased
our horses from them, required an able force and was work requir-
ing much time and privation. The duty of raising these troops
for this expedition was assigned to Col. M. T. JOHNSON, of Tarrant county, to whom was issued orders on the 17th of March to
raise a sufficient number of mounted rangers to repel, pursue and
punish the Indians then ravaging the north and northwestern settlements of Texas, with "full liberty to dispose of the force under your (his) command at your (his) discretion." In pursuance
of this order Colonel JOHNSON raised five companies of eighty-
three men, commanded by Captains SMITH, of McLennan; DARNELL, of
Dallas; WOODS, of Fannin; FITZHUGH, of Collin, and JOHNSON, of
Tarrant. These companies rendezvoused at Fort Belknap, where
they were joined by two companies under command of Captains ED.
BURLISON and W. C. DALRYMPLE, and on the 23d of May the expedition started for the Indian country. The several reports of Colonel JOHNSON, from old Fort Radsminke, the 30th of July. The
others penetrated the Indian's country beyond this line of Kansas,
and after enduring many privations, returned to Fort Belknap,
where they were disbanded by order of the executive.

Although no Indian depredations were at that time reported,
the executive, to guard against their repetition, ordered Capt.
L. S. ROSS, of McLennan, on the 11th of September, to raise a
company of seventy men and take his station beyond Fort Belknap,
where he arrived on the 17th of October. On the 6th of December
information reached the executive of the most appalling outrages
committed by Indians in Jack and Parker counties. Orders were
immediately sent forward to Capts. THOS. STOCTON, of Young, and
JAMES BARRY, of Bosque county, to raise, each, twenty-four men,
and proceed to co-operate with Captain ROSS, in protecting the
settlements. These troops did not then enter service, but on the
17th day of December an order was issued to A. B. BURLISON to
raise seventy men, which was followed by orders to Capt. E. W.
ROGERS, of Ellis, on the 26th of December and to THOMAS HARRISON,
of McLennan, on the 2d of January to raise, each, seventy men,
all of whom had now gone forward to Fort Belknap, where Col. W.
C. DALYRYMPLE, of Williamson county, acting under commission as
aide-de-camp to the executive, had been ordered to repair to effect an organization of troops and with means for their efficien-
cy.

It affords the executive pleasure to state that the Indians
who committed the late depredations in Jack and Parker counties
have been overtaken and killed by a force under command of Captain ROSS, whose report will be submitted.

SOME HISTORY OF VAN ZANDT COUNTY

The above from Governor SAN HOUSTON's message is given at length to show the alarming condition of our frontier, January, 1861.

Because the writer has been unable to secure Captain (afterwards governor), ROSS' official report of the capture of CYNTHIA ANN PARKER, he will give an account by VICTOR M. ROSS, as published in the first edition of a paper edited by him, at Myrtle Springs, Van Zandt county, about 1890.

GOVERNOR LAURENCE S. ROSS

Was born in Davenport, Iowa, September 27, 1838. While yet an infant in his mother's arms the family moved to the frontier post at Waco, in the new Republic of Texas. He attended Baylor University and in 1859, graduated from Wesleyan University at Florence, Alabama. During the summer of 1858 he, with a small command, had a battle with the Comanche Indians on the head of the False Wichata, in which ninety-five Indians were killed, three hundred and fifty horses captured and a small white girl picked up and no trace of who she was could be found, so Governor ROSS adopted her into his own family and raised her up to womanhood's estate, when she married. In that action Governor ROSS was seriously wounded.

When he returned to Texas, after graduation in 1859, Governor HOUSTON put him in command of a small force up in the Pan-Handle of Texas; the story of that campaign has been fully recounted above. In 1861, he entered the confederate army, joining his brother's company as a private. He was soon made a major of the regiment, then lieutenant colonel and six months later, colonel. In 1862 he was made a brigadier general. He participated in one hundred and thirty-five engagements, of more or less importance. After the war he was a planter in the Brazos bottom. In 1875 he was a member of the constitutional convention, and in 1881 was chosen state senator; in 1886 he was elected governor of Texas, and re-elected in 1888. In 1891 he was made president of the A. & M. College, at College Station, Texas, which position he held until his death, January 3, 1898. He was buried at Waco.

ROMANCE OF HISTORY--RECLAMATIONS OF WHITE CAPTIVES

(Dictated by Governor Ross.)

"In 1858 Major VAN DORN, with the Second cavalry, United States troops, one company of infantry to guard his depot supplies, and 135 Indians under my command, made a successful campaign against the Comanches, and by a series of well directed blows restrained their ravages upon the people for a long time. But in 1859-60 the condition of the frontier was again truly deplorable. The people were obliged to stand in a posture of defense and were continually in alarm and hazard of their lives,-- never daring to stir abroad unarmed; for small bodies of savages, quick-sighted and accustomed to perpetual watchfulness, hovered

on the outskirts and springing from behind bush or rock surprised
his enemy before he was aware of danger, and sent the tidings of
his presence in the fatal blow; and after the execution of the
bloody work, by superior knowledge of the country and rapid movements, safely retired with the bloody scalps to their inaccess-
ible deserts. While under these distresses and discouragements
the brave frontiersmen resolutely held their ground. Their loud
complaints induced the state government to organize and sent out
a regiment under Col. M. T. JOHNSTON, to take the field for public service, but these efforts proved of small service. The expedition, though at great expense to the state, failed to find an
Indian, until, returning, the command was followed by the wily
Comanches, their horses stampeded at night and most of the men
were compelled to reach the settlements on foot, under great suffering and exposure."

It will be seen by Governor HOUSTON's statement above that
most of the troops ordered to concentrate at Fort Belknap, in
Young county, did not comply with their orders and report to Captain ROSS, for duty. However, Captain ROSS determined on a vigorous campaign into the Indian country, and so he says:

As I could take but forty of my men from my post, I requested Capt. N. G. EVANS, in command of the United States troops, at
Camp Cooper, to send me a detachment of the Second cavalry. We
had been intimately connected on the VAN DORN campaign, during
which I was the recipient of much kindness from Captain EVANS
while I was suffering from a severe wound received from an Indian
in the battle of the "Wishata." He promptly sent me a sergeant
and twenty men. My force was further augmented by some seventy
volunteer citizens under command of the brave frontiersman, Capt.
JACK CURETON, of Bosque county. These self-sacrificing patriots,
without hope of pay or reward, left their defenseless homes and
families to avenge the sufferings of the frontier people. With
pack-mules laden down with necessary supplies the expedition
marched for the Indian country.

On the 18th of December, 1860, while marching up Pease River
I had some suspicion that Indians were in the vicinity, by reason
of the buffalo that came running in great numbers from the north
towards us; and while my command moved in the low ground, I visited all neighboring high points to make discoveries. On one of
these small sandhills I found fresh pony tracks, and being satisfied that Indian videtts had just gone, I galloped forward about
a mile to a higher point, and riding to the top, to my inexpress-
ible surprise found myself within 200 yards of a Comanche village,
located on a little stream winding around the base of the hill.
It was a most happy circumstance that a piercing north wind was
blowing, bearing with it clouds of sand, and my presence was un-
observed and the surprise complete. By signalling my men as I
stood concealed, they reached me without being discovered by the
Indians, who were busy packing up preparatory to a move. By this
time the Indians had mounted and moved off north across the level
plain. My command with the detachment of the Second cavalry had
outmarched and become separated from the citizens' command, which

left me but sixty men. In making disposition for attack, the
sergeant and his twenty men were sent at a gallop behind a chain
of sand hills, to compass them in and cut off their retreat,
while with forty men I charged them. The attack was so sudden
that a considerable number were killed before they could prepare
for defense. They fled precipitately right into the presence of
the sergeant and his men; here they met a warm reception, and
finding themselves completely compassed every one fled his own
way and was hotly pursued and hard pressed. The chief of the
party, PETA-NOCONA, a noted warrior of great repute, with a young
girl about fifteen years of age mounted on his horse behind him,
and CYNTHIA ANN PARKER, with a girl child about two years of age
in her arms and mounted on a fleet pony fled together, while
Lieut. TOM KELLIHER and I pursued them. After running about one
mile, KELLIHER ran up by the side of CYNTHIA's horse, and was in
the act of shooting when she held up her child and stopped. I
kept on after the chief and about a half mile further, when within about twenty yards of him, I fired my pistol striking the girl
(whom I supposed to be a man, as she rode as one and only her
head was visible above the buffalo robe that covered her body)
near the heart, killing her instantly, and the same ball would
have killed both but for the shield of the chief, which hung down
covering his back. When the girl fell from the horse she pulled
him off also, but he caught upon his feet, and before steadying
himself my horse, running at full speed was very near on top of
him, and was struck with an arrow which set him to pitching or
bucking and I with great difficulty kept my saddle; and in the
meantime narrowly escaped several arrows coming in quick succes-
sion from his bow. Being at such disadvantage, he would have
killed me in a few moments, but for a random shot form my pistol,
made while I was clinging with my left hadn to the pommell of my
saddle, and which broke his right arm at elbow, completely dis-
abling him. My horse then became quiet and I shot the chief
twice through the body, whereupon he deliberately walked to a
small tree, the only one in sight, and leaning against it, began
to sing a wild, weird song. At this time my Mexican servant, who
had once been a captive with the Comanches and spoke their language as fluently as his mother tongue, came up in company with
two of my men. I then summoned the chief to surrender; but he
promptly treated every overture with contempt, and signalized
this declaration with a savage attempt to thrust me with a lance
which he held in his left hand. I could only look upon him with
pity and admiration; for as deplorable as was his situation, with
no chance of escape, his party utterly destroyed, his wife and
child captured in his sight, he was undaunted by the fate which
awaited him. As he seemed to prefer death to life, I directed
the Mexican to end his misery by a charge of buckshot from the
gun which he carried. Taking up his accoutrements, which I subsequently sent Governor HOUSTON to be deposited in the archives
at Austin, we rode back to CYNTHIA ANN PARKER and KELLIHER, and
found him bitterly cursing himself for having run his pet horse
so hard after an "old squaw." She was very dirty, both in her

scanty garments and person; but as soon as I looked on her face I said: "Why, Tom, this is a white woman. Indians don't have blue eyes."

On the way to the village, where men were assembling with the spoils and large callado of Indian ponies, I discovered an Indian boy about nine years of age secreted in the grass. Expecting to be killed, he began crying, but I made him mount behind me and carried him along; and when in after years I frequently proposed to send him to his people, he steadily refused to go, and died in McLennan county only a few years ago.

After camping for the night, CYNTHIA kept crying, and thinking it was from her fear of death, I had the Mexican tell her that we recognized her as one of our own people and would not harm her. She said two of her boys were with her when the fight began, and she was distressed by the fear that they had been killed. It so happened, however, they escaped--one of them, Quanah, is now a chief; the other died some years ago on the plains. I then asked her to give me the history of her life with the Indians, and the circumstances of her capture, which was done in a very sensible manner; and as the facts detailed corresponded with the massacre at PARKER's fort I was impressed with the belief that she was CYNTHIA ANN PARKER. Returning to my camp, I sent her and child to the ladies at Camp Cooper, where she might receive the attention her situation demanded; and at the same time dispatch a messenger to Colonel PARKER, her uncle at Weatherford; and as I was called to Waco to meet Gov. SAM HOUSTON, I left directions for the Mexicans to accompany Colonel PARKER to Cooper in the capacity of interpreter. When he reached there her identity was soon disclosed to Colonel PARKER's entire satisfaction and great happiness.

The following truly affecting circumstances attending the early captivity of CYNTHIA ANN, was related to my father by Col. LEW WILLIAMS, an old and honored Texan.

In 1840 Colonel WILLIAMS, MR. SLOATE, a trader, and JACK HARRY, a Delaware Indian, packed mules with goods and engaged in an expedition of private traffic with the Indians. On the Canadian river they fell in with the Pi-han-ka band of Comanches, with whom they were peaceably conversant; and with these Indians was CYNTHIA ANN PARKER, who from the day of her capture had never seen a white person. She was then about fourteen years of age and had been a captive nearly five years. Colonel WILLIAMS found the Indian into whose family she had been adopted and proposed to redeem her; but the Comanche told him all the goods they had would not ransom her, and at the same time the fierceness of his countenance impressed upon Colonel WILLIAMS' mind a lively idea of the danger of further mention of the matter; but old Pi-han-ka prevailed upon the Indian to let them see her. She came and sat down by the root of a tree, and while their presence was doubtless a happy event to the poor stricken captive, who in her doleful captivity had endured everything but death, she refused to speak a word. While she sat there musing, perhaps of the distant kindred and friends, and the bereavement at the beginning and progress of her distress, they employed every persuasive art to evoke some expression. They told her of her playmates and relatives and asked what message she would send these loved ones. But she had doubtless been commanded to silence, and, with no hope or prospect of return, she was afraid to appear sad and dejected, and by stoical effort, in order to prevent future bad treatment, put the best face possible on the matter. But the anxiety of her mind was betrayed by the perceptible tremor of the mouth, showing that she was not insensible to the common feelings of humanity.

BENJAMIN F. PARKER, of Elkhart, Anderson county, was a primitive Baptist preacher; and many were the meetings of that faith and order that he attended in Van Zandt county. These meetings were invariably for two days dur tion. "Uncle Ben," as he was familiarly known, never tired of telling about how things were "fore-ordained and predestined before the foundation of the world." He was honest to the manner born.

His last visit to Van Zandt county, as I remember it, was after the death of JAMES DOUTHIT, a veteran of the battle of San Jacinto, whose headright of one league and labor of land, because of his services in the army of the republic, was laid adjacent to Canton; and "Uncle Ben" was appointed by the district court of Anderson county to block up said grant, as per orders of the court. He brought with him his ancient compass and spent several days in surveying, and telling of early days in Texas.

Parker county was created by an act of Texas legislature, approved December 12, 1855. The law referred to, donate three hundred and twenty acres in the center of the county for the "County Town." In the spring of 1856, ISAAC O. HEDLEY, assisted by DAVID O. NORTON, laid out the town of Weatherford. (DAVID O. NORTON was living in Van Zandt county when it was organized.) In the legislature in 1855, was ISAAC PARKER, then a representative from Tarrant county, which embraced the territory of what became Parker county. JEFFERSON WEATHERFORD, of Dallas, was the member of the senate. Both gentlemen were active in the legislation from which the county of Parker and the town of Weatherford originated and from PARKER's family and WEATHERFORD derived their names.

To ISAAC PARKER, Captain ROSS directed that CYNTHIA ANN PARKER be delivered, and sent his Mexican servant along with her as interpreter. Soon after he received her from Camp Cooper, he went to Austin as a member of the secession convention; and it was said that CYNTHIA ANN, in care of some of the Austin ladies, was for a time an onlooker of that august body. ADRIAN ANGLIN, who was at or near the Parkers fort massacre, grew up and became one of the noted Methodist preachers of his day. His headright league on which he settled was in Henderson county, just southeast of where CYNTHIA ANN PARKER lived in Van Zandt county.

SILAS M. PARKER

In the early fifties, the subject of this narration, a brother of BENJAMIN F. PARKER and father of CYNTHIA ANN PARKER, bought out a pre-emption claim of three hundred and nineteen acres of land on the south line of Van Zandt county from JAMES REID, be tween Kicapoo and Slater's creek, and settled thereon. In those days, so long as land was not patented, it was not subject to taxation. Most members of the legislature owned considerable land and they shaped legislation accordingly. So the records of Van Zandt county show that pre-emption, Patent No. 365, of Vol. 15, issued to SILAS M. PARKER, assignee of JAMES REID, in Henderson and Van Zandt counties, about 12½ miles N. 35° E. from Athens, April 17, 1857; Abstract No. 720, signed by E. M. PEASE, Governor and S. CROSBY, Commissioner of the Gen'l Land Office.

Not long after CYNTHIA ANN returned to civilization, her father brought her to his home in this county and she remained under his roof until the death angel called her hence. This, however, was in Anderson County, Texas, to which SILAS M. PARKER had moved and her death occurred in 1864. During her residence in Van Zandt county she was closely guarded, for the reason she never ceased to mourn the loss of her two children from whom she was separated in the battle of Pease River; and she long cherished the hope that time and tide would once more reunite them. Her daughter, PRAIRIE FLOWER, preceded her in death; and so life's charms to CYNTHIA ANN, seemed to have flown to some distant clime. However, during her stay in this county, in common with nearly all women of the day, she learned to card and spin, and was delighted to see a new web of cloth taken from the loom that PRAIRIE FLOWER might have a new garment. Most people that knew her here have passed over the river, but several yet remain with us.

REMEMBERED BY CONGRESS

Forty-five years after her death, the congress of the United States, by the act of March 5, 1909, (35 Stats, page 802), contains the following item of appropriation:

For a monument to CYNTHIA ANN PARKER, mother of QUANAH PARKER, chief of the Comanches, one thousand dollars, to be expended under such regulations as the secretary of the interior may prescribe.

The act of June 25, 1910, (36 Stats, page 797), authorizes an expenditure for removing the remains of CYNTHIA ANN PARKER and her daughter from Texas to Oklahoma, as follows:

The secretary of the interior is authorized to use out of t the sum of $1,000 appropriated in the act approved March 3, 1909, for a monument to CYNTHIA ANN PARKER, not exceeding two hundred dollars for necessary expenses of removing from Texas and re-interring in Oklahoma, the bodies of the said CYNTHIA ANN PARKER and her daughter, PRAIRIE FLOWER.

After this appropriation was made available for that purpose, the remains of CYNTHIA ANN PARKER and her daughter, PRAIRIE FLOW-ER, were disinterred from their place of repose in Anderson county, Texas, and re-interred in the burying ground of QUANAH PARKER, at or near Cache, Oklahoma.

QUANAH PARKER

Was a son of CYNTHIA ANN PARKER, having been born in a large rendezvous camp on Elk Creek, Indian territory, which is now Oklahoma. QUANAH's father, NO-KO-NIC, was a chief and daring leader of one of the fierce tribes of Comanche Indians. He oft-times headed a band of warriors, who ravaged the frontier of Texas and Mexico. As has been detailed, his mother was led into captivity, at Parker's Fort massacre, in Texas, in 1836. When grown, she became the second wife of NO-KO-NIC, and to their union three children were born, two boys and a girl, of which QUANAH was the youngest. The war parties of Comanches, with which QUANAH was always prominent, had for a number of years been routed, pressed and pursued by the Texas rangers and United States troops until about 1874, when largely through QUANAH's influence, they realized that it was useless to longer fight the white soldiers. They came into Fort Sill and surrendered to General McKIENZIE, of the United States army. After this QUANAH learned that his mother was a white woman. Through the advice of the commander of the post at Sill, he was moved to insert an advertisement in a Fort Worth paper, asking for a picture of his mother. This was sent him by Governor ROSS, of Texas, who led the charge that resulted in his father's death and the capture of his mother. From this picture he had a large oil painting made, which graced his home until his death at Cache, Oklahoma.

QUANAH did not inherit his right as a ruler among the Comanches, and because of his selection as chief of Comanches, he had many a tilt with other tribes which opposed elevating a "half-breed" to so high position.

By invitation, QUANAH visited Wills Point and appeared before an audience of several hundred people, but it is not known that he was appraised that his mother once made her home in Van Zandt county.

He spoke English broken; could neither read nor write; he was the father of fifteen children; with the exception of two oldest, they received a liberal education and all seemed reticent in manners. He was the proud husband of seven wives. Only three of them were his acknowledged helpmates at the time of his death. He, his wives and children, at the time of his death, owned 3,000 acres of land, 200 head of cattle and 25 horses. He lived in a modern eight-room house, which was well furnished, including late musical instruments, on which some of his children were noted performers.

Some incidents in the life of QUANAH PARKER are worth relating. Once upon a time the great chief of the Comanches paid Fort Worth a visit in company with Yellow Bear, another chief of some renown, and the Fort Worth Gazette had this to say of their guests:

SOME HISTORY OF VAN ZANDT COUNTY

A sensation was created on the streets yesterday, by the news of a tragedy from asphyriation, at the Pickwick Hotel, of which two noted Indians, QUANAH PARKER and YELLOW BEAR, were the victims.

The circumstances of the unfortunate affair were very difficult to obtain because of the inability of the only two men who were possessed of definite information on the subject to reveal it; one on account of death and the other from unconsciousness. The Indians arrived here yesterday from the territory on the Fort Worth and Denver incoming train. They registered at the Pickwick, and were assigned an apartment together in the second story of the building. Very little is known of their subsequent movements, but from the best evidence that can be collected, it appears that YELLOW BEAR retired alone, about 10 o'clock, and in his utter ignorance of modern appliances, he blew out the gas. PARKER, it is believed, did not seek his room until 2 or 3 o'clock in the morning, when not detecting from some cause the presence of gas in the atmosphere, or not locating its origin in the room, he shut the door and scrambled into bed, unmindful of the deadly forces which were then operating so disastrously. The failure of the two Indians to appear at breadfast or dinner, caused the hotel clerk to send a man around to wake them. He found the door locked and was unable to get a response form the inmates.

The room was then forcibly entered, and as the door swung back the rush of the deathly perfume through the sperture told the story; a ghastly spectacle met the eyes of the hotel employes. By the beside, in a crouched position, with his face pressed to the floor, was YELLOW BEAR, in a half nude condition,--Indian fashion night clothes. In the opposite corner, near the window, which was closed, PARKER was stretched at full length upon his back. YELLOW BEAR was stone dead, while the quick gasps of his companion indicated that he was in but a stone's throw of eternity. The chief was removed to the bed, and through the untiring efforts of Drs. BEALL and MOORE, his life has been saved. Finding QUANAH sufficiently able to converse, the reporter of the Gazette questioned him as to the cause of the unhappy occurrence, and elicited the following facts: "I came," said the chief, "into my room about midnight and found YELLOW BEAR in bed; I lit the gas myself; smelt no gas when I came into the room; when I went to bed I turned the gas off; I did not blow it out; after a while I smelt the gas, but went to sleep; I woke up and shook YELLOW BEAR and told him 'I'm might sick and hurting all over.' YELLOW BEAR says, 'I'm mighty sick, too.' I got up and fell down and all round the room, and that is all I know about it." "Why didn't you open the door?" asked the reporter. "I was too crazy to know anything," replied the chief.

It is indeed, a source of congratulation that the chief will recover, as otherwise his tribe could not be made to understand the occurrence, and results detrimental to those having interests in the territory would inevitably follow.

From which report it is safe to say, that at least one Indian took the Fort Worth limited gas route to the happy hunting ground.

GOES HUNTING WITH PRESIDENT ROOSEVELT

While THEODORE ROOSEVELT was president, he arranged with JACK ABBERNATHY, the great hunter and wolf catcher, then United States marshal, of Muskogee, Oklahoma, to go on an extended hunt in what was then known as the "Big Pasture," in western Oklahoma. Chief QUANAH PARKER was let in on the deal, and in this way, he slept out on the range with the president for a week or ten days, killing game and chasing wolves; and Chief QUANAH, ever afterwards, in his broken English, delighted to refer to this as one bright oasis on his journey of life.

Since the above was written, I have secured the following statement from T. J. CATES, of BEN WHEELER, which I add with pleasure:

I well remember CYNTHIA ANN PARKER and her little girl, TECKS ANN; she lived at that time about six miles south of BEN WHEELER, with her brother-in-law, RUFF O'QUINN, near Slater's Creek; she looked to be stout and weighed about 140 pounds; well made and liked to work. She had a wild expression and would look down when people looked at her; she could use an ax equal to a man; and she liked to work and disliked a lazy person. She was an expert in tanning hides with the hair on them, or platting or knitting either ropes or whips. She thought her two boys were lost on the prairie, after she was captured, and tried to starve to death. This dissatisfied her very much and she wanted to go back to the Indians. She would take a knife and hack her breast until it would bleed, then put the blook on some tobacco and burn it and cry for her lost boys. Almost every Sunday my wife would carry the little Indian girl TECKS ANN, visiting. She was pretty and smart and was about three years old the last time we saw her. She died and was buried in Old Asbury graveyard, about eight miles south of BEN WHEELER, but I can't remember the year. Poor CYNTHIA ANN was grieved over the loss of her child and she then moved to Anderson county, where she soon died of la grippe, as well as I remember. She was an open-hearted, good woman, and always ready to help somebody.

Taxable values of Van Zandt county in 1909, $7,542,480. Scholastic population in 1909, 6266; state apportionment, $39,-162.50. Specified crops in 1908: Cotton, 24,006 bales; Corn, 796,394 bushels. In 1909: Horses and mules, 9368; value, $585,-836. Cattle, 16,111; value, $155,064. Sheep, 74; value, $118. Goats, 157; value, $159; Hogs, 8239; value, $26,178. June 30, 1909; Banks, nine; capital, $390,143; deposits, $412,498. Assessor's rolls for 1909: Railroads, 32.55 miles; value, $288,424; value of rolling stock, $88,456; intangible assets, $620,180. Telegraph lines, 55.95 miles; value, $29,900.

CHAPTER 5

American Flag One of the Oldest Among Nations. Stars and Stripes
Not Our First Emblem. Banner of Today, With Increase In
Number of Stars and Stripes, Established in 1777.

Your flag and my flag, oh! how it flies today,
O'er your land and my land, and half a world away.
Rose red and blood red, its stripes forever gleam,
Snow white and soul white, our good forefathers' dream.
Sky blue and true, its stars forever bright,
A glorious guidon of the day, a shelter through the
       night.

Your flag and my flag, oh! how much it holds,
Your land and my land secure within its folds.
Your heart and my heart beat quicker at sight:
Sun kissed and wind tossed, the red, the blue, the
       white.
The one flag, the great flag, the flag for me and you,
Glorified all else beside, the red, the white, the
       blue.

                                        Nesbit.

    There were many forms of early flags, especially colonial
types used by the individual colonies and militia regiments before the United States flag was established by the continental
congress on July 14, 1877, a date now celebrated as flag day
throughout the country. This act required that the falg be of
thirteen alternate red and white stripes, and that the Union be
thirteen white stars on a blue field, but it did not define how
many points the stars should have, how they should be arranged,
or make provision for additional ones.
    At the time of the adoption of this resolution, WASHINGTON
is said to have observed, "We take the star from heaven, the red
from our mother country, separating it by white stripes, thus
showing that we have separated from her, and the white stripes
shall go down to posterity representing liberty."

                    FIRST DISPLAY OF FLAG

    The first display of the Stars and Stripes is believed to
have been on August 6, 1777, when the new flag was hoisted over
the troops at Fort Schuyler, Rome, New York. JOHN PAUL JONES is
said to have been the first to fly the Stars and Stripes over the
high seas, on the Ranger, 1777.
    From the time of the Revolution the Stars and Stripes in the
flag have varied. There were thirteen stars during the Revolution, fifteen in the war of 1812, twenty-nine in the Mexican war,
thirty-three and thirty-five in the Civil war, forty-five in the
Spanish war and forty-eight today. The stripes were changed
first from thirteen to fifteen, and then back again to thirteen.
It may be surprising to know that our national flag is among the
oldest flags of the nations, being older than the present British

Jack, the French tricolor and the flag of Spain, and many years older than the flags of Germany and Italy, some of which are personal flags or those of reigning families.

The flag of the highest historic and sentimental value to the whole country is in the National Museum collection. It is the original Star Spangled Banner, which flew over Fort McHenry on Baltimore Harbor during the bombardment on September 13-14, 1814, and was the inspiration of FRANCIS SCOTT KEY's immortal poem, now sung as the national anthem. This great historic souvenir of the war of 1812 has lately been preserved by quilting on heavy linen, and will ever remain one of the country's most precious relics. From 1795 this form continued as the standard flag until President MONROE's administration, when congress enacted that it should hereafter be of thirteen stripes, with the addition of a star for each new state, commencing July 4, 1818.

USED FIRST IN GARRISONS

It seems for many years, the army did not carry the Stars and Stripes in battle, though it had been in general use as a garrison flag. The land forces during this period and before it carried what was known as national colors or standards of blue with the arms of the United States emblazoned thereon, comprising an eagle surmounted by a number of stars, with the designation of the body of troops. In 1834 war department regulations gave the artillery the right to carry the Stars and Stripes, the infantry and cavalry still using the national standards, and those remained the colors of the infantry until 1841 and of the cavalry until 1887, when that branch of the army was ordered to employ the Stars and Stripes. From its adoption in 1777, however, naval vessels universally displayed the national flag.

Many styles and forms of the Stars and Stripes flag were in existence up to 1842, and it was not until during President TAFT's administration that definite specifications were drawn up. An executive order dated October 29, 1912, tended to standardize the Stars and Stripes, and yet further specifications in sizes were found necessary by President WILSON.

The history of the flag indicates that the Stars and Stripes was not carried by our troops in battle until the period of the Mexican war, 1846-47.

GIVE RULES GOVERNING DISPLAY OF UNITED STATES FLAG--
EMBLEM SHOULD BE LOWERED AT SUNSET AND
NEVER TOUCH GROUND.

Rules governing the displaying of the United States flag have been issued by the War Department, as follows:

The flag should never be hoisted at night.
Raise the flag at sunrise or after.
Lower the flag at sunset.
The flag should never be allowed to touch the ground.

The flag must not be used as a staff, whip or covering. Its position is aloft.

When draping the flag against the side of a room or building, place the blue field always to the north or east.

When displayed with other flags, the national emblem should be placed at the right.

Good taste required that bunting be draped or hung with the red at the top, followed by the white and the blue in accordance with the heraldic colors of the flag. It is a mark of disrespect to allow the flag to fly throughout the night. A flag flown upside down is a signal of distress.

The falg, marred, should be burned and a new one hoisted in its place.

The flag should be hoisted from every public building, the courthouse, for instance.

"The Star Spangled Banner" is the American national anthem. It should never be played unless the entire piece is rendered and the audience is expected to stand. At such a time as this it behooves all American citizens to observe the rules of our national banner and anthem.

SEVERAL TEXAS FLAGS

Historians say that in September, 1835, Mrs. A. B. DODSON made and presented to her husband's company a tricolored flag of calico--blue, white and red. The square, next the flagstaff, had a white star in the center; the white came next, then the red. Its shape was similar to the Mexican flag, and the single star was designated to show that for Texas alone the star of liberty was rising. This was more like that ultimately adopted than any other made during the revolution. Another flag was made about the same time by Mrs. JOHN LYNCH, who followed the suggestion of Capt. WM. SCOTT. It was solid blue silk with a large white star painted thereon, and the word Independence below. In September of the same year another Lone Star flag was made by Miss TROUTMAN (afterward Mrs. POPE of Alabama), reaching Texas in December. This was of plain white silk, with an azure star of five points on either side. On one side was the Latin inscription, "Ubi libertas habitat, ibi nostra patria est." On the other side, "Liberty or Death." "Captain BROWN's Flag of Independence" bore stripes like the United States flag with the interlineation of the word "Independence" protected by a bloody sword in the hand of an uplifted arm.

CHAPTER 6

NACOGDOCHES AND HENDERSON COUNTIES

A Biographical Sketch of General J. Pinkney Henderson.
Henderson County: Its Creation, Origanization and
Historical Record and Data.

NACOGDOCHES

As a preliminary to writing the history of Van Zandt county,
it seems proper to briefly sketch the territory from which the
county was carved, that the reader may know how the county appeared before its organization. To this end and for this purpose I will briefly notice Nacogdoches, of which Van Zandt county
was once a part, so that the reader can more readily trace it
back to the discovery of America.

About the year 1690, DON ALONZO DE LEON, governor of Coahuila, a state in the province of Mexico, a Spanish colony by conquest, in which was established a number of Missions in east
Texas. Among these was Nacogdoches, located at the confluence of
the Bonita with La Nana Creeks, in what is now Nacogdoches county,
Texas. The settlement in and around this mission was necessarily
slow, for numerous causes, chief among these were owing to the
fact that tribes of hostile Indians threatened it on all sides;
coupled with the further fact that under Spanish rule foreigners
were prohibited, under penalty of death, from entering the settlement. A few Catholic missionaries and Indian proselytes,
eked out a miserable existence by killing such game as they could
take with crude instruments they possessed and cultivating small
patches of maize and raising some stock. In 1778, GIL Y. BARBO
erected the famous Stone Fort at that place, which gave better
protection to those under its shelter; and about that time some
wealthy families reached there from New Orleans and efforts were
made to open up semblances of roads through the primeval forests,
that had obtained up to that time. The early settlers lived in
a very primitive manner. There were no grist mills; no cotton
gins and no accessible markets through which the outer world
could be reached. The East Texas missions were moved to locations on the San Antonio river in 1731.

Col. JUAN ALMONTE, in a report on Texas, in 1834, has this
to say: "There will be exported during this year about 2000
bales of cotton, from the Nacogdoches department. There are ma-
chines for cleaning and pressing cotton in the department of Nacogdoches and Brazos." In the year that this report was made,
Texas was divided into three departments, viz.: Bexar, Nacogdoches and Brazos, each embracing an immense territory. The first
cotton ginhouse in Texas was erected in 1825, on the Grose plantation; the next, near the mouth of Cow Creek, in Brazoria county,
by the AUSTINS; the third by ROBERT H. WILLIAMS, in Matagorda
county. Cotton was then packed in fifty and one hundred pound
sacks; hence ALMONTE's estimate of 2000 bales in Nacogdoches.

Nacogdoches county was one of the original counties after
annexation. It was designated as a land district and Hopkins

county was created from Lamar and Henderson counties, March 25, 1846. So it will be seen that Henderson county, which I will next take notice of, was created one month later and extended to the Hopkins county line on its north boundary.

J. PINKNEY HENDERSON, SAN AUGUSTINE, TEXAS

The man for whom Henderson county was named, was born in Lincoln county, North Carolina; studied law and was admitted to the bar before he was twenty-one years old. Soon thereafter he was aide-de-camp to Major General DORRETT, of the North Carolina militia and soon thereafter was elected colonel of his regiment. HENDERSON came to Texas when she was under Mexican rule. When Gen. SAM HOUSTON became president of the Texas republic, he appointed Mr. HENDERSON attorney general. Afterwards he was chosen secretary of state of the infant republic. He was sent as minister plenipotentiary to the United States in the winter of 1843-4, and together with ISAAC VAN ZANDT, of Texas, and JOHN C. CALHOUN, secretary of state of the United States, on the 12th day of Spril, 1844, concluded a treaty of annexation, by which Texas was to be annexed to the United States, which was rejected by the United States senate. In 1837, he was sent as minister plenipotentiary and envoy extraordinary from the Republic of Texas, to the courts of France and England. He secured valuable treaties with both of these governments. His visits abroad won him many affable friends. After annexation he was chosen as one of the delegates to the constitutional convention, that framed the constitution of the new republic. At the first election held under the new constitution, many new counties were created, among them the county of Henderson, which was named for him. In 1846 war was opened between the United States and Mexico and Governor HENDERSON was commissioned a major general in the United States army; and the legislature voted him a leave of absence, and he went to the front and commanded the Texas troops with such ability at Monterey, Mexico, during the three days battle, that on the capitulation of the city by the Mexicans, General TAYLOR appointed him as one of the three commissioners on the part of the Americans to negotiate the terms of surrender of the city. At the re-organization of the army he resigned and returned to his duties as governor of Texas. Congress voted him a sword as an evidence of the government's gratitude for his gallantry.

After the conclusion of peace between the United States and Mexico, and his term of office had expired, he removed to Nacogdoches and entered into a co-partnership with Gen. THOMAS J. RUSK, and they jointly practiced law together until the death of Senator RUSK.

Mr. HENDERSON was, in 1857, elected United States senator, and while he was filling this office he died in Washington, in June, 1858, and was buried at Marshall, Texas.

During his residence in Paris, as a diplomat from Texas, he met Miss FRANCIS COX, a daughter of Mr. JOHN COX, of Pennsylvania, whose temporary residence was in Paris, and in 1839 they were

married at London. They have two children now living; one married a German count who lived on the Rhine, and perhaps is now,
if not too old, in the ranks. The other, a Mrs. ADAMS, lived in
New Jersey when I last had a communication from her.

General HENDERSON held quite a good deal of real estate in
Van Zandt county, among which was an interest in the SAM BELL
tract, which covered the salt lands at Grand Saline.

General HENDERSON's services to Texas will long be remembered by a grateful people.

HENDERSON COUNTY

Van Zandt county having been created from Henderson county,
it is proper to give the origin of Henderson county and some of
its records before Van Zandt county was created.

Henderson county was created from Hudson and Nacogdoches
counties, April 27, 1846 and named for Governor J. P. HENDERSON.
Located in east Texas, the Neches River forms its eastern and the
Trinity its western boundary. Organized July 13, 1846. Said
county then embraced a territory of about 3,600 square miles,
about 2,265,000 acres of land. It contains today an area of 940
square miles. In addition to is present territory, it originally
covered all of Kaufman, all of Rockwell, all of Van Zandt, all of
Wood and nearly all of Rains counties.

The following historical record data was prepared by Judge
W. L. FAULK, an old citizen of Henderson county and may be relied
upon.

THE COUNTY SEAT QUESTION.

By commissioners appointed for that purpose the county seat
was located at Buffalo, on the Trinity River. In 1843 (1848) the
counties of Kaufman and Van Zandt were created from territory of
Henderson county and commissioners were appointed to locate a new
county seat in Henderson county. Centerville was selected by a
popular vote. A. F. McCARTY filed a protest against the removal
of the county seat from Buffalo to Centerville, but the commissioners' court ordered the public records of the county to Centerville and several terms were held there, but on November 19,
1849, the commissioners' court again met in session at Buffalo.
On August 24, 1850, another election was held to locate the
county seat of Henderson county, at which Athens received twenty-
seven votes majority and the records were moved there, and the
term of the commissioners' court of said county was held there in
October, 1850, since which time the county seat has remained at
the town of Athens and quiet has prevailed.

The first court that the records show was held in Henderson
county, was at Buffalo. The term began on December 13, 1847.
The Hon. AMOS CLARK, judge of the sixth judicial district, presided. The first case, although numbered sixteen, brought to that
term was an action to trespass to try title. The petition is
very lengthy, and is signed by OCHILTREE, JENNINGS and HYDE, at-

torneys for petitioner. It doesn't seem to have been answered until May 17, 1849. The answer consists of a short general demurrer and plea of not guilty, signed by REAGAN and REAVES, attorneys for defendant. The case was styled JOHN J. SIMPSON vs. WYATT PARHAM.

The first regular minutes that we find was a court held at Buffalo, on November 12, 1849, BENNETT H. MARTIN, district judge; A. J. FOWLER, district attorney; NICHOLAS H. GRAY, sheriff and WM. W. BRIGGS, clerk, by his deputy, JAMES T. ROYAL.

The following are the names of the jurors ordered to be summoned: JAMES HOOPER, MARION GARDNER, M. M. CLARK, G. B. MASON, JULIUS BARKER, SAMUEL WHITEHEAD, WM. CARTER, JAMES W. BOON, WM. W. STIRMAN, WM. A. BROWN, JAMES SMITH, JNO. S. DAMRON, JNO. BAKER, ANDREW F. McCARTY, JOHN H. KISO, JOHN V. WADKINS, MORRIS WARD, NATAHIEL S. BRATCHER, WM. WARD, G. N. SAWYER, ASA DALTON, WM. WALDRIP, WM. AVANT, HUGH T. MOORE, MILES D. BLUE, JACKSON PHILLIPS, WM. T. BREWER, J. JONES, JOSHUA B. LUKER, JEFFERSON MILLER, BARKLEY M. BALLARD, JAMES L. GOSSETT, JOHN B. WHITE, ISAAC VANHOSER, JAMES DUNCAN, THOMAS BOX.

The first criminal case that appears on the minutes is State of Texas vs. JAMES L. GOSSETT, NICHLAI HANSON charged with affray.

The first gaming case is State vs. NICHOLAS GRAY, charge, betting at "twenty-one." That game must now be obsolete, as we never hear of such a game.

The first indictment for murder that is shown on the record is the State of Texas vs. F. C. BUTLER.

The first man that was found guilty was JAMES DUNCAN for an assault and battery and was fined $1.00. J. W. OCHILTREE was foreman of the jury.

The adjourning order of the fall term, 1849, is as follows: Ordered that court adjourn until court in course.

The spring term 1850, of the district court was also held at Buffalo, by the same officers as at the fall term, 1849. The names of all the jurors are perfectly familiar to the compiler of this, although many of them ne never saw. It appears that the name of ALSEY FULLER was on the record more than any other person as a litigant on both the civil and criminal docket and as a petit and grand juror.

The fall term of the district court, 1850, was held at Athens, being the first district court ever held there, was begun on the 2nd day of October, 1850. O. M. ROBERTS was district judge; A. J. FOWLER, district attorney; JAMES BALL, sheriff; WM. C. BOBO, deputy; JOHN LEDBETTER, clerk. Some of the very familiar names to me, who constituted that term, are HENRY BOLES, BERY AN HIGHTOWER, FLEMMING BALL, JOHN C. DUNN, JOHN S. LEDBETTER, LEROY PARKS, WM. BOLES, SR. M. M. CLARK, J. B. LUKER, FELIX PARKS, R. H. PEARSON, C. CHOAT, MILES D. BLUE and S. J. SCOTT.

I notice the record shows that at that term of the court two prominent attorneys, THOMAS J. JENNING and WM. B. OCHILTREE, were tried for gaming, but shown not guilty. The jury returned the following verdict in each case: "We, the jury, find the defendant not guilty.--E. L. SMITH, foreman. We all knew the foreman,

Uncle ELI SMITH, as well as we did our own daddies. He was the father of our W. C. SMITH now at Malkoff. At that same term of court NICHOLAS GRAY beat his case of betting at twenty-one." Uncle ELI signed his verdict as foreman and said not guilty. It seems that FOWLER was not as lucky as our present district attorney, handsome JERE CROOK. The Hon. O. M. ROBERTS adjourned the court in his own handwriting in these words.

Court is ordered to adjourn.

O. M. ROBERTS,
District Judge, Presiding.

ATTEST:
J. LEDBETTER, D. C.

The minutes of the spring term, 1851, are, of course, modern to some of the old settlers. The jury for that term was selected on the 30th day of November, 1850, and one of them is near and dear to the writer of this, I will give some of their names: WM. K. FAULK, B. T. HIGGINS, J. P. SULLIVAN, W. C. HOLLAND, MARION GARDNER, M. DARNOLD, BERYAN HIGHTOWER, ASA DALTON. These jurors were selected by JOHN LEDBETTER, district clerk, E. J. THOMPSON, county clerk, and ELI L. SMITH, justice of the peace. This term was held by BENNETT H. MARTIN, district judge, and the fall term, 1851, and spring term, 1852, was also held by him. The spring term, 1853, was held by Hon. JOHN H. REAGAN. His handwriting then is almost precisely what it is now. He held every court thereafter, spring and fall terms, until the fall term of 1857, which was held by Ho. R. A. REEVES, district judge. At that term of the court Col. T. J. WOOD acted as special judge to try the case of CRAVENS vs. DUMAS.

I find in the office of the county clerk of our county that on the 25th day of January, 1847, the citizens of old Buffalo, the then county site of Henderson county, organized a debating society. Mr. JOHN H. REAGAN was called to the chair and the secretary says he made a good speech showing the mental improvement and moral influence of a debating society. JAMES BOGGS was the secretary at that meeting which met at the house of Mr. PERKINS. After appointing a committee to draft constitution and select names for the society the meeting adjourned to meet at the residence of JAMES PERKINS on February 6, 1847, at early candlelight. The manner of adopting the constitution, the various discussions on it and the by-laws are faithfully recorded by the secretary. The constitution and the by-laws are copied fully on the minutes. It was named the Buffalo lyceum. The question selected for discussion, "Was it better policy of the United States to invade Mexico than to have compromised?" The speakers were as follows: Affirmative: JAS. STEVENSON, B. GRAHAM, I. D. SCOTT, JAMES DUNCAN; negative, J. H. REAGAN, L. B. SANDERS, J. P. MOORE, A. B. GARDNER. The minutes show that the question was not discussed until September 27, 1847, and that "the merit of the question was decided in favor of the negative." Several of the defaulting members were fined five cents for nonattendance. These minutes are kept up for several pages at the beginning of a book containing commissioner court records. Some of the questions discussed by that society are right interesting, and are as follows:

"Was it good policy in the government of Texas to Grant colony contracts?"

"Whether it is better policy to clean out the Trinity River now or wait until we raise a quantity of produce to ship off?"

"Is the hope of reward greater than the fear of punishment?"

"Is the revenue system for the collection of taxes better than the protective?"

"Are the works of nature more pleasing to the eye than the works of art?"

"Should capital punishment be abolished?"

CHAPTER 7

VAN ZANDT COUNTY

Governor George T. Wood; Colonel Charles De Morse; Biographical
Sketch of Isaac Van Zandt; Creation and Organization
of Van Zandt County.

GOVERNOR GEORGE T. WOOD

It was GEORGE T. WOOD who approved the bill creating the
county of Van Zandt. He was a native Georgian, and came to Texas
in 1836, soon after the battle of San Jacinto. He became a planter in Polk county. He was a quiet, unassuming man of considerable force of character, as was evidenced by his being elected to
congress of the republic, brigadier general of militia; colonel
of a regiment of volunteers, and lastly governor of the State of
Texas.

Governor WOOD commanded a regiment at the battle of Monterey,
Mexico. To show what small influences exerted weight in those
days, it was said that Governor HENDERSON made WOOD governor of
Texas by omitting to mention the latter's gallant conduct in the
report of the battle of Monterey. Be that as it may, Governor
WOOD was a polished gentleman, a good lawyer and made Texas a
good governor. After his term of office expired he retired to
private life and died in Panola county, Texas, in 1856. Wood
county was named for him.

COLONEL CHARLES DE MORSE

Col. CHARLES DE MORSE was elected public printer and hauled
the manuscript copies of proceedings of the laws from Austin to
Clarksville and printed them on a Washington hand press, for the
sessions of 1848, including the act creating Van Zandt county.
Col. DE MORSE was born in Massachusetts, grew to manhood in New
York and came as a volunteer to Texas in the "Morehouse Battalion," arriving too late to participate in the battle of San Jacinto, though in hearing of the guns. He served in both the army
and navy of the Republic of Texas, and held various positions at
Austin from 1839 to 1842.

In 1842 there was a shake-up on account of the public archives of the republic being ordered by President HOUSTON, from
Austin to Houston for safe keeping. This was resisted by some of
the Austin people, who resorted to arms to encompass President
HOUSTON in his effort to carry out his mandate, and the records
were boxed up and held in hiding until the officers of the republic returned and resumed their duties at Austin. Colonel DE
MORSE was in all things anti-Houston and President HOUSTON was
the same to Colonel DE MORSE. So Colonel DE MORSE took leave of
Austin and repaired to Clarksville, Red River county, and founded
the Northern Standard, a weekly journal, which he continued to
publish until his death back in the eighties. He was a member
of the constitutional convention of 1875, and candidate for congress at the first election under the new constitution, but fail-

ed of election.

ISAAC VAN ZANDT, MARSHALL, TEXAS

The subject of this memoir was born in Franklin county, Tennessee, July 10, 1813. His parents were JACOB and MARY VAN ZANDT. His father was a native of North Carolina, the youngest son of JACOB VAN ZANDT, who, about the beginning of this century, moved out of the Moravian settlement in that state and established himself as an agriculturist in Franklin county, Tennessee. His mother's father, SAMUEL ISAACS, about the same time migrated from South Carolina and settled in Lincoln county, Tennessee, and adjoining county, to that of Franklin. On both sides he came of revolutionary path of ancestry. His grandfather VAN ZANDT, participated in several of the battles that won our independence of the British crown, and his grandfather ISAACS, all through the war, was a zealous and active follower of the fortunes of MARION in all of his dashing and hazardous raids against the English foemen, and their home allies, the traitorous tories.

All through his boyhood and youth, ISAAC VAN ZANDT was a victim of ill health, and for this reason his attendance at school was desultory, and not as fruitful of educational benefit to him as it would otherwise have been. But his enforced absence from the schoolroom gave him an opportunity to indulge at home his relish of good books. He read with an ardent yearning to acquire knowledge of the subjects treated of in the volume he perused, and thus, perhaps, fully compensated himself for all the loss sustained by being compelled to forego scholastic instruction. With English literature and general history he became quite conversant.

At the age of twenty he married Miss FANNIE LIPSCOMB, a relative of the late Chief Justice LIPSCOMB, of Texas, and commenced merchandising at Salem, in his native county, having his father for a partner. This business, however, continued only for a few months; for, his father died in 1834, the concern had to be wound up so as to facilitate a speedy distribution of the paternal estate among the heirs. As soon as this had been done, ISAAC VAN ZANDT promptly sold for cash his portion of the estate, consisting mainly of land and negroes, and in 1835 went north and invested the proceeds of his patrimony in a stock of goods. This stock he shipped to Coffeeville, Mississippi, and there resumed the mercantile business, expecting to be lifelong merchant and nothing else. This was the flush time in Mississippi.

Bank paper was abundant; everything vendible was bought and sold at high valuations; the credit system was in vogue and everybody were deeply into debt. At length the bubble burst and the culmination came in the shape of broken banks, bankrupt tradesmen and a financially ruined people. Having invested all he was worth in the Mississippi mercantile adventure, when the crash came, in 1837, VAN ZANDT found himself well-nigh penniless. He struggled for a time against the tide of misfortune, made every possible effort to collect the debts due him, and pay off those he owed, but his debtors, in most cases, neither by persuasion nor court process could be induced to meet his demands against them, and this failure to meet their obligations to him made him impotent to meet his creditors. Even bedding woven by his wife was sold to meet the debts of the husband. As long as he had anything that could be turned to the credit side of his indebtedness, it took that direction and he had the proud consciousness of knowing that he had held back nothing to which, either by the law of the land or that of moral obligation, his creditors had a right to claim. While residing at Coffeeville, his talent for public speaking was first developed. He became a member of a debating club, consisting of the young lawyers and others of the little town, and to his own surprise, as well as that of others, he soon displayed a rare readiness of speech and unusual acuteness of argument in the discussions that occurred. This almost purely accidental discovery of a latent, and hitherto unused talent, determined his future career in life, for, shorn of all his property, he had no resource but his native gift of intellect. He determined to turn his attention to legal studies, took up the elementary books of English law, and by assiduous application to a perusual of them, in somewhat less than a year, so far mastered their contents as to obtain, on due examination, admission to the bar. In this manner his reverse of fortune proved to have been a blessing in disguise, his commercial disaster leading him to a pursuit for which his natural abilities eminently fitted him. By this change of vocation he speedily won back more than he had lost pecuniarily as a merchant, and at the same time achieved an honorable distinction among his fellowmen, far surpassing that which ordinarily comes to the most successful follower of mere trade. This success came to him in Texas, whither he migrated, carrying with him his family, in 1838. His first home in the young republic was in Panola county, at that time but lately organized and very sparsely settled. An humble, lonely log cabin there sheltered him and his loved ones for some months. He did not locate himself in that county with the intention of abiding there permanently; but for economic reasons, and that, before offering himself as a general practitioner of the law, he might have a quiet retreat, where he might, by private study, make himself familiar with the statutes of the republic, and the modes of procedure in its courts. During their residence in that county, the hardships and privations of frontier life in their sternest forms were the daily experience of himself and family; but his wife, who, as well as he, had been nursed in the lap of plenty, met the severe allotment with fortitude, and so cheerfully bore herself through the ordeal of want and discomfort, that no sense of discouragement ever oppressed him. She was, verily, a helpmeet to him in those days of adversity, and to her unmurmuring accommodation of herself to her changed circumstances, and the words of cheer and hope that came to him from her lips, he was greatly indebted for the after success that crowned his struggle with adverse fortune. Had a querulous, discontented spirit influenced his life beneath that lowly roof in Panola county, the energies of her husband might have been sapped, and the outcome of his career might have been very different form what it was--an outcome that she now looks back upon with just pride and pleasure. She richly merits the quietude and affluence she now enjoys in the evening of her days, under the shade of the tree she helped her husband to plant, during the dark time of their earlier Texan life.

In 1839 ISAAC VAN ZANDT moved to Harrison county and engaged in the active practice of law. Success attended him from the start, and he rose rapidly to the front among his legal competitors. Soon the minds of the people around him turned upon a suitable man to represent them in the congress of the republic. To the sessions of 1840-41, with great unanimity they sent him as their delegate to the lower house of that legislative body, and the zeal he manifested in this new sphere of action, not only in behalf of the interests of his immediate constituents, but of those of the people at large, endeared him to the whole country, and the ability he displayed in the committee rooms and on the floor of the house commanded the respect and admiration of his co-legislators. He speedily became a marked man both at the bar and in the halls of legislation.

His next official position was that of charge d' affairs to the United States, which was conferred upon him by President HOUSTON, in 1842. During the two years that he resided at Washington City, as the diplomatic agent of the republic, he labored assiduously with the government to which he was accredited, to bring about the annexation of Texas to the United States, and when this measure had become a certainty in the near future, he resigned the office and returned home.

In 1845 he was a delegate to the convention that completed the work of annexation, and framed the first constitution of the "Lone Star" state. In that body there were many brilliant intellects, and in the galaxy his was an orb of no mean magnitude. Some of the members were far older than he, and among them, no doubt, could have been found a profounder jurist than he as yet had time to become; but on questions of state policy, and what was needful as a component element of the organic law they were framing, he displayed a wisdom that left its impress upon the instrument that came from their hands, and won for him the prestige of unusual statesmanship.

In 1847, he was before the people of Texas as a candidate for the office of governor, and while making an active, and what promised to be a successful canvass of the state, he was stricken down with yellow fever at Houston and died there on the 11th day of October. In fact, during the canvass his election was recognized as a certainty. His remains were transferred to Marshall, and by loving hands laid in the city cemetery, where to his memory they have reared a monument that will tell to the stranger where sleeps a man whom all Texans of his day delighted to honor.

In person he was above the average stature, erect and well proportioned. His head was covered with abundant locks, that were as black as the raven's plumage; his dark gray eyes sparkled

with intelligence, and his look habitually wore the impress of
frankness and benignity. His carriage was easy, graceful and
dignified, and his manners were urbane and courteous. In a word,
none could come near him and not feel that they were in the presence of a true gentleman.

This sketch would be incomplete with no mention of the fact
that ISAAC VAN ZANDT was a Christian. From his early youth he
had been a member of the Baptist church, and his exemplary walk
in life indicated that revealed truth had been heartily accepted
by him, and been allowed to mold his heart and character. The
serene composure of his dying hours, and the devout expressions
of Christian hope and resignation that characterized them, grand-
ly witnessed that:

> The chamber where the good man meets his fate,
> Is privileged beyond the common walks
> Of virtuous life--quite on the verge of Heaven.

THE REV. AMBROSE FITZGERALD

The Rev. AMBROSE FITZGERALD was the first clerk of the county court of Van Zandt county; was a son of SAMUEL and MARY FITZ-
GERALD; was born in the state of Missouri, on the 12th day of
March, 1827. At the age of twelve years, he moved with his parents to Meigs county, east Tennessee, where under adverse conditions, alternating between hard labor and attending the rud common schools then prevailing in that country, received a common
school education, which he improved by continuous study as circumstances would admit until in latter life he was quite well accomplished. Barely budding into manhood's estate (not quite 19)
he was married to MARY ANN O'KELLEY. At this time, financially
speaking, his greatest asset was a good store of self reliance.
Summing up his courage, he procured a wagon and a yoke of oxen;
he placed his possessions in the wagon, including his "girl wife"
and was off for the "promise land" of Texas. Having seen so many
people on the road, I may be pardoned if I suggest a partial in-
ventory of the contents of that wagon: A flintlock rifle; a supply of bar lead; a pair of bullet moulds; a quantity of powder;
a steel handmill; a supply of fishing tackle; a pole axe, hung in
a crude fashion to the wagon tongue, a well filled tar bucket
swung underneath the coupling pole, just behind the rear axle of
the wagon, and a dog that alternated between following the tar
bucket and riding with the family.

Such is the pen-picture of hundreds of "prairie schooners"
this writer has seen wending their way westward through deep
tangled wildwood, with little that might be called roads, and
bridges were almost unknown, and but few cabins along the wayside,
as an evidence of human habitation.

Brave indeed were the pioneers that left father, mother and
friends behind, to erect a shelter in the wilderness of Texas, as
did Rev. AMBROSE FITZGERALD, who must have pitched his tent in
what is now Rains county, about two and one-half miles northeast

of where the town of Emory now stands, in Mercer's colony, in Nacogdoches county, receiving a land certificate for 640 acres of wild Texas land, he and his girl wife set to building themselves a home, about the year 1846. That year Henderson county was organized, and so they were in another county. In 1848, Van Zandt county was created, just seven days before FITZGERALD reached his twenty-first birthday. At the first election held in the county four months later, he was elected clerk of the county court; qualified and entered the duties of his office.

The first couple to enter into a marriage contract in Van Zandt county was THOMAS CUNNINGHAM and MAHALA BROWN. The new clerk delighted to tell of his action when called upon to issue the license for this couple to become man and wife. He felt that it was a solemn affair, and so he drew up a bond, and had the prospective bridegroom furnish good and sufficient securities to the effect that he would do and perform all duties incumbent upon him as a dutiful husband. JESSE J. GAGE, a minister of the gospel, performed the ceremony, and the newly wedded couple went forth as man and wife. We have no record that Mr. CUNNINGHAM ever forfeited his bond.

In 1850 Wood county was created from Van Zandt county, and as Reverend FITZGERALD's home was in Wood county, he was elected first clerk of the county court of that county, and continued in that office until war spread its sable mantle over the land of our fathers; then he resigned his clerkship to accept a captain's commission in Col. R. B. HUBBARD's regiment confederate army. After peace was once more restored, Reverend FITZGERALD was again elected clerk of the county court of Wood county, Texas. Rains county was created from Wood, Hunt, Hopkins and Van Zandt counties, June 9, 1870; organized December 1, 1870. Very soon thereafter, Reverend FITZGERALD was elected assessor and collector of taxes for that county and later was elected county and district clerk of the same county, which position he held during the remainder of his life.

Reverend FITZGERALD was ordained a minister of the Baptist church in early life, and it was said of him, that he baptized more converts during his ministry than any other preacher officiating in so sparsely a settled county. One thing that delighted him very much, was administering the ordinance of baptism to Governor JAMES STEPHEN HOGG. Governor HOGG learned the art of a printer in the office of the National Index, H. C. MANNING, managing editor, and he purchased a small press and published a paper at Longview for a time, then moved his press to Quitman and commenced the publication of the Wood County Democrat. Soon after this he became converted and received the ordinance of baptism as above stated.

Reverend FITZGERALD became a Free and Accepted Mason in early life and was numbered among those high up in that order, was exemplified by the resolutions drawn by a committee and adopted by his lodge, after his death, which occurred at Emory, Texas, June 15, 1893; aged 65 years.

Reverend FITABERALD was married three times; his second wife

SOME HISTORY OF VAN ZANDT COUNTY

being Mrs. MARY W. BAXTER, of Quitman, Texas; his third being
Miss CARRIE SMITH, of Upshur county, Texas. In all, seventeen
children were born of these unions, seven of whom still survive.

EARLY SETTLERS

The People That Helped to Organize Van Zandt County.
The following is as complete a list of those who were here
in 1848, when the new county was organized, as it is possible to
obtain. At that time it embraced, in addition to its present
territory, all of Wood county, and by far the largest portion of
Rains county:

H. C. ADAMS	ADAM GREER	E. OLSON
C. C. ARRINGTON	SAMUEL GREER	OLA OLSON
SAMUEL BURK	P. M. GUNDERSON	C. C. OHELLY
L. H. BAUGHMAN	WALTER GREER	C. P. PARKER
LEONARD BROWN	ROBERT GUINN	R. R. POWERS
JOHN BALDWIN	G. A. HILL	JOHN PILES
ALLEN, BLAIR	DAVID HAVINS	WILLIAM PILES
PETER S. BENTON	JOHN HAVINS	JOHN PIERCE
JONATHAN BROWN	B. Y. HIGGINS	JOAB D. RAINS
JOHN RED BROWN	VICTORIA HOBBS	MARK RUSHING
HENRY CREAGLE	JAMES HILLHOUSE	C. E. RIVERS
JOHN COHEE	THOMAS HORSELEY	DAVID ROBINSON
OBEDIAH COOK	A. J. HORSELEY	WILLIAM ROSE
JOSEPH CROCKETT	JOHN M. HAYS	JOHN H. RIERSON
ISOM CLARK	JOHN JORDAN	J. M. HERMAN
THOMAS CUNNINGHAM	WM. D. JOHNSON	H. STARK
JESSEE COMPTON	ASNAN KNUDSON	JACKSON SMITH
JOSEPH COX	WM. D. LEGGETT	JOHN SIMPKINS
JOHN G. COX	E. LUNDERMAN	HENRY STOUT
THOMAS T. COX	T. L. LEDBETTER	JOSEPH SIMPKINS
J. W. CHRESTMAN	J. R. MARRS	BENJAMIN STRANER
ANDREW DONLEY	JOHN MARRS	SAMUEL SLATER
JOHN DONLEY	ALNEY T. McGEE	REDDEN S. SMITH
MARY DAVIS	S. MANSON	JOHN TOLLETT
CHARLES DUNCAN	WM. McCARROL	ASLAC TERGERSON
M. FITZGERALD	JOSEPH MOODY	TERKIN TERGERSON
A. FITZGERALD	ALLEN MILLER	JAMES TUMLINSON
JOHN FREEMAN	ROBERT MITCHELL	MRS. R. R. VARNER
JOSEPH FISHER	D. R. McINTURFF	MATTHEW WILEY
OLA GUNDERSON	A. B. McINTURFF	JOEL WAPER
WALTER C. GREER	JOHN MOORE	JAMES D. WRIGHT
GAINS GREER	ASLAC NELSON	JOSEPH WILLIAMS
JOSEPH GREER	D. O. NORTON	GILBERT YARBROUGH
GEORGE GREER	F. D. OHELLY	

AN ACT TO CREATE THE COUNTY OF VAN ZANDT,
MARCH 20, 1848.

Be It Enacted, etc. That all the territory heretofore comprised within the county of Henderson, and not now comprised within the counties of Henderson and Kaufman be, and the same is hereby constituted and made a new county to be called Van Zandt. That said county shall be organized in conformity with "Act for the organization of several counties in the State," approved 11th day of April, A. D. 1846.

That Jordan's Saline in said county be the countyseat of said county, until otherwise provided by law; and that this act take effect from and after its passage.

Kaufman county was created by the same legislature by act of February 26, 1848, nearly one month before Van Zandt, hence Van Zandt was apportioned all the remainder of Henderson county not apportioned to Henderson and Kaufman counties.

VAN ZANDT COUNTY

Van Zandt county was created from Henderson county, March 20, 1848, and named for ISAAC VAN ZANDT. It is situated in the northeastern part of the state on the Sabine River, which stream forms its northern boundary. Organized August 7, 1848, as originally created it contained about 1,715 square miles of territory. In 1850 Wood county was created from Van Zandt, taking about 838 square miles of its territory, leaving its present territory 877 square miles. Canton, near the geographical center of the county, is the countyseat. Other principal towns in the county are: Wills Point, altitude above sea level, 537 feet; Edgewood, 465 feet; Grand Saline, 408 feet; Silver Lake, 394 feet; Ben Wheeler, (named for the first mail carrier in the county), Edom, Martins Mills, Roddy, and Stone Point. All of these will be noted elsewhere.

Surface of the county rolling; mostly well watered and timbered. Other water courses are, the Neches River, which has its source in the county and forms part of its eastern boundary; McBee, Gilliland, Mill, Saline, Dry and Village Creeks flow into the Sabine River; Horseley, Murchison, Slater, Cream Level and Kickapoo Creeks flow into the Neches River; Twin, Lacy, Caney and Cedar Creeks flow into the Trinity River. Good well water is found generally over the county.

Rev. AMBROSE FITZGERALD, first county clerk of Van Zandt county, has this to say regarding the first election ever held in the county, on August 7, 1848:

Nearly, if not quite, every voter of the county exercised his privilege on that occasion, polling in the aggregate eighty-seven votes all told. The following were the county officers elected: GILBERT YARBOROUGH, chief justice (nearly corresponding to that of the county judge of present); JOHN JORDAN, THOMAS HORSELY, JOSEPH FISHER and ISHAM CLARK, county commissioners; P. S. BENTON, sheriff; JAMES D. WRIGHT, district clerk; A. FITZGERALD, county clerk; W. C. GREER, assessor of thres (?); CARY L. RICE, county surveyor; PETER KAYRANDALL, county treasurer.

Under the provisions of the law the retarns were to be made to the chief justice of Henderson county. Consequently, J.

JORDAN, commissioner-elect at the time principal owner of the
Saline, and the writer herof, each resuated on a mustang, with
lasso attachment and packed with the usual camp equipment common
in those days, set out with our election returns to the capitol
of Henderson county, which we found to be a clapboard shanty, an
apolpgy for a town called Buffalo on the bank of the Trinity
River. We delivered our treasure to the Hon. JOHN DAMEROM,
chief justice, receiving our certificates of election, and being
sworn into our respective offices, we returned to complete our
county organization. On this trip we saw an abundance of game,
????????? deer, antelope, turkeys, wolves, etc., and a small
herd of buffaloes crossed our path the evening before we passed.

MAIL SERVICE

The one branch of government service most appreciated by
all, is the mail service; so it is becoming that I give the early mail service of the new county.

In these days of fast mails, telephones, electric cars and
carriages, wireless telegraph, etc., when it seems like the
world is being run by lightning, it is well to recall the tardy
mail system in vogue in those good old days when everything was
free and easy. Maj. J. M. RUSH, a native of Tennessee, came to
Texas in 1847 from Mississippi and settled in Tyler, and secured
from the government mail route No. 6,233, from Tyler via old
Flora to Buffalo on the Trinity River three times a week, ninety-
two miles, at a contract price of $565 per annum. About this
time BENJAMIN F. WHEELER, a native of Adair county, Kentucky,
came to Texas from New Orleans. At the age of 15 years he went
to work on flatboats on the Mississippi and gradually went up
until he was on some of the fastest packets on the river in the
days of fast boats and fast living on the Mississippi. "I run
the river," he said, "for fifteen years." On reaching Tyler he
contracted with Major RUSH to carry the mail from Tyler to Buffalo on the above route horseback and was therefore, the first one
to carry the mail into the new county. His route was by Jordan's
Saline, and on the 17th day of May, 1849, ALLEN T. McGEE was appointed postmaster at Jordan's Saline, being the first postmaster appointed in the new county, and that too at a place where
the countyseat had been located nearly one year after the county
officers had qualified and entered upon the duties of their respective offices. The second postmaster appointed in the new
county was JAMES BUNDY, on the same route, January 29th, 1850.
This office was located on the west side of Crooked Creek, on
the old Shreveport and Dallas road and was called "Barren Ridge."
The third postmaster appointed was on the same route, JAMES M.
HARRISON, who was appointed postmaster at Four Mile Prairie,
June 10, 1850. The fourth postmaster appointed in the county
was GEORGE H. FAIN, at Canton, April 7, 1852, which place had
been the countyseat since 1850. This office was supplied by
mail over route N. 6,347, from Gum Spring, via Mount Carmel and
Garden Valley, fifty miles, once a week and back at $320 per

annum. J. J. STEEL of Gum Springs (now Starrville), was contractor.

The countyseat of Henderson county having been moved from Buffalo to Athens, Maj. J. M. RUSH, then secured a contract to carry the mail from Tyler to Athens, thirty-two miles, and back once a week, for $311 per annum, route No. 6,350. On this route in this county, near where Chief BOWLES was killed, a postoffice named Hamburg was established and on the 29th day of April, 1852, JAMES COLTHARP was appointed postmaster.

By reason of BEN WHEELER having carried the mails into Mercer's colony and having to stop overnight in the colony, he was awarded a colony certificate of 640 acres of land, which he laid at Creagleville in this county. He and Major RUSH were associated together in contracting and carrying the mails until their contracts were suspended by the change brought about because of the war between the states. Mr. WHEELER would not enter into a contract to carry the mails for the confederate government because he said he had so often taken the oath as carrier of the mails to support the constitution of the United States.

JUDGE BENNETT H. MARTIN

Judge BENNETT H. MARTIN presided over the first district court at Jordan's Saline, December 25, 1848. The county of Van Zandt was created from territory of Henderson county, Texas, by act of the second legislature of Texas, March 20, 1848, and was organized in August, 1848.

I regret that I have not been able to secure much data regarding this able and upright jurist. Unconditional land certificate No. 64 was issued to B. H. MARTIN, by the board of land commissioners of Red River county for 640 acres, on February 3, 1845, based on and by virtue of conditional certificate No. 98, issued by the board of land commissioners of the same county to B. H. MARTIN, on January 4, 1841; he having arrived in Texas, in December, 1840, and was head of a family. Judge MARTIN was appointed judge of the ninth judicial district of Texas, by J. PINKNEY HENDERSON, first governor of Texas, after the annexation of Texas to the Union. Vol. 3 Laws of Texas by Gamble, 1847 to 1854, says that the ninth judicial district was composed of the counties of Grayson, Collin, Denton, Dallas, Kaufman, Henderson, Anderson, Houston and Van Zandt. I think this is error, at least as to Dallas county, which was in District No. 6, for which Judge WILLIAM B. OCHILTREE, was appointed judge. Judge MARTIN opened the first district court in Grayson county, November 6, A. D. 1846; Judge MARTIN opened and presided over the first term of the district court of Collin county on the 14th day of June, 1848. He opened and presided over the first district court of Kaufman county, December 18, 1848, and next at Jordan's Saline as stated above.

Judge NAT M. BURFORD had a street in front of his residence in Dallas named Martin Street, in honor of Judge BENNETT H. MARTIN. I am not sure where he lived, but he was a favorite among the lawyers of his day and time, and I regret that I cannot give a more extended notice of him.

EARLY COURT IN KAUFMAN COUNTY

Statement of Capt. Joseph Huffmaster

Judge BENNETT H. MARTIN was never a resident of Kaufman county, but this county was a part of a large judicial district, and Judge MARTIN resided in some county east of Kaufman county, probably San Augustine or Nacogdoches. He held district court in Kaufman county soon after the county was organized. The term at which he presided was held under some trees about five miles north of the town of Kaufman, and to the left of the road leading to the present town of Terrell. That point was considered the center of the county, the county of Rockwall not at that time having been detached from Kaufman county. While he was holding said court, a man was tried for murder, the charge against him being the killing of his own wife. The offense was committed down on the Trinity River. The defendant was found guilty by a jury of murder in the first degree. There was no jail in the county at that time and the night after the trial the prisoner was in charge of a constable and several men as guards. During the night the guards were discussing the propriety of taking the prisoner out and hanging him to a limb of a tree. The constable getting an intimation of this, got his horse and rode with great rapidity to the old "Terrell Homestead," where Judge MARTIN was spending the night. In a very excited manner he aroused the family and called for Judge MARTIN. The judge appeared and inquired what was the matter, and the constable replied, that it was his opinion that the guards were going to take the prisoner our and hang him "verbally." This amused the judge very much, and the prisoner was not hung, but was sent to Palestine jail for safekeeping until the day appointed for his execution. From this jail the prisoner made his escape and has never been heard of since.

Another incident occurred during Judge MARTIN's court in which a man was on trial for stealing hogs. He was defended by Judge NAT BURFORD of Dallas. After they were through with the evidence and the district attorney had made his argument in the case, BURFORD broke out in a hearty laugh, which he kept up for a short time, when the judge inquired of him what he meant, and he replied that it was a funny scene to him to see the defendant going through the brush on crutches and running down wild hogs in the East Fork bottom. This was the only argument he made in the case, but it struck the jury exactly right and they came in with a verdict of not guilty.

ANDREW JACKSON FOWLER

ANDREW JACKSON FOWLER was a son of GODFREY and CLARA WRIGHT FOWLER. He was born in the old Fowler home, near Princeton, in

SOME HISTORY OF VAN ZANDT COUNTY

Caldwell county, Kentucky, November 11, 1815. At the time when
the republic was lashed to furious frenzy over the glorious news
from the battlefield of New Orleans, it would have seemed per-
sona non grata, not to have christened him ANDREW JACKSON. Notwithstanding he was born in the then deep tangled wildwoods, he
was a booklover and close student, and graduated from LaGrange
college, Alabama, in the class of 1836, the year Texas dressed
herself up in the habiliments of a republic for the first time.
He studied law under his brother, Judge WYLEY PAUL FOWLER, of
Smithland, "Mount Elm," a bluff on the Ohio river, near the
mouth of the Cumberland, for two years and then in company with
his brother, Col. JOHN H. FOWLER, they settled, respectively, in
Lamar and Red River counties. JOHN FOWLER served in the congress of the Republic of Texas, in the senate; and "JACK" FOW-
LER, as he was so well known to me, served in the same body, in
the lower house, in 1841-42, he representing Lamar county. On
the 10th day of February, 1840, he was married to Miss MARTHA
GLENN, at old Fort Houston, near Palestine, in Anderson county.
Judge FOWLER was a great teacher in his day and time and delighted in the profession. He spent the best days of his life in the
schools and colleges of Texas. He was professor of ancient languages in the Wesleyan college founded by his brother, Rev. LIT-
TLETON FOWLER, at San Augustine, Texas. He was also teacher of
science in Hill college, founded by himself, near Athens, in
Henderson county and later Rush Creek academy, in Navarro county,
also founded by himself. The Civil war coming on put a period
to the last enterprise.

Judge FOWLER was a pronounced Union man of the SAM HOUSTON
school. However, when war spread her sable mantle over Texas,
his friends elected him lieutenant colonel of BASS' regiment and
he qualified and donned the gray, which he wore with becoming
dignity, until the surrender.

When the first district court of Van Zandt county convened
at Jordan's Saline "JACK" FOWLER appeared as District Attorney,
on Christmas day, 1848. After the Civil war ended and matters
once more settled down to normal conditions, Governor DAVIS appointed him judge of the tenth district, composed of the counties of Anderson, Henderson, Kaufman and Van Zandt, and he served until the adoption of the constitution in 1876.

Judge FOWLER died at his home at Lindale, Texas, March 31,
1886. He left two children: N. G. FOWLER of Lindale and Mrs.
DORA FOWLER ARTHUR of Kingsville, Texas. The last of which I am
indebted for most of the information concerning the FOWLERS.

THE FIRST TERM OF THE DISTRICT COURT

The first term of the district court of Van Zandt county, in
the ninth judicial district of Texas, was held on the 25th day
of December, 1848, with the following officers:

Hon. BENNETT H. MARTIN, district judge;
ANDREW J. FOWLER, district attorney;

SOME HISTORY OF VAN ZANDT COUNTY

PETER S. BENTON, sheriff;
JAMES D. WRIGHT, clerk of said court.

THE FIRST GRAND JURY EMPANNELLED

THOMAS CUNNINGHAM, THOMAS HORSELEY, AMBROSE FITZGERLAD, THOMAS COX, GILBERT YARBOROUGH, JAMES HILLHOUSE, BENJAMIN STRANCHNER, MAURY B. IRVINE, ALLEN BIXIR, ABRAM FITZGERALD, JAMES M. HAYS, LILBURN H. BAUGHMAN, ABRAM McINTURFF, JOHN CHRESTMAN, JOHN GORDAN and JOHN MARRS.

The court appointed GILBERT YARBOROUGH foreman and R. D. MITCHELL bailiff.

Ordered by the court, that seventy-five dollars be allowed the clerk of the district court of Van Zandt county, for the purpose of furnishing the office of said clerk with a seal and the necessary stationery for his office.

DR. JAMES DURHAM WRIGHT

Dr. JAMES DURHAM WRIGHT came out from Kentucky in 1847 and settled on Saline Creek about three miles above the Saline prairie. He was the first doctor to settle in Van Zandt county. On the organization of the county he was elected the first district clerk of the county. He had migrated hither to settle in CHARLES FENTON MERCER's colony, but when the colony line was run, he learned that he was east of the line, and hence not included within its limits, so he moved to the southwest and settled on the southwest line of the Cherokee country. Taking up a pre-emption on that line, of 320 acres, and locating his colony certificate of 640 acres north of and adjoining his pre-emption, and reaching east and bordering on the Mercer colony line. After Canton was laid out he moved there and was the first doctor to locate in that town. He was a charter member of the first Masonic lodge granted in the county, to wit, Castillion Lodge A. F. & A. M., at Canton. He was appointed to go to Nacogdoches to transcribe the surveyors records for the county. He built a double logcabin on the spot now occupied by Dr. M. L. COX's residence and occupied it for a time and then returned to his pre-emption and resumed the practice of medicine. On March 7, 1860, he married Miss DELILAH MANNING, who was born in Clermont county, Ohio, August 13, 1830. Her father, MILO MANNING, was born December 2, 1805, on the Chemung branch of the Susquehana River, in Pennsylvania; and her mother was born in or near Montpelier, Vermont, March 11, 1811; they were married in Penalton county, Kentucky, January 20, 1828, and moved from that state and county to Texas in April, 1857, locating in Van Zandt county in the autumn

NOTE: The following were county officers: GILBERT YARBOROUGH, Chief Justice; THOMAS HORSELEY, County Commissioner; AMBROSE FITZGERLAD, County Clerk, and JOHN JORDAN, County Commissioner, being one-fourth of the easel.

of 1858

In 1861, Dr. WRIGHT moved to Erath county. Several Indian raids were made through Erath county during Dr. WRIGHT's stay there; the last in 1868. He lost a good many stock, for which his wife was paid by the government, after the doctor's death. This raid was a fierce one; in it the Comanches passed through Cook and Denton counties, and murdered the SHEGOG and MENASCO families; and McDOW in Erath county, JACOB LOFF in Parker; EDWARDS and wife and SMITH in Burnett county, in Young county they shot and scalped a herdsman and then crushed his skull with a tomahawk, and with all this he lived six days. In 1871 Dr. WRIGHT and family moved to the then frontier town of Commanche and homesteaded 160 acres of land, on which he died several years later. His wife survived him a few years and ided in their Commanche home at that town.

SOME EARLY COURT PROCEEDINGS

BE IT REMEMBERED, That on this the 25th day of June, A. D. 1849, there came on to be holden a district court in and for the County of Van Zandt. Present and presiding, PETER S. BENTON, sheriff, and JAMES D. WRIGHT, clerk of said court.

When the following proceedings were had: The Hon. B. H. MARTIN, judge, and A. J. FOWLER, district attorney, both having failed to be and appear at the courthouse; therefore, it ordered that court adjourn until tomorrow morning, nine o'clock.

Tuesday morning, 9 o'clock, court met pursuant to adjournment; presiding, the Hon. B. H. MARTIN, judge; A. J. FOWLER, district attorney; PETER S. BENTON, sheriff, and JAMES D. WRIGHT, clerk of said court; when the following proceedings were had:

The sheriff returned into open court the venire facias heretofore issued according to law, on the seventh day of April, 1849, with a certificate of personal service according to law, on and before the twelfth day of June, on the following named persons to serve as jurymen at the present term, to wit:

1.	MARVEL JONES	17.	MOSES JONES
2.	JOSEPH COX	18.	G. C. PEARSON
3.	FRANCIS D. O'KELLY	19.	J. Y. KUYKENDALL
4.	JOHN HARPER	20.	WILLIAM PILES
5.	I. N. SULLIVAN	21.	WILLIAM D. JOHNSON
6.	JESSIE YARBROUGH	22.	JACOB LACY
7.	SAMUEL SLATER	23.	JOHN HAVENS
8.	TRAVIS SCOTT	24.	JEREMIAH SPLAWN
9.	W. TANKERSLY	25.	C. BECKETT
10.	SILAS DUNCAN	26.	R. S. SMITH
11.	LEONARD BROWN	27.	JOHN RICE
12.	JOHN COTHERAN	28.	JOHN COHEA
13.	MARK RUSHING	29.	JOSHUA FISHER
14.	DAVID TUMLINSON	30.	ADAM GREER
15.	DAVID ROBERTSON	31.	DANIEL RENTER
16.	JAMES BUNDY	32.	JOHN PILES
		33.	A. T. HOSLEY

And that JONATHAN WELKINS, JOHN DONEG, and whereof were not to be found.

Whereupon the sheriff and clerk in open court proceeded to draw the following named persons to compose the grand jury, to wit:

1. SAMUEL SLAYTOR
2. JOHN HARPER
3. JESSE Y. KUYKENDALL
4. LAWSON PIERSON
5. JOHN M. SULLIVAN
6. JOSHUA FISHER
7. DANIEL REUTER
8. JACOB LACEY
9. JEREMIAH SPLAWN
10. MARK RUSHING
11. JESSE YARBROUGH
12. SILAS DUNCAN
13. FRANCIS D. O'KELLY
14. MARBLE R. JONES
15. LEONARD BROWN
16. WILLIAM D. JOHNSON

17. JOHN HAVENS

Whereupon, SAMUEL SLATER was elected and sworn as foreman of the grand jury, and his fellows being also sworn according to law, daid grand jury was charged by the court touching their oaths and then retired under the charge of the bailiff, JOHN MARES, who was duly sworn as such.

Monday, June 24, A. D. 1850

BE BE IT REMEMBERED, that on this the 24th day of June, A. D. 1850, there came on to be holden a district court for Van Zandt county; present and presiding, the Hon. BENNETT H. MARTIN, judge of said court; ANDREW J. FOWLER, district attorney; PETER S. BENTON, sheriff, and JAMES D. WRIGHT, clerk of said court; when the following proceedings were had, viz:

The sheriff returned the venire facias into open court, heretofore issued according to law, on the second day of April, 1850, with a certificate of personal service according to law, on and before the 15th day of June, A. D. 1850, on the following named persons to serve as jurors at the present term, viz:

1. JACOB LACY
2. JOHN PILES
3. HUGH NEAL
4. THOMAS COX
5. JOHN HAVENS
6. JOHN CHRESTMAN
7. ROBERT MARRS
8. JOHN BROWN
9. DANIEL REUTER
10. OBEDIAH COOK
11. JOHN H. SULLIVAN
12. ALLEN BLAIR
13. DAVIS FREEMAN
14. MANUEL JONES
15. MOSE JONES
16. JACOB D. RAINS
17. JESSE Y. KUYKENDALL
18. JOSEPH MOODY
19. SILAS DUNCAN
20. MARK RUSHING
21. JONAS ERVIN
22. THOMAS CUNNINGHAM
23. REUBEN JOHNSON
24. JOSEPH COX
25. ABRAM McINTURFF
26. DAVID TUMLINSON
27. WILLIAM ROSE
28. JOHN COTHERAN
29. JOHN COHEA
30. SAMUEL SLATER
31. WILLIAM TANKERSLY
32. JOHN HARPER

33. WILLIAM PILES

106

The following named men not found in the county: JAMES DENSON, ANDREW DONLEY and JOHN SCOTT.

Whereupon the sheriff and clerk in open court proceeded to draw the following named persons to compose the grand jury, to wit: 1. ROBERT MARRS; 2. DANIEL REUTER; 3. HUGH NEAL; 4. WILLIAM ROSE; 5. WILLIAM TANKERSLEY; 6. JOSEPH COX; 7. ALLEN BLAIR; 8. JOSEPH MOODY; 9. OBEDIAH COOK; 10. DAVID TUNLINSON; 11. JESSE Y. KUYKENDALL; 12. JOHN BROWN; 13. MOSES JONES; 14. JONAS ERVIN.

Whereupon, ALLEN BLAIR was selected and sworn foreman of the grand jury and his fellows having also been sworn according to law, the said grand jury was charged by the court, touching their duties ,and then retired under the charge of their bailiff, CAREY L. RICE, who was duly sworn as such.

BE IT REMEMBERED, That on the 7th day of September, 1850; there came on to be holden a district court of the county of Van Zandt; Hon. O. M. ROBERTS presiding, in exchange with Hon. B. H. MARTIN, judge of said court; A. J. FOWLER, district attorney; B. W. ANDERSON, sheriff, and ALLEN BLAIR, clerk of said court; when the following proceedings were had, to wit:

The sheriff returned the venire facias into open court, heretofore issued according to law, on the 3rd day of September, 1850, with a certificate of personal service, according to law, on and before the 25th day of September, A. D. 1850, on the following named persons to serve as jurors for the present term, viz:

MORGAN CARTER, WM. PILES, ABRAM McINTURFF, A. J. HORSLEY, JAMES HOOPER, PETER S. BENTON, JAS. GRAY, LAWSON RYASON, OBEDIAH SIMMONS, JOHN BENTY, WM. COLTHROP, MADISON RAWLES, ADAM SULLIVAN, JOHN MOORE, JAS. KING, WYATT PARHAM, SAMUEL HARRISON, CALAMS BECKETT, JAS. TUMLISON, WM. ROSE, DAVID TUNLISON, JAS. SCROGGINS, JAS. KUYKENDALL, WM. McBEE, HAZEL P. FORD, BERRY STRECENER, JAS. M. ALLEN, JOS. ROSIN, ISAAC ANDERSON, ALSEY FULLER, WM. FLATT, HENTY MARRS, WILLIAM WILSON.

The following named persons not found in the county; JUSTEN PRICE, JOHN CARTER, WESLEY NEAL.

The following named persons not having appeared, to wit: WM. PILES, WM. COLTHROP, A. J. HORSLEY, HAZEL P. FORD, ALSEY FULLER, J. L. RIRSON, PETER S. BENTON. And it appearing to the court that they had a lawful excuse were accordingly excused by the court.

The following named persons having answered to their names were placed upon the grand jury, to wit: SAM HARRISON, foreman; ABRAM B. McINTURFF, MADISON RAWLES, JAMES KING, COLUMBUS BECKETT, JAMES TUMLISON, DAVID TUMLISON, JAMES ALLEN, ISAAC ANDERSON, JAMES HOOPER, WILLIAM FLATT, JOHN BENTY, WILLIAM ROSE, JAMES GRAY.

The grand jury having been sworn, were charged by the court concerning their duties, retired. The docket was then called over by the court, and no cases being ready for trial: ordered, that court adjourn for one hour.

Court met pursuant to adjournment. The grand jury came into open court and reported, there was no business before them; whereupon, the court ordered twelve of the grand jurors to take seats as petit jurors.

This venire having been duly called, the following persons answered to their names, to wit: JOHN R. ALLEN, A. J. HORSELY, J. W. ELLIOTT, LEWIS MILLER, DAVID OWENS, C. P. PARKER, MADISON RALLS, MARCUS PHILLIPS, O. SIMMONS, JOHN BATEMAN, JOHN ELLIS, W. W. TANKERSLY, J. R. MARTIN, JOHN PILES, THOMAS L. COX, JAMES GILLILAND, ADAM SULLIVAN, STEPHEN INGRAM, WILLIAM BECK, WYATT RANEY, DAVID TOMLINSON, WILLIAM ROSE, WILLIAM CLARDY, JAMES MOORE, D. R. McCOY, WILLIAM McINTURFF, ELIJAH JAMES; out of which number the grand jury were duly drawn and empannelled and sworn and charged according to law as a grand jury for the body of the county of Van Zandt, to wit: J. R. MARTIN, foreman; O. SIMMONS, JAMES MOORE, DAVID OWENS, DAVID TUMLISON, J. W. ELLIOTT, WM. McINTURFF, STEPHEN INGRAM, JOHN BATEMAN, WM. ROSE, LEWIS MILLER, JAMES GILLILAND, JOHN ELLIS, JOHN R. ALLEN, MARCUS PHILLIPS, who, after having received the charge of the court, retired to consider of their indictment.

Ordered by the court, that a special venire issue, directing the sheriff to summon sixteen good and lawful men to serve upon the petit jury during this term of the court.

The sheriff returned into court the special venire executed and the following named persons were placed upon the petit jury, to wit: ADAM SULLIVAN, A. J. HORSLEY, D. R. McCOY, C. P. PARKER, WYATT RANEY, MADISON RALLS, W. TANKERSLY, JOHN PILES, THOMAS L. COX, WILLIAM CULLREON, A. BIVINS, P. S. BENTON, JOHN NORMAN, JAMES BATES, G. R. TACKETT, WILLIAM BECK, M. E. PACE, SAMUEL R. BARBER, JOAB BRUTON, SIRAS SULLIVANT, E. R. M. BRUTON, Z. P. SHERLY.

J. L. AUSTIN filed his application in writing for a license to practice as attorney and counsellor at law. Whereupon, it was ordered by the court, that STEPHEN REEVES, THOMAS LEWELLING and GEORGE ROSENBAUM be and they are hereby appointed as a committee to examine the said applicant; that the examination take place on tomorrow.

Ordered by the court that the criminal docket be taken up Wednesday morning, next.

No other cases being ready for trial, by consent of parties, the case of the State vs. JACOB RAINS, for assault and battery on the body of JACOB LACY was taken up, and the defendant pleaded not guilty, and after argument case was submitted to the jury. The jury retired and having consulted together returned a verdict, to wit: We, the jury, find the defendant not guilty, and the defendant is discharged. No other business appearing before the court ready for trial; ordered, that court be adjourned until 9 o'clock tomorrow morning.

The clerk having omitted to enter the fine imposed by the court on the absent venire in the proper place, whereupon enter the fine at the foot of the minutes. Absent without excuse: MORGAN CARTER, OBEDIAH SIMMONS, ADAM SULLIVAN, JOHN MOORE, WYATT PARHAM, JAS. SCOGGINS, WM. McBEE, BERRY STRACANER. And ordered by the court that they be fined $5 each and that scire facias issue for them to show cause at the next term of the court.

BE IT REMEMBERED, That on the 7th day of April, 1851, there

came on to be holden a district court for the county of Van Zandt.
Present, the Hon. B. H. MARTIN, judge of said court; and JOHN H.
GRAY, district attorney, pro tem; and L. I. SOLESBY, sheriff;
ALLEN BLAIR, district clerk, by his deputy, J. R. C. HENDERSON,
when the following proceedings were had, to wit: The sheriff re-
turned the venire facias in open court, heretofore issued accord-
ing to law, on the 24th day of February, 1851, for the present
term, viz.: WILLIAM FLATT, JOSEPH COX, R. JOHNSON, DRURY KOEN,
ANTHONY PARHAM, MORGAN CARTER, C. B. MOORE, JAMES KING, I. A.
ASBARRY, LAW MOORE, OBEDIAH SIMMONS, A. B. McINTURFF, JOHN SPEARS,
THOMAS HOOPER, THOMAS COX, M. C. PACE, L. B. LANGFORD, A. SULLI-
VAN, THOMAS SPEARS, JAMES C. GILLILAND, HENRY BREAGLE, MADISON
ROBINSON, JOHN PILES, JOHN MOORE, L. V. ARNOLD, N. S. BRATCHER,
MOSES JONES, C. C. McKINNEY.

The following was excused from serving for serving the for-
mer and present term: I. A. WILSON, STEPHEN INGRAHAM, H. O. HEN-
SON, JAMES GILLILAND, W. H. BUNDY, WM. H. McBEE, JARRELL HAYES,
TIMOTHY TOWNLY and O. SIMMONS.

The grand jury being drawn, sworn and charged as follows, to
wit: C. C. McKINNEY, foreman; JOHN SPEARS, THOMAS HOOPER, THOMAS
COX, M. C. PACE, L. B. LANGFORD, A. SULLIVAN, THOMAS SPEARS, JAM-
ES C. GILLILAND, HENRY CREAGLE, MADISON ROBINSON, JOHN PILES,
JOHN MOORE, L. V. ARNOLD, N. S. BRATCHER, MOSES JONES.

The following were drawn for venire: DRURY KOEN, ANTHONY
PARHAM, MORGAN CARTER, C. B. MOORE, JAMES KING, I. A. ASBERRY,
LEVI MOORE, OBEDIAH SIMMONS, A. B. McINTURFF, WILLIAM FLATT, JOS-
EPH COX and R. JOHNSON. Under the charge of P. S. BENTON, bail-
iff, the grand jury retired.

It was then ordered by the court, that BERRY ANDERSON, JOS-
EPH NEAL and MARTIN MORGAN be fined each ten dollars, and that a
scire facias issue for failing to attend as jurors. Court then
adjourned until tomorrow morning, 9 o'clock.

BE IT REMEMBERED, That on the 11th day of April, A. D. 1853,
there came on to be holden a district court in and for the county
of Van Zandt; present and presiding the Hon. JOHN H. REAGAN,
judge of said court; GEORGE ROSEBAUM, district attorney pro tem;
B. S. BEESON, sheriff, and McDONALD MOORE, clerk, by his deputy,
J. R. C. HENDERSON, when the following proceedings were had, to
wit:

The sheriff returned the venire facias into open court,
heretofore issued according to law, on the 28th day of February,
A. D. 1853, with a certificate of personal service according to
law, on the following named persons to serve as jurors at the
present term, viz.: JOHN R. ALLEN, A. J. HORSLEY, J. W. ELLIOTT,
LEWIS MILLER, DAVID OWENS, C. P. PARKER, JACKSON PHILLIPS, MADI-
SON RALLS, MURCUS PHILLIPS, O. SIMMONS, JOSEPH JAMES, JOHN BATE-
MAN, JOHN ELLIS, W. W. TANKERSLEY, J. R. MARTIN, ROBERT GODFREY,
JOHN PILES, W. W. ROBERTS, THOS. L. COX, JAMES GILLILAND, ADAM
SULLIVAN, STEPHEN INGRAM, WYATT RANEY, BENJAMIN WHEELER, WM.
ROSE, DAVID TUMLINSON, THOS. SPEARS, L. H. HOBBS, WM. B. CLARDY,
JAMES MOORE, D. R. McCOY AND M. McINTURFF.

The following named persons were not found in the county,
viz.: WM. B. CLARDY and CHESLY LEE.

CHAPTER 8

TRANSPORTATION

The first settlement in North Texas was made on Red River, at a point near the lower boundary of Lamar county, about five hundred miles above Natchitoches, by a trading company under the direction of M. FRANCOIS HARVEY in 1757. He built a fort which he named St. Louis de Carioretto, erected a flagstaff and mounted two small pieces of artillery. Several French families settled there and cultivated corn, tobacco and garden vegetables. This is the earliest navigation of which I have any record on Red River.

By a treaty made and entered into by and between the United States and Spain, 1819, the western boundary of the United States was definitely fixed in the Gulf of Mexico, off the mouth of the Sabine river; however, the dividing line was not run until 1839, the year the Cherokee Indians were driven out of East Texas. And then only one hundred and six miles north of 33d parallel line to a point on Red River, fixing the southwestern boundary line of the Louisiana purchase by commissioners appointed by the United States and Mexico. These commissioners concluded their services on the 24th day of June, 1840, and, as strange as it may appear, that is as far as that line was ever run. After this the United States erected forts along the line of her western frontier as a means of protecting the same and her border citizenship. Among these I will mention Forts Jessup in Louisiana, opposite Nacogdoches, and Fort Towson in Oklahoma, at or near the mouth of the Kiomitia River, nearly opposite Paris, Texas. As a basis of supply for these forts, Captain HENRY SHREVE, whose home was Saint Louis, Missouri, was sent with a crew and snagboat to clear Red River for steamboat navigation from its mouth to the nearest point to Fort Towson. The first important service for his snagboat was encountered at Loggy Bayou, the outlet from Lake Bisteneau into Red River. The mouth of this bayou is one hundred and ten miles below Shreveport, Louisiana. Here he found a heavy drift-pile, really the lower end of the great raft in Red River. He cleared the river of all obstructions to a point a short distance above where the present city of Shreveport now stands, which was then the principal village of the Caddo Indians. In 1837, the Shreveport Town company was organized, which founded Shreveport. Captain SHREVE being a charter member and large shareholder. Captain SHREVE did not proceed higher up the river than about the mouth of Twelve Mile Bayou, five or six miles above Shreveport, because he discovered that the river had, in its spring and winter overflows, out channel, principally Cow, Black and Stump Dam bayous, around this raft and filled the great reservoir of what is known as Caddo Lake, although the different sections are known by local names, such as Sodus or Soda Lake, Ferry Lake, Smithland Lake and Clinton Lake. These channels were navigable and it was not necessary to remove the raft.

This brings us to the entrance to the stream in Texas known as Cypress Bayou River. This stream originally flowed into Red River, but the great raft had entirely obliterated its mouth.

Navigation was established up the mouth of the Kiomitia River in high water during the winter and early spring. Jefferson was a great landing, and I have seen many boats tied up at the mouth of Mill Creek opposite Clarksville, loading horses, cattle and cotton.

The shipping points in Texas for Van Zandt county were Port Caddo, a port of entry during the days of the republic of Texas, and Jefferson. Though most of the business from this section went to Shreveport, in Louisiana, from the fact that that city had large wholesale houses and commission merchants with extensive warehouses, and the inland freighting was done with long teams of oxen and they could get loading both ways.

INLAND ROADS

A military road was provided for by the congress of the republic, from the mouth of Bois d'Arc, on Red River to the Nueces River at the crossing of the Presidio road, in 1839. This military road was to be sufficiently cleared and bridged to admit of passage of wagons. Blockhouses, or garrisons, were to be maintained at various points. In the vicinity of each fort three leagues of land were to be surveyed in lots of 160 acres each, two of which lots were to be reserved to the government and two were to be given to each soldier of the regiment on duty along said road for its protection and improvement. The remainder was to be distributed among such ablebodied citizens as would settle upon and cultivate it for the space of two years. The frontier regiment was to consist of eight hundred and forty men, to serve for three years, unless sooner discharged. The regiment was to be divided into fifteen companies of fifty-six men each, and to be stationed along the road as follows: Fifty-six men at Red River; one hundred and sixty-eight men at the three forks of the Trinity; one hundred and twelve men at the Brazos; one hundred and twelve men at Colorado; fifty-six men at the San Marcos; fifty-six men on the Cibolo; fifty-six men at the Rio Frio and two hundred and twenty-four men at Nueces. The troops were to cultivate a part of the three hundred and twenty acres reserved to the government for their sustenance. Beginning in 1840 this road was laid out and opened up by Capt. WILLIAM G. COOK (for a long time in the ranger service of Texas), after some delay and much hardships, from Austin to the mouth of Kiomitia Creek on Red River. It took in White Rock, in what is now Dallas county. In 1840-41 Birds Fort, twenty-two miles west of the present city of Dallas, was built and occupied for a short time by a company of three months; rangers, under Capt. JOHN BIRD. After the rangers left several families located there. Late in November, 1841, JOHN NEELEY BRYAN, a Tennesseean, who had spent some time in the settlements on Red River, camped and erected a tent on the banks of the Trinity, near the site of the present courthouse in Dallas, and remained alone until the succeeding spring, except when visited by persons looking at the country. He was the first settler in Dallas county. In the spring of 1842, several other persons having arrived in the meantime at Bird's Fort, the family of Capt. M. GILBERT being the first and next that of JOHN BEEMAN, the former in canoes and the latter in an ox wagon, abandoned the fort and removed to Dallas; that of BEEMAN to remain permantently. Other families followed until quite a settlement was firmly established. Their nearest markets were Houston, two hundred and seventy-five miles below, and Shreveport, over two hundred miles by the road on Red River, and in the beginning without roads to either place. The military road was changed from White Rock, four miles distant, to Dallas in 1843, and a village speedily sprung up at the latter place, as the road came to be one of the favorite routes of travel for imigrants to Peters' colony and for persons whose distination was points farther in the interior.

COL. JOHN C. McCOY

Col. JOHN C. McCOY was among the first settlers of Dallas; hauled lumber from Colthorp's Mill in Van Zandt county to build the first frame residence in Dallas. This house was located at Commerce and Lamar streets.

Much interest attaches to the Dallas home of Col. JOHN C. McCOY. It stood on the southeast corner of Lamar and Commerce streets, and which is now a solid block of brick business houses.

Colonel McCOY was born in Clark county, Indiana, September 28, 1819. He came to Galveston on New Year's Day, 1845, and went to Houston by steamboat. With Dallas as his destination he came by ox wagon transportation with supplies of sugar, flour, powder, lead, baggage, etc., to the weight of 7,000 pounds. With his companions Colonel McCOY marched beside the wagons with bowie knives and rifles in hand, as far as Cincinnati, on the Trinity River. At Cincinnati he and his associates built a flatboat six and one-half feet wide by thirty-six feet in length, and, with hooks and poles, ascended the Trinity River, crossing Budie Falls and other shoals, at which places they had to unload and reload the boat, then drag the boat over the rocks. It required twelve days to reach Fort Alabama. The boat was there abandoned and ox teams procured and the trip to Fort Houston was made without incident. The rest of the trip was made with a wagon and ponies and, "The next day," wrote Colonel McCOY, in his memoirs, "we took dinner with JOHN BEEMAN on WHITE ROCK CREEK. Thence we went west to Dallas, which consisted of a single pole cabin, ten by twelve feet in size, located on the east bank of the Trinity River and occupied by Col. JOHN NUFF BRYAN and wife."

Mail in those days came from Bonham once in two weeks, "mule back." Dallas was then situated in Nacogdoches county, nearly 200 miles from the countyseat.

Colonel McCOY was made a Mason at Bonham, in Constantine lodge No. 13, in 1848, and the same year assisted in organizing Tannehill lodge in Dallas. In 1849 Colonel McCOY built the first frame house in the country, and in December, 1851, married Miss CORA McDERMOTT, whose father lived in a logcabin in a grove one mile east of Dallas, at what is now Duncan and Worth streets.

SOME HISTORY OF VAN ZANDT COUNTY

Colonel McCOY was an old-time whig in politics, but became a democrat upon the disbandment of that party. He was the first lawyer to locate in Dallas and died at his home on the southwest corner of Main and Harwood streets, April 30, 1887. In 1894 the body of Colonel McCOY, with those of his wife and child, were moved to Oakland cemetery.

CAMP WORTH

June 5, 1849, a troop of the Second United States dragons, under command of Brev. Maj. RIPLEY A. ARNOLD, established a military post on the west fork of the Trinity River, which he named Camp Worth, in honor of Gen. WILLIAM J. WORTH, of Mexican war fame. This name was given the camp October 17, 1849. The name was changed to Fort Worth, November 14, 1849, and the post was abandoned September 17, 1853.

Now, during the occupancy of this fort, a road was opened up east to Shreveport through Van Zandt county, known as the Shreveport and Dallas road, being the first dirt road for wagons to travel to market. In 1846 SAM HUFFER blazed a trail from Nacogdoches by Fort Houston, near Palestine, to Jordan's Saline, now Grand Saline, but it could not be classed a road for transportation. The Dallas and Shreveport road passed near the present town of Wills Point and about one-half mile south of the present town of Grand Saline

THE TYLER AND PORTER'S BLUFF ROAD

In April, 1846, the legislature appointed W. B. DUNCAN, J. C. HILL, E. E. LOTT, JOHN DEWBERRY and JOHN LOLLER, commissioners to locate the county boundary of Smith county and also to locate the countyseat of the county. These commissioners did their work and did it well. Soon after they had concluded their work in this respect JOHN LOLLER opened up a road to the Neches River and put a corduroy bridge across the river where the long bridge is now jointly owned by Smith and Van Zandt counties. In 1845-6 SAM HUFFER settled a big spring near the present line of Henderson and Van Zandt counties, and near what is known as Big Rock; erected him a tent there and followed the occupation of surveying. He was employed in 1849 to lay out a road from Lollar's bridge on the Neches River to Porter's bluff on the Trinity River, and a wagonroad was opened up between these points and known as the Porter's bluff and Tyler road. After Canton was laid out in 1850, the Lollar's bridge road was extended via Canton to Kaufman. These roads wee the means of inland transportation by use of long ox teams in the early settlement of Van Zandt county.

CAMELS IN TEXAS

(From the Memoirs of ex-Governor FRANCIS R. LUBBOCK, who owned a ranch on Buffalo Bayou, near the San Jacinto battlefield.) Old Texans recollect that under the auspices of the Hon.

SOME HISTORY OF VAN ZANDT COUNTY

JEFFERSON DAVIS, then secretary of war under President PIERCE, a cargo of thirty-five camels were landed at Indianola, in the spring of 1856. After a short rest in that vicinity, they were driven up to San Antonio, and a few weeks later the herd of camels went into permanent quarters at Camp Verde, sixty miles southwest of that city. They were in charge of Major WAYNE, who tested with satisfactory results their capacity as swift burden bearers. The next spring forty more landed at Indianola and joined the herd at Camp Verde. In the fall of 1858, a couple of ships, presumably British, anchored at Galveston under suspicious circumstances. They were first thought to be slavers watching a chance of secretly landing their human freight, but the ships turned out to be laden only with camels; at least no evidence appeared that they had any African negroes aboard to sell as slaves. Happening to be in Galveston at the time, I went to see the camels (about forty in number) after they had been landed and penned. Mrs. WATSON, an English lady, owner of the herd, was hunting some reliable person to whom she might intrust its care till finally disposed of by sale or otherwise. I was introduced as a proper person to the lady, and her agent, SENOR MICHADO. A few preliminaries once settled, as to the extent of my obligation for their safety, I contracted with SENOR MICHADO on satisfactory terms to assume the custody and maintenance of the camels when delivered at my ranch. Accordingly a steamboat was chartered on which MICHADO brought the animals to the mouth of Sim's Bayou for delivery. The landing took place in the presence of a crowd of spectators, among whom were SIM ALLEN, JULES BARON and myself. On finding themselves once more on solid ground, they showed their high spirits by jumping, rearing and frisking about like sheep. Observing these capers, BARON remarked that he did not believe that any one could lasso a camel. ALLEN quickly affirmed the contrary, and finally bet BARON ten dollars that he could rope one himself. ALLEN mounted his horse, lasso in hand and with a sharp swing, on first trial threw it over the head of a large camel and brought him safely to the ground after a short struggle. BARON, lately in from Louisiana, had not learned that Texans generally accomplished what they undertook.

MRS. LOOSCAN WRITES ABOUT CAMELS

Houston, January 29, 1899

Judge C. W. RAINS,
        Austin, Texas.
        Dear Sir: I am in receipt of your letter of recent date, requesting that I write out my recollections of camels once pastured near Governor LUBBOCK's ranch, on Sim's Bayou. I think it was in the summer of 1859 that about forty camels, in charge of four or five Arabs were pastured on the south side of the stream at the distance of about a mile from the residence. In company with ELLA HUTCHINS (now Mrs. SEABROOK SYDNOR of this city), JOHN BRINGHURST and CHARLEY GENTRY, all of Houston, I drove over from Harrisburg to see the camels. We were disappointed, however, in

our wish to have a ride on one of them, as the only gentle one was missing from the herd. After a good deal of time spent he was finally discovered mired up to his breast in mud in the bayou. All efforts to extricate him having proved fruitless, the ride was given up; the next day a yoke of oxen succeeded in pulling him out, but the strain was so great the camel did not long survive. Subsequently, when the camels were brought to Harrisburg, one of them was equipped with the peculiar pack-saddle commonly used on those animals. It was covered with rugs or carpets, and the shelflike saddle on one side was occupied by a gentleman friend and myself, while the other side was balanced by another gentleman. We rode about three-quarters of a mile, the camel being led by an Arab, who trotted on ahead, continually encouraging the camel by ejaculations to which he seemed to respond. The long strides made a swinging rough motion, by no means easy, but rapid, and when the ride had come to an end in obedience to command, the animal sank suddenly upon his knees; a headlong plunge for the riders would have resulted but for the rapidity with which the shole came to the ground. . . .

I am, respectfully,

ADELE B. LOOSCAN

A STORY OF A HALF CENTURY OF RAILROAD BUILDING WITH ITS TRIALS AND TRIUMPHS.

The Texas & Pacific railway was stretched across the great states of Texas and Louisiana to fulfill the demands of necessity of travel and railroad building transportation. Five decades ago saw the thin short rails that supported two little engines and a few rudely constructed freight cars, then, today, the modern twentieth century line that gives service that this age demands, comfort, dispatch, accommodation and luxury.

The old timer was here when I came. Ah, I remember him well; and he well deserves to be remembered. There were giants in those days; and there was need there should be. No vestibule trains, nor palace coaches waited to fetch them hither, no noisy procession with banners waiving and brass bands playing marched forth to honor their arrival. They journeyed, for the most part, afoot with a flint lock rifle in hand and a faithful dog at their heels. They picked their way through trackless canebrake and wooded waste across swift running, bridgeless streams. They had quitted what they regarded the overcrowded centers of the populous east to seek a home in the lonely wilds of the west.

Keenly alive to the idea of bettering their condition amid open air and arable lands, they built their logcabins and the smoke ascended in a lonely column. And, so I found them when I

(NOTE: Judge RAINS was once county judge of Van Zandt county. Governor LUBBOCK was an admirer of JEFFERSON DAVIS and was with him when captured in Georgia, after LEE's surrender. Author.)

came with open arms and a hearty welcome, with latchstring hanging out to all newcomers.

They had buried all their hatchets, all their animosities back in the states and were a care-free people. Hardships were toys in their hands and they played with them every day. JOHN DUBERRY was among the early settlers on the east side of the Neches River, in Smith county, and he built the first cotton gin there, and flatboated his cotton down the Trinity River to Galveston to market. Then came BURREL H. HAMBRICK in 1853 and built the first cotton gin in Van Zandt county on the west side of the Neches River in this county. His farm covered the battleground on which Chief BOWLES, the head of the Cherokees was killed in 1839 in the last Indian fight in this country, and his deed expresses the battleground tract. With JOHN P. VEASY, THOMAS HORSELY and others, they hauled their cotton to Magnolia on the Trinity, ten miles west of Palestine and shipped it to Galveston. Then more settlers came and Shreveport became our market, and so remained until the advent of the railroad.

More settlers came and they began to talk railroads and a bunch of enterprising men in Harrison county became inoculated with railroad virus and organized a company under the laws of Texas, known as the Southern Pacific Railroad company. In the latter fifties and with slave labor they commenced to build west from Swanson's landing on Caddo Lake toward Marshall. The work was necessarily slow, for it was almost done by hand. Some pioneers reached Tyler and they called a "big" railroad meeting to tell us all about it, and sent up circulars to Van Zandt and, of course, Van Zandt had to respond. She did herself proud on that occasion, as she always does.

COL. JACK WHORTON

Colonel JACK WHORTON was a native of Maryland, moved to Kansas, where he hung out a sign as a lawyer, having been admitted to the bar in his native state. Border ruffianism was holding the boards in Kansas at that time, and bleeding Kansas was bleeding too much to suit JACK WHORTON. So he pulled up stakes and wended his way to Van Zandt county and opened an extensive horse ranch on the Fitzhugh grant northwest of Wills Point, devoting his time to raising good stock. He secured the services of a brunch of Mexicans and lived for a time in a tent, but later built a double logcabin; living in rather unpretentious way, no one had surmised that he was the possessor of "store bought clothes," but on reading one of Tylers circulars, in 1859, he went down into an old trunk, fished out a factory made hat and pair of shoes and a full-blooded suit of broadcloth clothing, packed a pony with the usual camp equipage, and mounted a Mexican on one horse and himself on the best horse on the ranch, they set out to Tyler to the railroad meeting. That city was then small; houses there were not nearly so numerous as are feuds in Kentucky now or revolutions in Mexico. Tyler had selected EVERETT E. LOTT, RICHARD B. HUBBARD, LEMUEL DALE EVANS and GEORGE W. CHILTON to do the

talking on that memorable occasion, and they were each and every
one of them professional "gab slingers." However, the delegate
from Van Zandt with his Mexican servant had arrived and went
through a barbershop and a copper distilled refreshment stand and
all diked up in his "store bought" clothes he had made an impression that demanded notice. A consulation was held and it was decided to have the gentleman from Van Zandt county to open the
"meetin'." So Col. JACK WHORTON, from Van Zandt was introduced
to make a few preliminary remarks. Col. JACK opened up in good
style.

> And when the blazing sun was set,
> And the grass with dew was wet;
> Colonel JACK was still talking yet,
> The Tyler gang's goat to get.

However, the Marshall people kept hammering away until by
the outbreak of the Civil war, they had a miniature railroad in
operation from Swanson's Landing, on Caddo Lake, to Marshall. A
crude road it would now be considered, but it was a sure enough
railroad just the same, as wide as other railroads, if not so
long.

During the war, the track was taken up between Swanson's
Landing and Jonesville, and the rails, which were the old style
flat iron used in building the confederate gunboat WEBB, which
undertook to run the blockade at and below New Orleans and was
destroyed passing the forts below New Orleans. But this is another story.

After the dove of peace had once more spread her wings over
this glorious Union, Red River from the Mississippi to the mouth
of Kiomitia, a distance of one thousand miles, was floating
steamboats almost as thick as fallen leaves in Vallambrosia.
Cotton went to seventy-five cents a pound, or three hundred and
seventy-five dollars per bale, in currency, which was somewhat
under par. At that time, in the early seventies, all cotton
raised in north and east Texas was hauled to Red River, for shipment to New Orleans. Marshal again was connected to water navigation. This time new rails were laid from Shreveport to Marshall, and during the latter sixties, was extended west of Longview, where another halt was made. Then came the great era of
railroad building in the United States. It makes one's head
grow dizzy to think of the vast sums of money poured out in the
republic for the next thirty years in that one industry alone.
For thirty years we paid out one million dollars per day building
railroads--think of it, think of it! The state of Texas donated
thirty-eight million acres of land to railroads--just think of
that. Of this vast amount, the Texas & Pacific Railroad received
five million, one hundred seventy-three thousand, one hundred and
twenty acres.

Now we will get back to our subject of transportation in Van
Zandt county, as that is what I am trying to tell about.

In 1872, the Texas & Pacific Railway company purchased or

secured control of the sixty-six miles of trackage between Shreveport and Longview and let a contract to the California Construction company, of which Gen. GRENVILLE M. DODGE was president, to commence active construction of the Texas & Pacific. Col. THOMAS A. SCOTT is considered the "father of the T. & P. railray," at that time being president of the Pennsylvania Railway.

In October, 1872, active work was commenced at four different points; at Marshall the rails went north, in the direction of Texarkana, and this line was completed on December 31, 1875. Work was also commenced at Longview, building west in the direction of Dallas, and at Dallas easterly towards Longview, and the two ends of track met on August 16, 1873, in the Grand Saline creek bottoms, about two and one-half miles below where the first log courthouse was built in Van Zandt county. Then there was completed a through line from Shreveport to Dallas. And though the track was not in best condition, service was put on and at the first siding on the prairie, a car was set out for a temporary depot. Within a few days a train going west stopped at the depot, and a cowboy reined up alongside of it to take in the situation. He was mounted on a small pony. The riders hair and boot tops, into which his trousers were stuffed, nearly met. He wore a sombrero and long gauntlets and his boots were decorated with murderous-looking spurs. From one side of his saddle horn hung a cow whip, while from the other dangled a Spanish gourd covered with buckskin, and from his saddle hung a rawhide lariat. A newcomer to Texas stuck his head out of the car window and took a long, fond look at the first prairie his eyes had ever beheld. Then he inquired: "Isn't this exhilirating?" "No, sir-ee," answered the cowboy in defense of his town, "this is Iola." And so the matter stood for some time, when the old timers petitioned the postmaster general to name it Wills Point, and so it stands today.

About this time, in company with Dr. J. D. WRIGHT, the first district clerk of Van Zandt county, I called at Uncle JOHNNIE CHRESTMAN's, where we spent the night. Uncle JOHNNIE lived a few miles west of Grand Saline on the old Shreveport-Dallas road, and after we had cared for our horses I thought I would congratulate Uncle JOHNNIE on his good fortune in having at last secured a railroad so near to him. In the best words I could command I broached the subject. But, oh, my, this brought Uncle JOHNNIE to his feet with clenched fist and set teeth, it was like shaking a red rag in the face of a gentleman cow. He said the country was ruined, that the railroad had built across his fishing hole where he had spent thirty summers and there would never be any more game in Van Zandt county and that there was nothing more worth living for.

But I must get back to railroad building. In the year 1872, in October, construction of the Trans-Continental line of the Texas & Pacific was begun at Sherman, and was completed, on July, 1873, eastwardly to Brookston, fifty-four miles east of Sherman and eight miles west of Paris, and Brookston remained the terminus of that line until December, 1875, when the construction of the line was recommenced by building east from Brookston and west from what is now known as Nash, but formerly known as T. C. Junction, five miles west of Texarkana. The two ends of the line met at a point three miles west of DeKalb on August 18, 1876, thus completing the line from Texarkana to Sherman.

Prior to the Civil War, the Memphis, El Paso & Pacific Railroad company was chartered by the state, and more or less grading was done on this line between Paris and Texarkana, and from the latter place to Jefferson during the sixties and seventies.

The Texas & Pacific was extended from Dallas (Eagle Ford) to Fort Worth and reached the latter place July 19, 1876. The line from Sherman by the way of Whitesboro to Fort Worth was completed in the year 1881. An extension of the road westward form Fort Worth was completed in January, 1880, and the track was completed to Sierra Blanca in 1881, at which time a contract was made with the G. H. & S. A. Railway permitting the joint trackage between Sierra Blanca and El Paso, a distance of ninety-two miles, thus completing a line from Shreveport and Texarkana to El Paso.

The line was then connected up to New Orleans. The last report I have shows that the Texas and Pacific railroad had a capital stock of $38,000,760,110, owned by 916 persons.

Texas is now cross-sectioned with railroads and they are our best friends. If we have a short crop of anything in one portion of the state they carry the products there from the fields of another section. And they carry our products to the markets of the world. They are great civilizers, in that they transport the mails so rapidly that the great daily newspapers, by the use of them and the rural delivery service, reach the farmers generally on the day of publication.

The incoming population of educated, progressive and hustling people have built up institutions of learning, churches, libraries and created modern and effective governments, both state and municipal.

The days of the desperado, the landshark and the cattle thief have ended, and though this has been done within the past quarter of a century, it is nevertheless fully accomplished.

Western Texas, which was the last refuge of that ill-favored class, is clear of them. The country which a few years ago was open to be grazed by any man's cattle is now under fence and divided in great pastures. The north and south lines of railway stopped the driving of stock north over the great trail.

With ranches under fence and the trail abolished, the occupation of the wild, irresponsible cowboy was at an end. Competition came and the cowman had to get down to business and look after the details of his affairs. From a man who saw civilization only once a year, when he drove his cattle to market, he has become a keen business man. He has no more use for a six-shooter now than a broker in wall street, and, like the broker, his whole a-tention is riveted on the daily reports of the market. Many of them are millionaires, with palatial homes in place of the dugout of thirty years ago. The long horned steers have gone and the white-faced Herefords have come in their stead.

SOME HISTORY OF VAN ZANDT COUNTY

LAND DONATIONS TO RAILROADS OF TEXAS

(Compiled by Hon. W. L. McGAUGHEY, who formerly lived in the neighborhood of Watkins schoolhouse. He also taught school in Van Zandt county.)

The following shows the name of the railroad and the number of acres donated to each:
Austin & Northwestern Ry. Co., 392,320 acres; Buffalo Bayou B. & Col., 896,640 acres; Columbus Tap, 49,280 acres; Chicago, Texas & Mes., 411,520 acres; Central & Montgomery, 279,040; C. C. S. D. & R. G. N. G., 721,600 acres; Denison & Southeastern, 215,680 acres; Dallas and Wichita, 414,080 acres; Denison and Pacific, 426,240; East Line & Red River, 1,184,000 acres; East Texas, 231,040; Eastern Texas, 294,400 acres; Galveston Houston & Harrisburg, 611,840 acres; Galveston Brazos and C. N. G., 158,720 acres; Georgetown, 103,040 acres; Gulf Col. & Santa Fe, 3,637,120 acres; Galveston Harrisburg & S. A., 1,432,960 acres; Gulf West T. and P., 302,720 acres; Houston, E. & W. Texas, 839,680 acres; Houston and G. N., 2,311,040 acres, H. & T. C., 4,769,280 acres; Houston Tap and B., 512,000 acres; Henderson and O. B., 153,600 acres; I. & G. N., 3,352,320 acres; Indianola, 179,840 acres; Longview & Sabine Valley, 108,800 acres; M. K. & T. Extension, 325,120 acres; Memphis, El Paso & Pacific, 262,400 acres; Rusk Transportation, 79,360 acres; Southern Pacific 599,040 acres; Sabine and East Texas, 432,640 acres; San Antonio and Mexico, 276,489 acres; Texas Western N. G. 430,720 acres; Texas & Pacific, 5,173,120 acres; Tyler Tap, 470,400 acres; Texas T., 351,360 acres; Texas Central, 1,806,080 acres; Texas-Mexican, 735,000 acres; Texas & St. Louis, 1,614,080 acres; Texas & New Orleans, 1,228,800 acres; Waxahachie Tap, 116,480 acres; Waco & Northwestern, 481,280 acres; Washington Coutny, 245,229 acres; making a grand total of 38,826,880 acres.
REMARKS: Of the 60,667 certificates, about 6000 were barred.

General Land Office, Austin, April 12, 1892
I, W. L. McGAUGHEY, Commissioner of the General Land Office of the State of Texas, hereby certify that the foregoing statement in regard to land certificates issued to railway companies is true and correct according to the records of this office.
In testimony whereof, I have hereunto set my hand and affix the impress of said office, the date last above written.

W. L. McGAUGHEY,
Commissioner General Land Office.

THE FOWLERS

Before dismissing the matter of railroads, I feel like I ought to pay a tribute to one of the well deserving employe's of The Texas & Pacific Railway company; one that was with us until it seemed that he was a part and parcel of us. I refer to LIT

FOWLER, so long a conductor on the T. & P. He was a grandchild of the Rev. LITTLETON FOWLER, who came to Texas during the days of the revolution. His headright certificate for 640 acres of land is laid on the headwaters of Little Saline Creek in Van Zandt county.

LITTLETON MORRIS FOWLER

LITTLETON MORRIS FOWLER was a son of LITTLETON and MISSOURI FOWLER; he was born in the FOWLER home near McMahon chapel, in Sabine county, then in the Republic of Texas, October 15, 1841. He grew up under the ordinary environments then prevailing in the infant republic. At the age of five years he lost his father. In 1857 he entered the McKinzie institute, a Methodist school near Clarksville, in Red River county, Texas, where he remained until 1860. In the fall of 1862 he inlisted in the Fourteenth Texas cavalry, C. S. A., in the company of JOHN L. CAMP, serving throughout the remainder of the war. At the close of this bloody conflict, he went to Tuscaloosa, Alabama, where he married Miss AUGUSTA ISABELLA LYNCH, to which union, six children, four daughters and two sons were born. In 1872 he removed to Texas and settled on his father's old home place, near McMahon chapel, in Sabine county, where he was born. Here he entered the ministry, joining the old East Texas conference, in 1872. He remained a member of conference until his death, which occurred at Henderson, Texas, January 20, 1917, after a long useful life.

LITTLETON AUGUSTA FOWLER

Was a son of LITTLETON MORRIS and AUGUSTA LYNCH-FOWLER; he was born in Tuscaloosa, Alabama, March 21, 1869. He came to Texas with his parents when he was eight years of age. He began work with the I. & G. N. Railroad when he was only nineteen years of age, and continued in the railroad service until his death. He entered the service of the Texas & Pacific Railroad as brakeman, in January, 1893, and was promoted to conductor in June, 1898, and remained in the service in that capacity during the remainder of his life. For a number of years his home was in Wills Point, where he was married to Miss CLOTA MOUGHON, the daughter of Dr. and Mrs. W. C. MOUGHON. To this union there was born three children, to-wit: FLORINE FOWLER, ADA LOUISE FOWLER and HARRIS FOWLER, all of whom survive him and reside with their mother in Fort Worth. For a number of years his run was out of Wills Point, but later the division point was changed and his run was out of Fort Worth, in which city his death occurred on Tuesday morning, May 23, 1916. He was laid to rest in White Rose cemetery, at Wills Point. So that at least one of the FOWLERS found a last resting place in Van Zandt county.

FANNIE FOWLER-CAIN

Was a daughter of LITTLETON MORRIS and AUGUSTA LYNCH-FOWLER, and a sister to LITTLETON AUGUSTA FOWLER. She was living in Van Zandt county when she was married to Rev. D. L. CAIN, a member of the Texas Methodist conference, at Ben Wheeler, November 9, 1897. They lived in Canton from December, 1901, until July 18, 1903, when Reverend CAIN died and was laid to rest in Canton cemetery. So it will be seen that two of the FOWLERS were married in Van Zandt county.

POPULATION OF VAN ZANDT COUNTY BY DECADES AND FOR THE YEAR 1909

    1850, 1,348; 1860, 3,777; 1870, 6,494; 1880, 12,619; 1890, 16,225; 1900, 25,481; 1909, scholastics, 6,266; 1909, population at 5½ persons to scholastic, 34,463.

CHAPTER 9

THE CAPITAL OF THE UNITED STATES

In the early days of the American republic, it was void of a home for several years, and the place of official meetings was changed, as time and circumstances dictated.

During the Revolutionary war, the congress of the confederation held its sessions generally at Philadelphia, then the most important city in the country. The exigencies of war sometimes forced it to withdraw to other places, but as soon as the dangers had passed, it returned.

At the close of the war the question of a permanent seat of government at once arose. The discussion of the subject was carried on with considerable acrimony, and the conflicting claims of various sections of the country seemed irreconcilable. Now one place, now another was chosen, only to be set aside at a subsequent meeting, and the final determination seemed as far off as ever. New York, Philadelphia, Baltimore, Harrisburg, Trenton, Georgetown, the banks of the Delaware above Philadelphia, all were more or less favored at one time or another. The constitution was promulgated and adopted, but the question of the national capital was still unsettled; it was left to the determination of the first congress under the new government, power being given "to exercise exclusive legislation in all cases whatsoever, over such district (not exceeding ten miles square), as may, by cession of particular states, and the acceptance of congress, become the seat of government of the United States."

The first congress of the United States met at New York, March 4, 1789, but on account of the nonarrival of some of its members, it was not ready for business until a month later. The second session of the first congress began January 4, 1790. Necessary public business took up much of the time, and the capital question was not mentioned until May, when a bill was introduced into the senate and favorably reported by the committee, locating the capital on the Potomac. When the bill came before the senate, June 28, 1790, locating the seat of government "on the River Potomac, at some space between the mouths of the eastern branch and the Concocheague." On the vote being taken, it stood sixteen yeas to nine nays. The bill came before the house July 9, 1790; it was passed as it came from the senate. Thirty-two yeas to twenty-nine nays.

July 16, 1790 (approved).

GEORGE WASHINGTON,
President United States

The cornerstone of the president's house was laid October 13, 1792; the cornerstone of the capitol was laid September 18, 1793. The seat of government was transferred from Philadelphia to Washington in October, 1800.

The invasion of the city of Washington by the British was a great calamity. On the 24th of August, 1814, the British, in numbers, reached Bladensburg, just outside the District of Columbia; had a small fight with some raw militia, and marched onto Washington; reached the eastern grounds of the capitol the same evening. According to the British statement, General ROSS had sent in a flag of truce before entering the city, intending to levy a contribution, but not destroy it. The flag was fired upon, and the destruction of the city followed.

The buildings burned were the unfinished capitol, with contents of the library of congress, and many valuable paintings and archives; the treasury; the white house; the arsenal, and some private buildings.

The loss to the government was over $2,000,000; and to private individuals about $500,000.

THE CAPITAL OF TEXAS

In the days of the Republic of Texas, the capital thereof was something like a band of Gypsies--very much on the move.

To begin with, the declaration of independence, March 2, 1836, was made at Washington, on the Brazos; temporary organization of government was at Harrisburg, where President BURNETT and cabinet moved a few days after adjournment at Washington, on the Brazos.

Santa Anna's approach caused President BURNETT to move with his cabinet to Galveston. After the battle of San Jacinto President BURNETT and cabinet left Galveston and established the seat of government at the mouth of the Brazos, at Velasco and Quintana. It was at Velasco that the treaties with Santa Anna were consummated while he was a prisoner of war.

The seat of government was transferred to Columbia, October, 1836; SAM HOUSTON was inaugurated president at this place. It was at Columbia that the first laws of the republic were enacted, and the government of Texas permanently organized.

From Columbia the seat of government was moved to Houston, where congress met in May, 1837. Houston remained the capital until 1839, when congress decided to locate the government at a city that should bear the name of Austin. Austin is the present capital.

Fearing an attack by the Mexicans, President HOUSTON called congress to meet at Houston (1842). Some time later President HOUSTON removed headquarters to Washington, on the Brazos, where, by proclamation, he convened the next session of congress. Here he delivered his valedictory, and here President ANSON JONES was inaugurated.

President ANSON JONES convened the convention at Austin, July 4, 1845, to consider the proposed terms of annexation made by the United States. On February 19, 1846, from the gallery of the old capitol at Austin, President JONES delivered his valedictory, and Governor HENDERSON was inaugurated the first governor of Texas. The seat of government has not been changed since that date.

It will be noticed, that after the government had been duly established at Austin, President HOUSOTN convened the congress at

SOME HISTORY OF VAN ZANDT COUNTY

Houston, and this aroused great indignation among the people in
and around Austin, and a great portion of the government archives
were seized and boxed up and held until after the election of AN-
SON JONES, as president of the Republic of Texas, and he convened
the convention at Austin, since which time Austin has been the
capital of Texas. The fact of the archives having been held in
durance vile has, in history, been styled the "Archive War."

THE COUNTY SEAT OF VAN ZANDT COUNTY

   A nomadic corporation established at Jordan's Saline by law.
Located at Canton by chance, accident or mistake. Moved to Wills
Point without warrant of law. Returned to Canton by order of
commissioners' court.
   Politics were abroad in the land then, but parties had not
been organized as they have since, yet a sample dish might be set
before the reader in an act of the legislature of 1850 creating
Wood county out of territory from Van Zandt county. A large family of grown men named ANDERSON settled on the west side of the
Sabine River near the northern line of Van Zandt county; one of
them ,BERRY W., was the second sheriff elected in Van Zandt county; another, ISAAC, had put in a hand ferryboat across the river
on the road from Cedar Grove to Jefferson and if, in the creation
of a new county the river covering the ferry was made the line,
the ferryman would have to pay a license to each county; if, however, the land on each bank was assigned to one county only one
license could be collected, so, in the act creating Wood county,
all the territory north of the Sabine River was assigned to Wood
county, except about three leagues covering the landing of the
ferryboat owned by IKE ANDERSON, and so it remained until Rains
county was created in 1870. "Fluence" was looked for then as
now. Van Zandt haveing parted with about half of her territory
by reason of the creation   county it became necessary
to locate a new countyseat, which was done by the holy trinity of
chance, accident and mistake. THOMAS MILLS, living in Kaufman
county was a settler in Mercer's colony, for which he received a
land certificate for 640 acres of land, which he transferred to
OBEY W. OWENS, on the 18th day of November, 1850. One-half of
this certificate was purchased by the commissioners' court of Van
Zandt county, on the 23d day of December, 1850. At that time the
district surveyor's office was located at Nacogdoches. ENOCH C.
TINNEN was a deputy surveyor and he was given the certificate to
locate as near the center of the county as he could find suitable
land on which to locate the countyseat. He located the certificate about two and one-half miles northwest of the present town
of Canton. The location was reasonably a fair one and the commissioners' court designated it as the Canton town tract, sent a
surveyor on the ground to block it into lots and blocks, but as
the district land office was at Nacogdoches and the maps in use
were far from perfect, the country a "wilderness of woe" and but
few bearings to govern a surveyor, in this instance the surveyor
commenced at the east corner of same, making a difference of

about two and one-half miles in locating the town and located it on land belonging to a private individual instead of the county of Van Zandt as was intended. After the town was surveyed the commissioners' court passed and had recorded the following:

Ordered by the court that JAMES BUNDY be appointed to build a courthouse in the town of Canton, the county seat of Van Zandt county, on the plan as follows, to wit: The wall to be eight feet high, width and length to be eighteen feet, cracks lined with boards, to be covered with four-foot boards nailed on, and a good puncheon floor, one door and shutter, and one window and shutter, the house to be completed against the 20th of December, 1850, and it is further ordered by the honorable court that the archives of Van Zandt county be moved as soon as the courthouse is finished. And, whereas, E. C. TINNEN proposes to obtain a patent for the town tract including the town of Canton for 320 acres of land for the sum of $50 to be paid on receipt of the patent county court by the treasurer of said county, it is evident by the court that the foregoing proposition be accepted, if the same be accepted within six months form the present date.

JAS. M. HARRISON,
C. J. Van Zandt Co.

JAMES BUNDY was then one of the county commissioners and lived about one mile southeast of the present town of Edgewood and died on his farm in the early fifties. His son, DAVID T. BUNDY, who did most of the work on the courthouse, lived then near Lindale, in Smith county. The house stood on the west side of the public square and was accepted by the court, and on the 11th day of February, 1851, the court ordered, "That JESSE A. AS-BURY be allowed $5 for removing the archives to the countyseat of Van Zandt county." Now, this is some of the Jeffersonian simplicity we hear the modern politician in his tailormade suit and derby hat preaching about.

The court also had another building erected that will be interesting to an up-to-date gentleman in kidgloves who has his cuffs and collars laundered by steam fifty miles from home, so we give the order of the commissioners' court describing the work:

Ordered that a jailhouse be built described as follows: Out of postoak timber ten inches square to be ten feet in the clear, in the (square) double walls, six inches between each wall to be filled with peeled round timbers, floor to be out of 10 inch square timbers to come under the plains, nine feet between the floors. Each floor must be 1st together and pinned with one and one-half inch wooden pins; a good framed roof covered with two foot boards well nailed on shingle fashion to show eight inches. The foundation must be rock two feet under the ground; sills twelve by thirteen inches to be put on rock. Underneath the floor to be filled with timbers three sides hewn to the top of the sill, the lower floor to be put across said timbers; door five high, two feet and six inches wide, to be a double door, the inner shutter to be iron grates two inches broad and one-half inch thick three inches apart. The upright and crossbars must be rivited with one-half inch rivits; the outer shutter to be out of one-inch oak plank and it double, one eightpenny nail in every square inch and then clinched on the inside; the inner door shutter to be hung with two of the crossbars so it will be firm and steadfast; each door to be cased with a bar of iron two and one-half inches wide and three-quarters of an inch thick, to be spiked with one-half inch spikes in the end of each log; one window of twelve inches framed out of iron bars two and one-half inches wide and three-quarters of an inch thick, with bars one inch square and one inch apart fastened on the inside of the outer wall and spiked with half-inch spikes three inches apart; the gable ends to be weatherboarded with good plank in workmanlike order; the outside door to be hung with good wrought hinges and to have a good jail lock.

JOHN NORMAN contracted to build the jail and AANAN KNUDSON, a Norwegian, living on Four Mile prairie, this county, subcontracted to get out the timbers and do most of the work. The building was completed in "good workman-like order," received and paid for by the court, then came the tug of war. On the 8th day of December, 1852, a patent to the 320 acres of land was issued by the state of Texas to the chief justice of Van Zandt county and in the spring of 1853, ENOCH C. TINNIN, who contracted with the court, appeared in court with the patent.

The county records had been located here since January, 1851, from which time to April, 1852, the inhabitants of the new town had received their mail at Barren Ridge, eight miles distant, but on the last-named date GEORGE FAIN qualified as postmaster at Canton and opened a postoffice here supplied by mail from Gum Spring, and Starrville, once a week.

And now the commissioners' court had received and paid for the patent to the Canton town tract (THOMAS MILLS' 320 acres), two years after the courthouse and jail had been built and one year after the postoffice had been opened, then the fact was disclosed that the land owned by the county was two and one-half miles from that occupied by the county buildings.

The people in the country favored a removal to the land owned by the county, but the town people were for remaining where they were. At the August election, 1852, ANDREW J. HUNTER was elected chief justice of the county and the town people admonished him to secure title to the land they occupied and he set about trying to do so.

JOHN GEORGE WOLDERT

JOHN GEORGE WOLDERT was born at Adorf in Saxony, July 18, 1814. Rebelling at the military tyranny of the kingdom, he fled to America, landing in New York, November 5, 1838; when, notwithstanding his extreme youth, became foreman in the guitar establishment of the celebrated Marton in Maiden Lane. In this place he did not remain long, however, but went to Charleston, South Carolina; remained there a short time only, when he received a pressing call to return to New York, from HENRY FISHER, who, at that time, was organizing a colony for Texas. Being master of four languages was the main cause of his employment with FISHER, but they soon disagreed and parted company. Mur. WOLDERT came to Texas alone, reaching the then small village of Galveston, November 5, 1839. Finding the yellow fever prevailing as an epidemic he remained on the Galveston Island only one day, when he started out on foot and alone through the wilderness for eastern Texas to find an old classmate, the celebrated Dr. SEIBOLD, who, on account of his political views, had been banished from his own country, and had taken up his abode with the Indians in the wilds of Jasper county. While on this journey he fell in company with the Hon. GEORGE W. SMYTH, one of the land commissioners of the Republic of Texas, who was then surveying the line between Texas and Louisiana. Mr. WOLDERT had been an expert civil engineer in the army of Germany and he prevailed upon him to assist in locating the line. This work was terminated on Red River and from there he set out again to find his way to Jasper county. While on his way he was captured by a roving band of Indians and carried to a point on the Colorado River near Bastrop, where he made his escape. After a few weeks of wandering alone in the deep-tangled wildwood he reached the hospitable home of Dr. SEIBOLD.

Texas possessed more wild land than anything else and Mr. WOLDERT took up land surveying as an occupation and located at San Augustine. In this way he soon became possessed of a large quantity of land, among which was the northeast half of the JESSE STOCKWELL league and labor. Here Judge HUNTER found him, in 1853, and explained the situation of the Van Zandt countyseat having squatted on his land. His home at that time was in San Antonio. In 1850 he had visited the World's Fair at London and from thence he had wended his way to his old home at Adorf, where he met and married Miss ALMA EDILINA RITCHTER; returned to America and established him a home in San Antonio, where there was a large German element and they naturally felt more comfortable among that element of society. At that time Mr. WOLDERT owned land in twenty-seven counties in east Texas, and because Van Zandt county was a squatter on a part of the JESSE STOCKWELL league, he executed a deed of gift to said county, "For countyseat purposes," to one hundred and sixty acres thereof.

In 1859 he moved to Tyler, where this writer made his acquaintance in 1870, and found him a great conversationalist and free and open-hearted man.

JOHN GEORGE WOLDERT came to Texas about the latter part of year 1839, and shortly afterward located at San Augustine. He was a practical surveyor and secured title to quite a quantity of land in Texas and, among other grants, the northeast half of the JESSE STOCKWELL league and labor, on which the town of Canton had been located. Judge HUNTER found Mr. WOLDERT at San Augustine and on January 25, 1853, he executed a deed of gift to Van Zandt county for 160 acres of land covering the county buildings and surrounding settlements. This satisfied the town people, but the country people longed to have the town located on the THOMAS

MILLS survey and the matter was discussed more or less at intervals, but no public demonstration was made until the spring of
1857, when, on the 18th day of May, the commissioners' court let
a contract to FREDERICK EZELL to build a brick courthouse on the
public square. The old-timers came to the front and said if the
courthouse was built they would never pay for it. The house was
built at a contract price of $6,355. The court paid out all the
available funds on the house, received it, moved the records into
it and issued script to Mr. EZELL for the remainder of his claim,
but at the August election, in 1858, the country people were
heard from. They elected a court, pledged not to pay the courthouse claims and this was followed in 1860 and so on from time to
time. During the war between the states the debt could have been
paid in confederate money and no one missed it, but there were
enough of the opposition left to hold the county offices and the
debt staved off. In 1871 the house was torn down by order of the
commissioners' court and a wooden building erected in its stead.
On the 29th day of May, 1877, an election was held throughout the
county for the removal of the county seat from Canton to Wills
Point and the legal votes as counted by the commissioners' court
was for Wills Point, 652, and for Canton, 310; so the court ordered the records removed from Canton to Wills Point, to which order
T. J. TOWLES, et al., filed a contest which was carried to the
supreme court. The records were moved to Wills Point. The fall
term of the district court was approaching and the contestants
became restless at the law's delay in the matter of settling the
courthouse question, and volunteers were asked for to bring the
records back to Canton. The boys enrolled. The day was set for
Monday so as to make a good week's work, and when the bugle
sounded at 10 o'clock on the day of rendezvous, Canton's three
hundred and ten were in line and the march commenced; then it was
that Wills Points' six hundred and twelve weakened. However,
over the house containing the records a United States flag about
the size of a regulation napkin fluttered like an aspen leaf in
a cyclone; the town was put in a state of defense; its streets
blockaded with wagons, boxes and any available material to prevent or delay an entrance by force. The governor was appealed to
and he promptly ordered out the Stonewall grays and Lamar rifles
under command of Colonels EBLIN and BOWER, and they hastened to
the relief of the 652 then in distress, at a siding on the Texas
& Pacific railroad, formerly called Iola, but now called Wills
Point. The writer was a noncombatant in this struggle, on account of his religious scruples, but he entered the fortified town
and was met by some of the 652 and implored to help them turn a
countyseat loose which they very much regretted having took up in
their hitherto peaceful town and at that time was causing them
much anxiety of mind and loss of sleep. Complying with these re-
quests, the writer visited Colonel ELBIN's headquarters at the
O'NEAL, now the Harris House, and tendered his kindly offices in
terminating the war. After a short consultation, it was agreed
that the writer repair to Canton, get as many of the 310 to meet
at the old courthouse as possible and Colonel ELBIN and Col. J.

C. KEARBY, of Dallas would come on later and arrange for an arm-
istice, pending the decision of the supreme court on the question
of removing the countyseat from Canton to Wills Point. The meeting was held and addressed by both EBLIN and KEARBY, and Canton
agreed to wait a reasonable time to hear from the supreme court,
meantime they wanted the 652 to know that they would keep their
powder dry.

After the supreme court had handed down its decision in the
case of ex-parte T. J. TOWLES, et al., the commissioners; court
of Van Zandt county met in special session at Wills Point and
promulgated and recorded the following order, to wit:

Whereas, the law under which the county seat was changed
from Canton to Wills Point is claimed by the supreme court to be
defective and repugnant to the present constitution, this court,
though not recognizing the binding force of a dictum of the supreme court, yet in the interest of public peace, now orders the
public records to be returned to Canton; and it is further ordered that the sheriff immediately transfer said records from their
place of deposit at Wills Point to the courthouse at Canton.

Then the 310 had a Fiesta de Grande; many fatted calves were
killed in honor of the prodigal's return. The Canton braves had
laid the foundation on which Admiral DEWEY built a victory without the loss of a man, and they did all eat and were filled, and
honorably mustered out of service; having gone through a six
months' campaign and never met a reverse.

On the 16th day of August, 1878, the commissioners; court in
session at Canton, passed and recorded the following order:

Whereas, it is the duty of this court ot co-operate with all
good citizens in their efforts to allay the hostile feelings between the different sections of the county, engendered in the
late public trouble. And, whereas, the allowance of certain accounts against Van Zandt county, known as war claims, would have
a contrary effect, postponing the era of good feeling which should
exist. It is therefore ordered by the court that said accounts,
amounting in the aggregate to the sum of $400, be rejected with-
out further consideration.

This was the last act closing the hostilities of war in
which the only bloodshed was that of fatted claves, the veterans
of which have never held a reunion nor asked for a pension.

We now return to the EZELL courthouse claims. On the 30th
day of April, 1880, a mandamus was issued out of the district
court of Van Zandt county, compelling the commissioners' court of
said county to levy and have collected a tax to pay these claims.
Thus it was after nearly all of the old-timers had played their
part on life's stage and crossed the river, another generation
paid the debt contracted by the commissioners' court of 1857.
This is not a case exactly in point of the sins of the fathers
being visited on their offspring, but another citizenship paid a
debt in which they never at any time had any interest.

After the payment of the EZELL claims, the people had hoped
that matters pertaining to the courthouse question in Van Zandt
county would settle down to a normal condition, but on the 4th

day of September, 1894, another storm appeared on the horizon. On that day the commissioners' court let a contract to OTTO P. KROEGER to build another brick courthouse in Canton at a contract price of $49,000, and issued courthouse bonds to amount of $50,000, apparently for the purpose of paying for the courthouse, but an election was pending for county officers and an anti-courthouse ticket was put in the field and elected on the first Tuesday in November. After which on November 12, the $50,000 courthouse bonds were burned and the court having accepted a bond from Mr. KOEGER in the sum of $50,000, to complete the work of building the house as per his contract, turned over to him $35,000 in Archer county bonds formerly held by the school fund of the county and on November 13th, one day after the burning of the $50,000 bonds the court issued $26,000 county bonds, $14,000 of these were turned over to the contractor, thus paying him in full for his work, which had now commenced. On November 17th, the old court met again and issued $35,000 in bonds, thus having burned $50,000 worth of bonds and issued $61,000 in bonds after the new court had been elected. About the 1st of February, 1895, a suit was filed in the district court of Van Zandt county styled Van Zandt county vs. OTTO P. KOEGER, et al., by reason of which suit the judge of the third judicial district court of Texas, on the 22nd day of January, granted an injunction against KROEGER and others pending the issue of the suit. At the spring term of the district court of Van Zandt county, the suit was dismissed. The courthouse has been completed and is now occupied by the county officials and peace for the time being reigns in Warsaw.

THE WILLS POINT WAR

Its Causes and Responsibility. Biographical Sketches of the Great Men Who officiated Therein, All of Them Confederate Soldiers. Burning Telegraphic Correspondence.

JUDGE C. W. RAINS

Judge C. W. REINS was born September 18, 1839, Upson county, Georgia, and came to Texas in early manhood. He was a Princeton man, but left there, when a junior, in 1858. He joined the confederate army early in the Civil war, entering the service under Capt. (later general) R. M. GANO, and remained in the service until the close of the conflict. After civil government was restored to Texas, he entered on the practice of law and came to Canton as a partner of J. J. HILL, then of Kaufman, and a law office under the firm name of HILL & REINS, and was employed in some hotly contested cases. Judge HILL came to Canton from New Orleans, during Governor THROCKMORTON's term of office, and later went to Kaufman, and was appointed to codify the law of Texas. Judge RAINS was county judge of Van Zandt county in 1876-1878, and ex-officio superintendent of public instruction of the county during his term as judge. After his term of office as judge expired in Van Zandt county, he lived for a time at Wills Point, and from there he moved to Quitman and was county judge of Wood county from 1886 to 1890. There he became personally well acquainted with JAMES STEPHEN HOGG, and when Governor HOGG went to Austin to qualify as governor, Judge RAINS moved to that city and was appointed state librarian, May 5, 1891, and served until January 18, 1895, during the whole of HOGG's administration. He then engaged in writing books and editing others for a short time and was again appointed librarian, and held the office until his death, which occurred at Austin, August 2, 1906. His remains were laid to rest at Round Rock, Texas.

Judge RAINS was a man of wonderful memory. In a casual conversation about common day events, he would store away every word one would say, and held it as a ready reference for all coming time. He was a forceful writer and seldom had to look up any authority he had ever read, although he was an incessant reader.

Judge RAINS gave this version of the countyseat question in Van Zandt county:

In 1877 the peace of the State was seriously threatened by a countyseat dispute in Van Zandt county, but happily the conservative good sense of the people there prevented any bloodshed.

In counting the returns of the election held for determining the countyseat, several boxes were thrown out on account of irregularities, and Wills Point was declared to be the legal countyseat. The records were accordingly removed from Canton to Wills Point, by order of the county commissioners' court. A few months later an armed force of about 500 men was organized at Canton, and led by Hon. T. J. TOWLES, a member of the legislature, and moved on Wills Point with a view of taking possession of the records and returning them to Canton by force, if necessary. Troops, sent by Governor HUBBARD, went to the aid of the county authorities, and as a result, the Cantonites returned to their homes and the records remained at Wills Point till they were returned to Canton by order of the commissioners' court, after a decision by the supreme court, that there was no law in force at the time for holding a countyseat election.

CAPT. THOMAS JEFFERSON TOWLES

Capt. T. J. TOWLES was born in Jones county, Georgia, December 29, 1849. When fourteen years of age he came to Van Zandt county, where he was reared and educated. In the month of June, 1861, he enlisted at Dallas in Company G, Third cavalry, and served through the entire war, being in all the battles participated in by his regiment. He was dangerously wounded at Newman, July 30, 1864. After the surrender Capt. TOWLES returned to Van Zandt county and became a planter. He was called by the people of Van Zandt county to the offices of sheriff, tax collector and twice was elected to represent the county in the lower house of the legislature, the 15th and 21st sessions. Shortly after being elected to the 15th legislature, a vote was taken throughout the county, on the question of the removal of the countyseat from Canton to Wills Point. After certain boxes was discarded and not counted because of some inefficient returns, the votes, as counted, gave the required number of votes to Wills Point, and the records of the county were removed to Wills Point. Ex-Parte T. J. TOWLES and others filed a contest. In the contest in the county, Wills Point received a favorable decision. From this decision T. J. TOWLES and others appealed to the supreme court of Texas, of which O. M. ROBERTS was chief justice. Pending this appeal, T. J. TOWLES headed a goodly number of citizens favoring Canton, and made a demonstration on Wills Point, as though to return records by force, if need be.

Captain TOWLES was married to Miss N. A. NOLAN, in Butts county, Georgia, February 14, 1864. Seven children were born to them, four sons and three daughters, of whom only the two youngest are living, Mrs. EVA TODD of Oklahoma, and Miss ALICE, who is living with her mother in Canton. Captain TOWLES died at his home in Canton some years since and was laid to rest in the Canton cemetery, with Masonic honors.

GEORGE W. TULL, SR.

GEORGE W. TULL, Sr., was associated in the election contest between Canton and Wills Point, in 1877, with T. J. TOWLES and others, and as I always understood it, financed Canton's side of the contest.

Mr. G. W. TULL, Sr., aged 90 years, 1 month and 21 days, died at his home in Canton, Monday, February 26, 1917, at 10:45 p. m. Funeral services were conducted at the Baptist church Wednesday afternoon at 2 o'clock by Rev. M. A. QUINDLEN, pastor of the Canton Baptist church, after which interment took place in the Canton cemetery. A large concourse of friends and acquaintances assembled with the family at the church and cemetery to pay a last tribute of love and respect to the deceased, and many beautiful floral offerings were in evidence.

GEORGE WASHINGTON TULL was born in DeKalb county, Georgia, January 4, 1827. His parents were STEPHEN and MARY TULL, and he was the third of six children. From Georgia the family moved first to Alabama, then to Mississippi and later to Tennessee. He attended the common schools of Tennessee but his school life was limited as at the age of ten, circumstances were such that he had to support himself and assume the responsities of life. He came to Texas at the age of twenty-five, stopping first in Kaufman county, then coming to Van Zandt county, and later going to Cherokee county, settling near where the town of Jacksonville now is.

In 1854 he went to California influenced by the gold fever that attracted so many people to that land of promise at that time. He went from California to Tennessee and remained here six months, returning to Texas on a mule. He had saved the money he accumulated during the four years spent in California gold fields and when he arrived in Texas the second time he had sufficient funds to begin a small business. He selected Canton as a location and established a mercantile business in the fall of 1858, the business being conducted continuously for a little over fifty-eight years, with the exception of a few years suspension during the Civil war. Mr. TULL stood with SAM HOUSTON in opposition to secession, but, when his adopted state joined the confederacy, he enlisted under the Stars and Bars and rendered dutiful service on the battlefield for the south.

On July 16, 1861, Mr. TULL married Miss SALLIE MOORE in this county and one child, now Mrs. ENNIS PEACE of Wills Point, was the result of that union, his wife dying October 7, 1862. April 12, 1866, he married Miss SARAH JANE WAGES, who died October 8, 1868, without leaving issue. October 11, 1869, he married Miss MARY JANE COWAN, and eleven children were born of this union, six of whom are now living as follows: W. N. TULL of Fort Worth, Mrs. W. R. ANDERSON of Greenville, Mrs. G. L. FLORENCE of Gilmer, Mrs. M. G. SANDERS, Miss ALLIE and G. W. TULL, Jr., of Canton. He is also survived by his wife, seven grandchildren and four great grandchildren.

Mr. TULL was converted in 1874 and united with the Baptist church, living a consistent Christian life since that time and being a useful member of his church. He was generous to a marked degree, and it is said that he has helped more poor people than any man in the county.

Mr. TULL was the oldest merchant in the county and had attained a measure of success rarely attained during so long a period of time.

JEROME C. KEARBY, ATTORNEY AT LAW

JEROME C. KEARBY, who rendered valuable services in helping to quiet the disturbance caused by the removal of the county records from Canton to Wills in the autumn of 1877, was born in Arkadelphia, Clark county, Arkansas, about the time Van Zandt county was created. He was the eldest of three children born to EDWARD PORTER KEARBY, whose father was a farmer in Kentucky, where Dr. KEARBY was born and educated as a physician. While yet a young man, Dr. KEARBY emigrated to Hot Springs county, Arkansas, in 1840; he was married to MARY PEYTON, of that county in 1844, and practiced medicine there until 1857. Mrs. KEARBY was a native of Tennessee. Dr. KEARBY moved from Arkansas to Denton county, Texas, where he engaged in the practice of medicine, and later studied law, was admitted to the bar, and moved to Van Zandt county and commenced the practice of that profession. He remained in Van Zandt county until Rains county was created, when he moved to Emory, where he was for a time judge, and died at Emory.

JEROME C. KEARBY attended the common schools (such as they were) in Denton county until the balck clouds of Civil war hung heavily over Texas. In 1861 he enlisted in Capt. O. G. WELCH's company, COOPER's regiment, Twenty-ninth Texas cavalry, and was later transferred to Col. CHARLES DE MORSE's regiment. His first inlistment was for one year and at the end of this enlistment he re-enlisted and served until the surrender. He was in the battles of Elkhorn, Cabin Creek, Honey Creek, Poison Springs and

SOME HISTORY OF VAN ZANDT COUNTY

Mansfield, Louisiana.

Mr. KEARBY returned to Denton county and began the study of law in the office of Judge WADDLE at McKinney, Texas, where he remained until the judge's death, which occurred in 1867. He then returned to Denton and resumed his studies with his former Colonel WELCH. He was admitted to the bar at Denton, Texas, in 1869. He then came to Canton, opened an office and began the practice of law in Van Zandt county. In 1871 he was married to Miss LULA ROBINSON, a native of Alabama and daughter of J. M. and ELIZABETH (O'HARA) ROBINSON, native of Alabama, but who removed to Van Zandt county in 1866. Mr. ROBINSON followed farming until 1880, when he died in Van Zandt county. His wife died eight years later. Mr. KEARBY built him a home in Canton, where he lived until 1874, when he moved to Dallas. There he formed a co-partnership with CHARLES JENKINS in the practice of law, and later with R. E. BURK; from 1876 to 1883, with JEFF WORD, Jr.; from 1884 to 1893, with JOHN M. McCOY, then with J. C. MUSE until his death, which occurred at Denton, Texas, July 24, 1905, where he was buried with Masonic honors.

JEROME CLAIBORN KEARBY was a states right democrat until that party nominated HORACE GREELY for the presidency, then he flew the coop, so to speak, and voted for VICTORY C. WOODHULL, because, he said, there was something in that and nothing worth while left in the democratic party to fight for. Now after forty years struggle, when nearly all who embraced that cause have been gathered to their fathers, the news comes to us from Washington on June 4, 1919, that the SUSAN B. ANTHONY amendment to the constitution of the United States had passed the senate and congress.

The amendment as it was enrolled, reads: Art.--Sec. 1: "The right of citizenship of the United States to vote shall not be denied or abridged by the United States or by any state on account of sex." Sec. 2. "Congress shall have power, by appropriate legislation, to enforce the provisions of this article."

Think of congress sweating over those lines for forty years. How I wish that JEROME KEARBY could have lived to read that dispatch. So long as Mr. KEARBY lived after that, he was a free lancer in politics. Mr. KEARBY was twice nominated for congress and once for governor of the state. He and LULA KEARBY had born to them four children, viz: VICTOR P., who read law in Van Zandt county; MAUD, who married J. W. MITCHELL, a prominent insurance man of Fort Worth; FAY, who married J. W. GORDON, who for many years managed the Thurber Colo mines; JAY, a lawyer for some time in Dallas. Mrs. KEARBY and children were members of the Congregational church. Mrs. KEARBY made her home with her daughter for many years.

GOVERNOR RICHARD BENNETT HUBBARD

RICHARD B. HUBBARD was born November 31, 1836, the year that the "Twin Sisters" made history in Texas. He was a native of Walton county, Georgia; was educated and graduated at Mercer university of Georgia, and later received the degree of L. L. B., at the law department of the universities of Virginia and Harvard, Massachusetts; settled in Tyler, Texas, in 1853. In 1855, he was elected one of the democratic delegates to the Cincinnati convention; was appointed district attorney for the western district of Texas by President BUCHANAN, in which capacity he served two years and resigned to represent Smith county in the legislature. He was a member of the lower house in 1859-60 and 61. When the Civil war came on he was commissioned colonel of Twenty-second Texas infantry and served until the surrender. He then returned to Smith county and lived on his farm near Lindale. In 1872 he was chosen elector on the GREELY ticket. In 1874 he was president of the state democratic convention. He was nominated for lieutenant-governor and elected. In 1876 he became governor of Texas and served until 1879.

In 1877 Judge C. W. RAINS of Van Zandt county, appealed to him for troops to defend the county records at Wills Point, on which a demonstration was being made by a force of citizens under Capt. T. J. TOWLES, then a member of the lower house of the Texas legislature, and whose home was at Canton. Governor HUBBARD responded by ordering two companies of infantry from Dallas under Lieut. Col. E. G. BOWER. The companies were known as the Stonewall grays and Lamar rifles, who reached Wills Point September 18, 1877.

Governor HUBBARD was appointed by President CLEVELAND as envoy extraordinary to Japan, where he served from 1885 to 1889. He returned to Tyler and followed private pursuits until his death at Tyler on July 13, 1901.

(Telegram)

Wills Point, Sept. 9, 1877

T. R. B. Hubbard, Governor:
    The Canton mob, under TOWLES, mustering about three hundred strong, are encamped about two and a half miles from here, waiting and expecting the Edom mob, under YOUNGBLOOD. The sheriff's posse numbers about ninety men, are fortifying around the courthouse. We need two hundred stand of arms. A collision is hourly expected.

C. W. RAINS,
County Judge Van Zandt Co.

(Telegram)

Wills Point, Sept. 17, 1877

Adjutant General Steele:
    We are invested by a mob in superior numbers. We need arms and troops. Send help or we may be badly damaged.
C. W. RAINS,
County Judge Van Zandt Co.

136

SOME HISTORY OF VAN ZANDT COUNTY

(Telegram)

Palestine, Sept. 17, 1877

Colonel E. G. Bower, Dallas, Texas:

I am in receipt of a telegram from the county judge of Van Zandt county at Wills Point that the town is invested by a mob with superior numbers to seize the county records and remove them to Canton. He expects an assault will be made with arms. You will proceed at once by special train, if no regular train is on hand, with at least fifty picked men of your companies to Wills Point and prevent bloodshed and preserve the peace. You will use your best judgment and act cautiously to prevent a conflict. Report to me regularly.

By Order of
GOV. R. B. HUBBARD,
Commander-in Chief

Wm. Steel, Adjutant General

(Telegram)

Tyler, September 18, 1877

Judge C. W. Rains:

Ordered a Dallas company under Colonel BOWER to go to Wills Point to prevent breach of the peace and prevent bloodshed. He will go by special train. Provoke no conflict if possible
WM. STEELE,
Adjutant General

Wills Point, September 18, 1877

Twelve M.—We have just arrived here, fifty strong, and there is no trouble, though some excitement. The people here are somewhat apprehensive, but mob has dispersed to their homes.
E. G. BOWER,
Lieutenant Colonel First Texas
Volunteers

(Telegram)

Wills Point, September 18, 1877

General Wm. Steele, Adjutant General:

No trouble here now. Colonel EBLIN has gone to Canton in company with a few citizens of this place and of Canton. He will counsel obedience to law, and I have strong hopes that there will be no further trouble of any kind. Gentlemen from Canton, however, say they intend to have a recount of the votes cast, and that all votes shall be counted. How long shall I remain?
E. G. BOWER,
Lieutenant Colonel First Texas
Volunteers

SOME HISTORY OF VAN ZANDT COUNTY

Dallas, Texas, September 26, 1877

General Wm. Steele, Adjutant General, Austin, Texas.

General: Enclosed I have the honor to submit rolls of officers and men of Stonewall greys and Lamar rifles, on duty at Wills Point, during the late disturbances there . . .

Colonel GEORGE NOBLE, superintendent T. & P. R. W. company placed a car at my disposal and permitted me to retain it at Wills Point during our stay, and in it we returned. I receipted him for the transportation . . .

I do not know whether or not any provision can be made for the pay of the men. Most of them are young men, who are earning their bread by daily labor, and they can not well afford to lose their time. If they can be paid it will go far towards improving the status and membership of the companies.

I desire to express my gratification that the services of the command were such as to justify the commendations of yourself and the commander-in-chief, and also that the conduct of officers and men was in every manner satisfactory to the citizens of Wills Point.

Very respectfully, your obedient servant,
E. G. BOWER,
Lieutenant-Colonel First Regiment, Texas Volunteers.

NOTE: The expenses for the services, rations and transportation in this case amount to $385.

ORAN MILO ROBERTS

ORAN MILO ROBERTS was born in Laurenes district, South Carolina, on the 9th day of July, 1815, just a few short months after JACKSON had fought the battle of New Orleans. While quite young he moved with his father's family to Ashville, North Alabama. The family lived on a stingy farm; they had rather a hard time trying to keep the hungry wolf from the door. At the age of sixteen, the subject of this sketch bid adieu to the plow and the hoe, and through the kindness of RALPH P. LOWE, Esq., and attorney of Ashville, he entered his office as a law student. That was the way most lawyers were made in those days. Later he entered the university of Alabama, and in 1836, at the age of twenty-one, he graduated. He studied law in the office of Judge PIOLEMY HARRIS, near St. Stephens, in south Alabama, and acted as private tutor to his sons to defray his expenses. He completed his studies in the office of WILLIAM P. CHILTON, of Talladaga. Commenced the practice of his profession at Ashville, and was soon elected a member of the legislature of the state. In 1841, the year that the Cherokee line was run, he came to Texas and settled in San Augustine. After Texas was annexed to the Union, Governor HENDERSON appointed him judge of the fifth district. Judge ROBERTS presided over the first district court ever held at Canton, in 1850, in a small loghouse where NOLEN BROTHERS' drug store now stands, on the west side of the public square, though he was not judge of Van Zandt county at the time. In 1857 he was elected associate justice of the supreme court, to fill the vacancy caused by the death of Judge LIPSCOMB, and held that position until 1862.

In 1860 Governor HOUSTON made a great speech at a Union meeting at Austin and the slave propagandist cast about for a man to offset that speech as much as possible. Judge ROBERTS was of the Calhoun school of politicians and chief justice of the supreme court of Texas, and he was selected and made a well-prepared speech filled with more fire than eloquence, which was delivered at Austin and many thousand copies of his speech was printed in pamphlet form and Texas was seeded down with them and many were sent out of the state.

On Monday, January 28, 1861, the secession convention met at Austin, and Judge ROBERTS was unanimously elected president of the convention. As almost anything is permissible in a biography, I will give his speech in full, upon taking the chair:

I bow to the sovereignty of the people of my State. All political power is inherent in the people. That power, I assert, you now represent. We have been congregated in obedience to the public will; by the spontaneous and voluntary concert of the people of this state, to consider and dispose of questions equally as momentous and more varied than those that were solved by our revolutionary forefathers of 1876. The crisis upon us involves not only the right of self government, but the maintenance of a great principle in law of nations—the immemorial recognition of slavery where it is not locally prohibited—and also the true theory of our general government as an association of sovereignties, and not a blended mass of people in one social compact. However grave the issues now presented may be, I trust this body will fully be adequate to their solution, in such manner as to preserve the right of the state. While not insensible to the great honor conferred upon me by this body of idstinguished citizens, I am aware that my selection is attributable more to my position in the judiciary of the state than my experience or knowledge of parliamentary deliberations. It is an indication to the world that this movement of the people of Texas has not originated in any revolutionary spirit of social disorder, and I doubt not that the moderation and wisdom of your deliberations and acts will demonstrate it.

In 1862 Judge ROBERTS resigned his judgeship and become colonel of the Eleventh Texas regiment of infantry in the confederate army. In 1864 while still commanding his regiment, he was elected chief justice of the supreme court to succeed Judge WHEELER, upon which he resigned his commission in the army and again qualified as chief justice.

At the close of the war he returned to Tyler and entered upon the practice of law. In 1866 he was elected to the state concention and made chairman of the judiciary committee. In August, 1866 he was elected to a seat in the United States senate, together with DAVID G. BURNETT, but the state of Texas was placed under military rule and they were not seated. From 1868 to 1870 he was professor of law in the high school at Gilmer, Texas. In 1874 he was appointed by Governor COKE to the office of chief justice of the supreme court, and, in 1876, he was elected to succeed himself in that position. In 1877 the case of ex-parte T. J. TOWLES, et al., a contested election from Van Zandt county, was taken to the supreme court and Judge ROBERTS wrote the opinion. It simply stated that since the adoption of the constitution, in 1876, no law had been enacted under which a legal election could be held for the removal of a countyseat. After that decision, the commissioners' court of Van Zandt county ordered the county records to be returned to their former place of deposit at Canton. In 1883 he was appointed by the board of regents of the state university as Professor of Law in the University of Texas. He held this position for several years, then retired to private life, making his home at Marble Falls until he died on May 19, 1898.

MICAJAH HUBBARD BONNER

MICAJAH HUBBARD BONNER was born in Greenville, Butler county, Alabama, January 25, 1828; removed with his father, Rev. WILLIAM BONNER, a Methodist minister, and his family to Holmes county, Mississippi, where he attended the common schools of the county, and later attended Lagrange College, in Kentucky. He was admitted to the bar at Lexington, Mississippi, in 1848, the year that Van Zandt county was created; came to Texas and commenced the practice of law at Marshall in an office constructed by himself. Afterwards removed to Rusk, Cherokee county, and formed a partnership with J. PINKNEY HENDERSON. This association continued until General HENDERSON was elected to congress, after which Mr. BONNER practiced alone for a time and then he and his brother, F. W. BONNER, became associated together and continued to practice law at that place until 1873. The lawyers of the seventh district, of which he was not a resident but which he had frequently attended on business in the supreme court at Tyler, elected him special judge for that district. Having received the appointment he moved to Tyler where he made his home until his death. In 1874 Governor COKE reappointed him to the same judgeship, which he held until the adoption of new constitution of 1876. At the fall term of the district court for Van Zandt county (1877), the records having been removed to Wills Point, he held one term of court in the Methodist church in that town. In this he was confronted with much difficulty. Only a short time previous to the day of opening court Governor HUBBARD had ordered two companies of state troops to Wills Point to preserve the peace. Capt. T. J. TOWLES and others petitioned Judge BONNER not to hold court. As I remember it, the petition was spread upon the minutes and Judge BONNER entered an order on the minutes, saying he would not try any contested cases but would hear any case submitted by agreement of the attorneys on both sides and would grant such orders that might be asked if, in his opinion, he was warranted in so doing. He dismissed the juries, and held court open for the purposes he had assented to. This was the only term of district court ever held at Wills Point. In 1878, Judge BON-NER was appointed by Governor HUBBARD as associate judge of the supreme court, to fill a vacancy caused by the resignation of Chief Justice MOORE, and at the ensuing election he was elected to succeed himself. At the expiration of that term he declined re-election on the bench and retired to the practice of law.

A WORD ABOUT THE EARLY SETTLERS

No immigrant brought his environment with him. He brought his ideas and experience, and had the advantage of the ideas and experiences of others from a far different section of the country. The early settlers were always courageous and resourceful. It required courage to break home ties and take a wife and family to an unknown land and wild country. They were energetic and inventive, and necessity of primitive conditions developed these faculties and gave them an unlimited field for operation. I am fully persuaded that this small book contains very nearly if not quite all the names of the early settlers who came to the county. Most of the book has been given over to biographal dissertations of those who planted themselves here in the wilderness and yet another volume the same size could be filled just as creditably out of the names herein contained.

CHAPTER 10

JORDAN'S SALINE

The first record that I have of white people visiting Jordan's Saline was on the 17th day of July, 1839, when the army of the republic of Texas, nominally under the command of Gen. KELSEY H. DOUGLAS, with Secretary of War ALBERT SIDNEY JOHNSTON, Adjt. Gen. HUGH McLEOD, Gen. THOMAS J. RUSK and General BURLISON, commanding divisions, after a two days' fight with the Cherokee Indians and associated bands.

This part of Van Zandt county had up to that time been a part of the Cherokee nation. Later on in this chapter will be given the commencement of the salt industry under the whites; how it has progressed up to this date; with a biographical sketch of SAMUEL Q. RICHARDSON; the salt plant built by him and consumed by fire. Also a full account of the Lone Star hotel, the first hotel ever built in the town.

One visiting the present city of Grand Saline now, with its two railroads, its two tremendous salt plants, its two strong banks, its newspaper plant, its telephone exchange, its two commodious gins, its great waterworks system, its electric light plant, its modern hotels, its wholesale and retail stores, its postoffice and rural mail delivery systems, its schools and churches, can have little idea how all these were built up in the wild-wooded waste, so I am pursuaded that the story from the ground up will be received by many with interest.

When the landsharks put one over on Gen. SAM HOUSTON and had the Cherokee reserve thrown open to location, there was a grand rush for these favored lands. A man by the name of JORDAN was a deputy surveyor and he had a brother, "JOHN," who entered into a partnership with ALNEY T. McGEE, and they bought several thousand acres of land script, which they placed in the hands of Surveyor JORDAN for location; among them a Smith certificate for one league, which was laid to cover the Saline prairie. FRED HAM had the SAM BELL league certificate located on the same tract. In 1845 JORDAN and McGEE entered into a co-partnership to go into a manufacturing business on the Sabine River. This paper was signed in old Nacogdoches and they had SAM HUFFER, an experienced surveyor, to blaze a trail from Fort Houston to the Saline prairie, which they hacked out so that they could travel it ot the Saline and hauled two kettles to that place and commenced making salt in a primitive way, which they continued until 1853.

Not long after the location of the landccertificates mentioned above were made, HAM commenced a suit at Nacogdoches to establish his right to the SAM BELL grant. He employed Gen. JAMES PINKNEY HENDERSON and Gen. THOMAS J. RUSK, attorneys, to represent him. The suit was kept in court until 1853, when a compromise was agreed to, by which JORDAN and McGEE were to raise their certificates on the saline prairie, including the JAMES MARSDEN 738 acres just south of the BELL tract and also including the old courthouse on Saline Creek where SAM ALEXANDER now lives, and allow the BELL certificate to patent; out of the southwest corner of which JORDAN and McGEE were to have 320 acres, not to cover any salt lands, and the BELL owners were to have the remainder of that grant. In this way HAM got the greater part of the BELL grant and Generals HENDERSON and RUSK received allotments as attorneys for HAM. After this, JORDAN and McGEE moved to Kings River, California. FRED HAM enlarged the salt plant by several kettles and had the business conducted until 1859, when he sold out to SAMUEL Q. RICHARDSON (a single man) who put in a considerable plant and put in a pump, which was operated by a mule located at the head of a fresh water lake on the Saline prairie. Mr. RICHARDSON cut sweetgum logs about sixteen feet long and bored holes through them and jointed them together, thus making a line of conductor pipe so as to deliver the water to his salt works out on the foothills on the southeast part of the Saline prairie. This was continued until the Texas & Pacific Railroad built through Van Zandt county. All this time salt was being made from surface water, that is to say, water from the bed of a lake that once covered the Saline prairie, and not from a well that penetrated the enormous salt rock that underlies several hundred acres of land in the now Grand Saline territory.

After the Texas & Pacific railroad was built Mr. RICHARDSON continued making salt over on the south side and hauled the dry salt to the depot for shipment. It occurred to him then that it would be cheaper to add another mule to his pump and deliver the water on the railroad tracks and reduce it to salt there. Now he began boring more logs and built him a plant on the tracks and laid a gumlog pipe line across the prairie to the new plant and commenced pumping water from the same old well through this log pipe line, which was laid on top of the ground, to his new plant. So he then loaded the salt on the cars at this factory. Think of pumping water through a string of logs for three-quarters of a mile, when a well fifteen or twenty feet deep would have reached the same muck at the bottom of the old lake right under his works! Later he put down a deep well trying to go through the immense saltrock under his works, but, as I remember it, he never went through the saltrock, but after that he pumped brine, 90 per cent salt, and increased the output of his works to several hundred--per day and of a decidedly better quality.

The last salt works put in by Mr. RICHARDSON was called the Grand Saline Salt company, and will be referred to later on.

A SHORT BIOGRAPHY OF JUDGE SAM Q. RICHARDSON
AND OTHER HISTORICAL FACTS

Judge SAMUEL Q. RICHARDSON was born in Frankfort--not on the Rhine-- but on the Kentucky River, in Kentucky, in 1828, the youngest of six children born to S. Q. and MARY HARRISON RICHARDSON, natives of Virginia. About the year 1790 they moved to Fayette county, Kentucky, where the father was a counselor at law. He later removed to Covington, the same state, where he was killed in 1834; the mother having died in 1833.

The subject of this sketch, S. Q., was raised in Bourbon county, Kentucky, and at the age of 17 years he left his old Kentucky home, going to Van Buren county, Iowa, where he followed farming. In 1848 he came to Texas, settling in the northwest part of Rusk county, where he started a mill, bu, like other things Mr. RICHARDSON had undertaken, was never completed. He served as deputy sheriff of Rusk county and in 1851-52 he was engaged as a clerk in Shreveport, Louisiana, for a short time. In 1853 he erected a mill at Henderson and in 1856 he removed to Tyler and erected a steam sawmill at that place. In February, 1859, he came to Van Zandt county, bought 4,000 acres covering what was then known as the Saline prairie and engaged in salt making. On the southeastern portion of said prairie he erected his furnace on an elevation at the foothill, putting down a well out on the prairie above the head of a freshwater lake and putting in a pump, which was operated by a mule on a dump above high water mark. He bored sweetgum logs, ten feet in length, with a large auger and jointed them together, laid them down as a conductor pipe to deliver salt water to his works.

He operated this plan until after the Civil war was in progress, then Mr. RICHARDSON enlisted in Van Zandt county, Texas, in Company I, Twenty-second infantry, for one year and served mostly in Louisiana and Texas. After his term of enlistment expired, he went north of Mason and Dixon's line and remained until peace was restored, when he returned to Van Zandt county and was appointed by Provisional Governor A. J. HAMILTON chief justice of Van Zandt county. He made an exceptionally good county judge. At the same time Judge RICHARDSON was appointed chief justice, JOHN J. STANGER, who lived in Edom country, a good man of German descent, was appointed tax assessor, but his farm had run down during the war, so he appointed Uncle BILLE TERRY to do the office work.

Uncle BILLIE was a fine bookkeeper, prided himself on keeping the nicest books to be found. An ink splotch on a page of his books would cause him to transcribe a whole page to another portion of his book, and he never wanted any one to see the defect. He made out a nice set of taxrolls, and I chanced to be at the hotel when he brought them in. Judge RICHARDSON had come in from his Saline home and had dispensed with some probate matters and came to the hotel for dinner, and Uncle BILLIE TERRY asked him when his court would be ready to examine his taxrolls. Judge RICHARDSON answered, "At 2 o'clock." "How long do you think it will take you, Judge," asked Uncle BILLE. "An hour, or possibly an hour and a half," answered Judge RICHARDSON. Uncle BILLE said after dinner to this writer: "I wonder if Judge RICHARDSON ever saw a set of taxrolls." I told him I could not say as to that, but I well knew Judge RICHARDSON; had worked for him on Saline, and for Mrs. RICHARDSON during his absence on account of the war, and he was the best mathematician I had ever seen, and it made no difference to him how many columns of figures were on the rolls, he would carry them all up at once at a rapid rate. So I was in court when Uncle BILLIE brought in his rolls. He had taken them to a saddler and had them covered with oil-cloth, and a neater set of rolls was never presented to a court.

Judge RICHARDSON took a copy of them, looked at them, whipped out his pocket knife and ripped the sewing loose. He spread one sheet on the table before him, ran up the figures on one side and turned over the other side, went about half way up it, found an error, handed it to Uncle BILLIE for correction and grabbed another sheet and every error he detected he would hand it to the assessor for correction until he finished the examination and approved the rolls and rode to his home on a mule by sundown.

Judge RICHARDSON was grossly imposed upon during the war. People went upon his saline property during his absence and erected miniature salt works, cut his timber and made salt at will, thus damaging him very materially. But he resumed the salt making after his return and continued the business until 1878, when he moved to Dallas and bought fifteen acres land out on the H. & T. C. railroad and put in an ice plant, which he operated for several years with success. He paid $100 an acre for the land and soon Dallas came out to him and he laid out RICHARDSON's Addition to Dallas and named it for himself. Also named a street Richardson. The city of Dallas has moved on out past this addition, and now it is in the center of the resident portion of that city.

Judge RICHARDSON built him a costly, commodious brick residence in his addition to Dallas and afterwards moved back to Grand Saline and put down the first deep well piercing the rock salt bed several hundred feet and put in a salt plant on the T. & P. railroad, which he operated until his death.

Judge RICHARDSON married in Van Zandt county, in March, 1860, to Mrs. MARY J. CASEN, widow of GREEN CASEN and daughter of EDMOND and NANCY (BLOU) WILLIAMS. She was a native of Georgia. Her mother died in her native state, and her father afterward came to Van Zandt county, in 1859, where he made his home with Judge and Mrs. RICHARDSON until his death in 1880. Of her marriage with Mr. CASEN, she had born to her four girls: ELIZABETH, who married A. G. RIDGELL; JENNIE, who married M. R. NORMAN; MARTHA, who married JACK O'HARA, and EMMA, who married JAMES CURY McCULLOUGH. Mr. and Mrs. McCULLOUGH now live in a nice comfortable brick residence at Grand Saline.

A. G. RIDGELL, M. R. NORMAN and wife, and JACK O'HARA are all dead.

Of her marriage to Judge RICHARDSON, MARY CASEN had born unto her four daughters: MARY, who married SAM LONG, now dead, of Dallas; SARAH, who married ALVA FIELDER, now dead, December 17, 1890, who built extensive salt works and laid out FIELDER's Addition to Grand Saline; FANNIE, who married W. B. SHADDEN in Dallas; DORA (deceased), who married J. M. SPAULDING.

MARY J. RICHARDSON died in Dallas in 1895. She was buried in Greenwood cemetery.

Judge RICHARDSON married a second time, Miss WILLIE WHITWORTH being his last companion. They were married in 1896. Judge RICHARDSON died in 1900. He was buried in Dallas. His last wife married W. R. COLLIER and they now live in Grand Saline.

Judge RICHARDON had one child, WILLIE McCOY RICHARDSON, by

his last wife who married EARL PERSONS, one of the most prosperous farmers and stock raisers in Van Zandt county. Mr. PERSONS and wife, WILLIE, are building one of the finest brick residences in the county at Grand Saline.

$100,000 FIRE LOSS AT GRAND SALINE

Plant of Grand Saline Salt Company Will Be Built As Soon As Possible.

(From the Grand Saline Sun. October 29, 1917.)

On Wednesday night of last week, at 8 o'clock, fire of unknown origin, but believed to be due to the explosion of a lantern or the careless dropping of a match, completely destroyed the plant of the Grand Saline Salt company, which is known locally as the "lower works."

The fire was beyond control when it was first discovered by men employed in the panroom and originated in a shelter of rest room which contained a radiator and had been provided for the men in which to change their clothing and warm while waiting for the salt carts to be filled by machinery. There were no electric lights when the fire occurred due to the fact that the city light plant and city waterworks were temporarily out of water and the salt plant was being lighted by lanterns and candles, and it is believed that the fire originated from some of the improvised lights.

The boilerrooms and boilers, the shops and the office buildings were saved intact, but the salt works proper was totally destroyed.

The loss is estimated at $100,000, partially covered by insurance.

The plant was owned by T. S. McGRAIN of this city and EMERSON CAREY of Hutchinson, Kansas. The pay roll before the fire amounted to from $1,500 to $2,000 a week but, owing to the shortage of labor here, every man who desired to work, according to Mr. McGRAIN, went to work at various places on the morning following the fire. Many of the men went to work for the W. B. CARRINGTON company on Thursday morning and there has been no suffering among the employees.

Mr. McGRAIN stated to a Sun reporter that he would rebuild the plant, in all probability, just as soon as the insurance is adjusted, and the work of rebuilding will be pushed as rapidly as the freight and material altuation will permit. However, owing to unavoidable delays resulting from the fire, his plans in regard to the construction of the new plant are not fully matured.

THE FIRST MODERN SALT PLANT AT GRAND SALINE

About the latter part of the eighties, Major PARSONS, of South Bend, Indiana, came to Van Zandt county to investigate the saline properties of the county, with the view of putting in a modern salt plant here. He had put in a solar salt plant at Colorado City, which turned out a quantity of salt, but it had quite a quantity of foreign substances in it, so it was only placed on the market for stock purposes. He saw the need of a plant that would turn out a good quality of salt for table and dairy purposes; to that end he visited Grand Saline and some other points in east Texas. At Grand Saline, Judge RICHARDSON had a monopoly of the salt land, as he thought, and would not sell to any one else land for the purpose of developing the salt industry at Grand Saline.

In order to secure a depot at Grand Saline Judge RICHARDSON had deeded to Gen. GRENVILLE M. DODGE of Iowa fifty acres of land where the town of Grand Saline now stands, but no one had dreamed of there being any salt under that place. General DODGE had laid out this land in lots and blocks, as they appear today, and conveyed the property to the Texas & Pacific railroad. A few lots west of the main street running north from the depot had been sold, but most of that part of the town still belonged to the Texas & Pacific railroad, and was a wildwooded waste. Major PARSONS was a man of much determination, so entered into a contract with the Texas & Pacific railroad for its holdings in the western half of the original town of Grand Saline, conditioned he could find salt out there. In this connection he secured a small room in the old depot in which to lodge during his putting down a test well and to remain long enough to build, in case he found salt; there being no hotel accommodations there at that time, in fact there never had been, notwithstanding the fact that the county-seat of Van Zandt county had a two years' stopping place in the immediate neighborhood. Major PARSONS put down a well on the right-of-way of the Texas & Pacific railroad and found solid salt rock and plenty of it out there in the deep tangled wildwood, and at once set about clearing away the brush, so that he could put in an up-to-now salt plant amid the hoot of the owl and the howl of the coyote. The plant was a large one and had a barrel factory and dairy salt plant as auxiliary parts thereof.

OLD HOSTELRY INTIMATELY CONNECTED WITH EARLY HISTORY OF GRAND SALINE

Old Lone Star Hotel Building Passes Away to Permit Necessary Improvements

(by Roy Walton)

The office force of the B. W. CARRINGTON Salt company has lately moved into new quarters--a neat structure recently completed and occupying the site and reconstructing the ground floor of the building at the corner of Spring and Frank streets, once known as the Lone Star hotel.

The hotel, a new eight-room frame building with east and west porches, was built by Major PARSONS at that time owner of the Lone Star salt works, and was built for the accommodation of

the employees of the plant. But, being the only hotel that Grand
Saline afforded for a long time, it soon became the stopping
place for the traveling public, and many traveling men throughout
the state still remember this pleasant hostelry, where, as the
town grew and their frequent visits demanded by the trade, they
were wont to find at the Lone Star hotel the "best the market afforded" for the accommodation of the outer and inner man.

Many times in those days there was set before the guests a
brace of ducks from the lake on the Saline prairie, or a platter
piled high with nice brown quail or squirrel, for game was plentiful in the woods and fields around Grand Saline, and good large
frying chickens sold here "two for a quarter."

Now a few of the citizens of the Salt City have spent some
pleasant days at the Lone Star hotel and many youthful day dreams
have been dreamt within its narrow walls. The hotel was the
first painted house in the salt city and was surrounded by the
first grass plot in town. It was also ornamented by the first
painted fence in town as was pointed to with a great deal of
pride by the citizens. It is not generally known that J. E. PER-
SONS, farmer, bank director and merchant for more than twenty-
five years, president of the Salt City company, is a painter, but
he painted the first painted fence in Grand Saline and he did a
good job, too.

Mrs. A. BRYAN was the first landlady to take charge of the
hotel and she remembers many notable guests, among them Miss HEL-
EN GOULD, who stopped here on one occasion and visited the salt
plant. Mr. and Mrs. BRYAN are the only residents of this city
now residing here who lived here in those early days, and can remember there were no streets blazed in all the town and that they
traversed a little crooked path through a dense wood when coming
from the depot, then a crude building, to the hotel.

The Lone Star hotel for several years was known as "the home
of brides." It opened its doors to Mrs. A. WILDERSPIN, a bride
from that "bonnie green isle across the sea"--the well beloved
"Aunt LUCY," who was then a slender slip of a girl with a comple-
xion like milk and roses, whose young husband, ANDY WILDERSPIN,
was superintendent of the salt works. This hotel was also the
home of Mr. and Mrs. J. A. FAZENDA. Mr. FAZENDA, at that time
foreman of the cooper shop, is now a prosperous wholesale grocery
merchant of Los Angeles, California.

It was at this hotel that LOUISE FAZENDA, famous and daring
movie actress of Long Beach, California, daughter of the above,
first saw the light of day, and to this home J. A. FAZENDA brought his little sister, MAY, now Mrs. A. C. RICK of Dallas, from
New Orleans--a child with a sad face and a sombre dress, for her
mother had just left her sunny southern home for one in the beautiful beyond--a house not made with hands. It was the early home
of Mr. and Mrs. U. J. FAZENDA, Mr. and Mrs. W. P. GIBSON, Mr. and
Mrs. J. E. PERSONS, Mr. and Mrs. H. P. BEAIRD, Mr. and Mrs. JEFF
EASON, Mr. and Mrs. O. A. TUNNELL, Mrs. TUNNELL being the lovable
daughter of Mr. and Mrs. S. C. NIBLACK.

The first band director that Grand Saline ever boasted of,

Prof. McCARTNEY, lived at the hotel. He had a good band, too.

On the night of July 18, 1892, this hotel accommodated about seventy-five guests form Mineola, the occasion being a dance given at the plant. The building was new and clean and a band from Tyler furnished music for the occasion. Major PARSONS and a Grand Saline matron, noted for her beauty, led the grand march, and the scene was one of great beauty.

The hotel was at one time the home of the first school teacher Grand Saline ever had, Miss FLORENCE HOWARD, a beautiful young girl from Evansville, Indiana, a niece of Mrs. PARSONS. To punish the bad boys of the school she would whip the palm of her own white hand, for she knew it would hurt them worse to see her suffer than if it were themselves who received the punishment. It is said it made those tenderhearted young gentlemen weep, and they have been weeping over the woes of the fair sex ever since.

The hotel was the lodging place of the veteran bookkeeper and timekeeper at the plant, AUGUST WUERICH, and his room was directly over his present office where he now works. It was in the room that is now th south office room where he proudly exhibited to the other lodges his daughter JULIA, upon her arrival from Colorado City, a tiny infant in very long clothes.

The hotel was at one time the home of Mrs. CHARLOTTE CURRY, who came with her family of girls from Arkansas, and it was from out this household that Dr. H. RATHER wooed and won a fair bride. The hotel was once the home of SIM FLORENCE and JUD RILEY, founders of the Grand Saline Sun, and at one time the abiding place of the present editor of this paper, who then a lad "rustled" barrels for the barrelling rooms at the salt plant and wheeled salt for the dairy room, and at the noon hour being in a very "humid" condition, would not go to the dinner table, but hastily dispatch his noonday meal on a barrel turned upside down in the kitchen.

But he old hotel and all those daydreams and youthful hopes are gone. The new office building presents a neat and substantial appearance surrounded by a fence and having nice concrete walks. The interior is beautifully finished in a delicate green plaster board and natural wood. Two substantial fireplaces with brick mantels will make it comfortable in winter and in summer it is cool and pleasant.

The CARRINGTON company and its superintendent, Mr. F. B. PHILLIPS, are to be congratulated on their neat quarters.

ELDER ELIJAH ROBISON KUYKENDALL. GRAND SALINE

Of all the people I knew in early days, who were here when Van Zandt county was organized, I only recall as living today, ELDER ELIJAH ROBISON KIYKENDALL of Grand Saline. He is one of the early settlers of the county. There are probably now none living who were here when he came in 1848. The family is of German extraction. On coming to America they first settled in North Carolina. JESSE was the grandfather and lived in North Carolina and came to Tennessee. PETER was the father's name and he was a Christian preacher and preached in an early day in Tennessee. He moved with his family to Van Zandt county in February, 1848. He settled about five miles southwest from the present town of Grand Saline. ELIJAH was born in Tennessee, December 14, 1836. The country was sparsely settled at that time. PETER S. BENTON, a tanner; J. D. WRIGHT, a doctor; JOHN CHRESTMAN, a farmer; JOS. COX and TOM COX, farmers, and ALLEN BLAIR constituted the settlement here. There was a settlement on McBee's creek, and Mr. Mc-BEE owned a mill, the first in the county. It was what is known as a treadmill, but it ground all the meal fro many miles around. The Shreveport and Dallas road ran through the county from east to west and the Porter's Bluff road ran through the southern end of the county. These roads were traveled a great deal by immigrants, stock drovers, adventurers, etc. There was a settlement then at the head of Saline Creek about five miles east from Canton. YOES, RAWSON, KING, and others lived there. Then, in what is now the Edom community, lived Uncle JOHN PILES, JOHN COTHERN, CLABE COTHERN, JOHN MARRS, and HENRY MARRS, JACK HORSELY and his father. The BRUTONS and HARRISONS lived on Four Mile prairie. The country was more sickly than now and the seasons were irregular. The range was excellent. The mast in the bottoms and the grass on the uplands were fine. The creeks were all bordered with cane in great variety. Fat cattle, fag hogs, fat horses were available winter and summer. Deer and turkey and prairie chickens were here in great abundance. Also there were bear, panther, wolves, catamounts and Mexican lions. The Indians were gone and the buffalo had retreated further west. There were some mustang ponies and a few wild cattle in the country. It was under conditions like these that young ELIJAH grew up. School advantages were limited.

J. J. KUYKENDALL, an older brother of our subject, was the first teacher in the county, also the first deputy sheriff. ELIJAH's school advantages therefore were limited but he grew up a robust youth. October 18, 1858, he married NANCY ANN BRATHCER. She lived until July 20, 1881. January 21, 1882, he married Mrs. M. J. SMITH who has been dead now for several years. In 1862, he volunteered into the confederate service and served until the surrender, in Texas, Louisiana and Arkansas. He lost his health during the war and travelled several years afterward. He regained his health, however, and has been a remarkably strong man for his years since. He became a Christian at the age of twelve and at the age of fifty entered the Christian ministry. He is a house carpenter by trade. He owns his home in Grand Saline and has acquired some other property in the city. He lives a blameless life before the people. He has a good record, is a typical old Texan and furnishes a worthy example of Texas life.

PAID FEE IN 1847

When one wanted to send a letter through the mails before July 1, 1847, the writer made arrangements to have it transported by the payment of a fee, and this was noted on the letter, but in that year it was decided to make the system more convenient by the issuance of postage stamps, so these could be kept on hand and the letter dropped into a receptacle that today serves as a street letter box. The first issue amounted to 860,000 stamps, placed on sale in New York. There was no glue on the reverse side of the stamp; homemade paste served that purpose. The number of stamps issued in 1918 was more than 13,000,000,000, and one of the branches of the Bureau of Engraving and Printing worked night and day turning them out. The first stamped envelopes were issued in 1852, and the first newspaper wrappers in 1861. Nearly 2,000,000,000 of these were issued in 1918. Postal cards did not come into use until 1873, when 31,000,000 were put on the market by the government. Last year there were 707,000,000 issued and sold. The government began registering letters in 1855, when the innovation worked well and 630,000 were so handled. Now there are 110,000,000 registered letters passing through the mails annually.

CHAPTER 11

HISTORY OF LOG CABINS IN THE LONG AGO

In the early settlement of Van Zandt county, a man with a small yoke of oxen hitched to a rudely constructed wagon, with a tarbucket on the end of the coupling pole just behind the rear axle, with a scanty lot of household goods in the wagon, a wife and several children, at least one faithful dog following behind, a bunch of cane fishing poles tied onto the outside of the wagon bows and a flintlock rifle tied to the bows under the sheet, who had wended his way through the deep tangled wildwood and canebrakes from Burcombie county, North Carolina, to Texas, in quest of a home, would offtimes tie up along one of the swift running brooks in Van Zandt county, unyoke the oxen whose feet were bleeding from long service, cut a small sapling, leaving a stump about five feet high, the top of which he hewed square with a poleaxe; to this he securely bolted a steel cornmill into the hopper of which was placed about a half gallon of kernels of Indian corn, which, after being put through the mill to its third reading, was passed to the cook, who in the meantime had built a roaring fire which burned down to large coals, and of the cornmeal she made a batter, spread it upon a board smoothly shaven with a drawing knife, and set on the edge inclining a little outward at the top, with a stone or something behind it to hold it in place in front of the coals, and soon a nicely baked pone of bread was ready for a meal, showing on its surface the fingerprints of the cook. While this was in process the head of the family had lifted a few goggleeyed perch from the stream and they were smoking in a pan of lard when dinner was announced and all would eat and were filled. As soon as the family could rest and clean up a little a grindstone was lifted from the wagon and a comly frame was made for it, into which it was then placed. The poleax, the broadax and drawing knife were sharpened and a maul with some "gluts" (wooden wedges), preferably out of dogwood were made. Then the crosscut saw was filed, and trees began to answer the roll call of the poleax and fall from their stumps.

These logs were cut in such lengths as to build a house 16 x 18, or 18 x 20 feet. There were two ways of building a logcabin, the most general was to hew the logs on the ground, but some elected to build the house and sketch it down (hew the logs afterwards). By the time the logs were ready for hauling, the oxen's feet were well enough to draw them together, which was done by securing one end of a logchain to the log and the other to the oxyoke, and in this way the logs were assembled for the building. Generally the logs were hewed before being put into the building, they were scalped on the outer up sides and lined, then with a poleax they were scored and juggled off so that the man with the broadax could hew them to the line. These logs would face from eight to ten inches. The ends were generally squared on the ground, so but little work was left for the men on the corners to fit them after they were passed upon the cabin. Two sidesills were hewn square to face from fourteen to eighteen inches. If stone could be found anywhere near the building site large rocks were hauled for the foundation, if not, then huge blocks were squared upon which to place the sills. When all was ready, the vox populi, for miles around were invited to come to the raising, and usually a quilting bee was pulled off the same day in company with the raising, for everybody was supposed to be at the raising, including the women, children and dogs.

The house was usually built in a day, that is to say, the walls were put up, then came the roofing which was made out of boards riven out of large trees which had been sawed into cuts four feet long and bolted into bolts ready for the froe. The sleepers that rested on the sills on which the floor was laid were round logs with the top hewed to a line to face eight or ten inches, the undersides of these logs being hewed at the ends for about two feet, so they would rest firmly on the sills. Floors were made of either dirt or puncheons. It was no unusual thing to leave out the sleepers and use the ground for a floor. In fact, if a man had two houses, the one used for a kitchen and dining room almost invariably had a dirt floor. Puncheons were broad pieces of timber, split from large trees with maul and wedge, and hewed to a smooth surface on the upper side with a broadax. They were usually about six feet long, from two or four inches thick and from ten to twenty inches wide. They were trimmed on the underside at each end so they would fit firmly on the sill. When these puncheons were once placed in position and the edges trimmed, they remained steadfast without nailing. These old puncheon floors were neither air-tight or ornamental. If there was no space between them open more than one inch they were considered as customary acceptable. Before nails came in use, the cracks between the logs were "chinked" with small bits of stone or blocks of wood made for that purpose and daubed with mud usually secured from postoak flats and plastered on by hand. The prints of the fingers were always indelibly stamped upon the daubing in every crack of the house. When the walls of the cabin reached the proper height, a longer log was put on at each end which extended about eighteen inches beyond the sides of the house at each of the four corners. On the outer ends of these logs was placed a half of a large log split, the flat sides hewed and the under sides were blocked out where they rested on the ends of the extended logs. These logs were called butting poles, and they marked the limit of the eaves. On the ends of the next round above the butting poles, side logs were placed about two feet out of the perpendicular of the side walls towards the center of the cabin. These logs were called the first ribs. On the first ribs rested the next two end logs which of course, were shorter than those that had gone before, by as much as the first ribs were drawn within the perpendicular of the side walls. These shorter logs were called end studs. On them rested two more ribs which were placed about two feet further out of the perpendicular wall on each side towards the center of the cabin. These were called second ribs, and so on until the frame of the cabin ended with a "ridge pole or center rib" at the cone. The first course of clapboards was placed on the first rib and the

153

top wall of the cabin. The ends of the boards extended over the wall about eighteen inches and butted against the butting pole, which was fastened to the long end logs on which it rested by wooden pins driven into auger holes. When the first course of boards was laid down sticks of wood split for this purpose, about two feet long and five or six inches square, called knees, were placed at intervals along the course of boards with one end resting at right angles against the butting pole. A log called a weight pole was next laid full length of the house on the first course of boards, just above the upper ends of the knees. The butting pole for the next course of boards was also a weight pole for holding on the first course of boards, and in like manner course after course of boards were placed until the cabin was covered. The heating apparatus was a huge open fireplace at one end of the cabin. Ordinarily a fireplace would admit logs five feet long. When the cabin was completed the old time fiddler was called upon to furnish "catgut and rosin," and they danced all night, 'till broad daylight, and went home with the girls in the morning.

COPY OF FIRST BOND ISSUED BY VAN ZANDT COUNTY

"No. 1. United States of America, The State of Texas. The County of Van Zandt, in the State of Texas will pay One Thousand Dollars to the bearer in United States GOLD COIN or in its equivalent in good and lawful money of the United States of America, on the 12th day of July, 1891, or before at the option of Van Zandt county, with interest at the rate of eight per centum per annum, payable annually on the 10th day of April. Principal and Interest payable at the Office of the County Treasurer of Van Zandt County.
" "This Bond is issued by authority of an act of the Legislature of the State of Texas entitled, An Act Authorizing the Commissioners' Court of the several counties of this state to issue Bonds for the Erection of a Courthouse, and to levy a Tax to pay for the Same," approved Feby. 11th, 1881; and the amendments thereto heretofore enacting by the Legislature of the State of Texas; and also by Authority of the Order of the Commissioners' Court passed on the 12th day of July, 1886.
"Done at the Town of Canton, in the County of Van Zandt, State of Texas, on the 12th day of July, 1886.

"J. G. RUSSELL,"
County Judge, Van Zandt County.
"Countersigned: W. D. THOMPSON, County Clerk, Van Zandt County."

CHAPTER 12

MILLS

"The shadows are deepening around the pond and the stream is singing itself to sleep. But yet there is a little grist in the hopper, and while the water serves, I will keep grinding. And by the time the sun is down and the flow in the race is not enough to turn the big wheel the grist will run out and I will have the old mill swept and tidied for the night. And then for home and a cheery evening, a quiet night, lighted with stars and pillowed with sleep. After that the dawning, and another day; fairer than any I have ever seen in this world of roseate mornings and radiant sunsets." -- Robert J. Burdette.

Very few indeed living today can comprehend the hardships, the inconceniences and the distressing needs, the pioneers underwent in settling in Grand Old Texas, seventy-five years agone.
The first mills were "steel hand mills," that had bolts to fasten them to a post, and had two cranks. A small amount of grist, might in time, be reduced sufficiently to enter into a pone of bread.

THE FIRST POWER MILL

The first power mill in east Texas, was put in by a colored man at old Nacogdoches, in 1837. This was run by waterpower and was considered a good gristmill, and done the grinding for a large scope of country. This colored man was free, and according to published reports, he made a good and well-respected citizen, and accumulated considerable property, and when GALONS, for that was his name, died, nearly the whole population attended his burial.
In 1848, Mr. AMBROSE CRAIN put in the first cotton gin at that place, and then cotton became the money crop.

THE FIRST CORN MILL BUILT IN VAN ZANDT COUNTY WAS BY WILLIAM H. M'BEE

After the "Twin Sister" made report of their actions at San Jacinto, on the memorable 21st day of April, 1836, the republic of Texas organized a government with a president and congress in due form. The congress passed a law confirming a title to all married men who entered Texas as homeseekers. Under this law WILLIAM H. McBEE went before the board of land commissioners of Fannin county, and made proof that he entered Texas as a homeseeker, in 1834, as a married man; and said board of land commissioners did, on the 2nd day of March, 1838, issue to him headright certificate No. 51, for one league and labor of land. Armed with this official document, Mr. McBEE went forth in quest of land in Texas upon which he could locate his certificate and build him a home. Beginning at Wills Point, thence running southwest to the Trinity river, a block of 115 leagues and labors surveys had been made under forged land certificates, which the

land office of the republic of Texas refused to patent. These
surveys covered land in Dallas, Kaufman, Collin, Rockwall, Hunt
and Van Zandt counties. On one of these abandoned surveys, Mr.
McBEE laid his certificate for one league and labor of land; patent issued to him October 25, 1850. Mr. McBEE moved his family
to his grant of land in 1844, which was then in Nacogdoches land
district. Two years later Henderson county was organized and he
was a citizen of that county. Two years later, in 1848, Kaufman
and Van Zandt counties were organized, and when the boundary line
between them was run, his grant was about equally divided between
those counties; however, his residence was established in Van
Zandt. Soon after he settled on his grant he built a treadwheel
mill thereon, which proved to be the first cornmill ever operated
within the confines of Van Zandt county. The power which drove
this mill was obtained by placing a few oxen on an inclined wheel
and as they walked, this wheel, which had cogs all the way around
on the outside of it, turned a smaller wheel which turned the
mill.

WILLIAM H. McBEE died on his grant in Van Zandt county, on
the 17th day of February, 1852. He was well respected and an
honorable citizen and helped to open up the old Shreveport and
Dallas road. He was buried in the old Cedar Grove cemetery, 550
feet above sea level. In addition to his land grant, he left a
creek to perpetuate his name for all time to come. A small rill
that had its source in the old village of Cedar Grove obtains the
proportions of a creek of huge size before it empties into the
Sabine River at Goose Lake. Also a district schoolhouse bears
his name.

The mode of living in primitive days was simple. The writer
recalls many visits to cabins of the early settlers where the
fire was never let die out and the black coffee was always hot
day and night. It was a prevailing custom, when anyone called at
these cabins, to hand them a cup and saucer, and as they held
these vessels, the cup was filled with piping hot black coffee,
which was served, as a general rule, without cream or sugar.
When you entered these cabins you passed under the old flint and
steel rifle, which was resting on buckhorn brackets, with the
bullet pouch hanging from one of these brackets.

An appropriate sign to put up over the door of the cabins
would have been. "Come in without knocking, and go out the same
way; and keep this up until old father time calls you hence without day." For these simple people were not schooled in knocking
as are the crafty people of this day and time.

In 1848, the year that Van Zandt county was created, and before the county lines were run, Mr. W. W. STIRMAN put up a water-
mill at or near Big Rock, on the south line of the county. This
was what was called an "under-shot" mill, which was turned by let-
ting the water through the dam on the wheel. This was a small
grist mill, but it beat the steel handmill all hollow, and did
the grinding for a large scope of country, because the country,
at that time, was sparsely settled.

Some ten years later, Mr. S. S. ROHRER came out from Maryland

and married the Widow HUFFER, and put in a much better mill, run
by water, in the same neighborhood. This mill was kept going almost day and night during the Civil war. He added a carding machine to it and carded wool rolls.

JAMES COLTHORP put in the first sawmill in the county, in
1850, and cut the lumber for the first courthouse built in Dallas.
This mill was three miles west of Loller's bridge and Mr. COLTH-
ROP was appointed postmaster, his office being called Hamburg.

BURREL H. HAMBRICK settled and opened up quite a plantation
on the west side of the Neches River, at the old battleground
where Chief BOLES was killed, in 1839, and put up the first cotton gin in the county. After the Civil war he, having lost his
slaves, abandoned his plantation and moved to Tyler. In company
with GEORGE HUMPHRY they put up a cotton thread mill with twelve
hundred spindles. Mr. HAMBRICK trusted pretty much everything to
Mr. HUMPHRY, and it was reported that they made 2% per month on
their investment. But in 1868, while Mr. HUMPHRY was out buying
cotton for the plant, a spark from the machinery went into the
lint room, and the plant was entirely consumed by fire. Mr. HAM-
BRICK lost something over twenty thousand dollars in this enterprise, from which loss he never recovered, and, when he died, left
but little estate. Such is the ever shifting tide of finance; no
one knows what a day may bring forth.

HYNSON's SPRINGS

All old-timers will remember Col. HENRY O. HYNSON, who lived
on the old Shreveport and Dallas road, this side of Marshall.
I? a horseback we put up at Col. HYNSON's, and driving a team, or
a herd, H son's Springs was a favorite camping place, where the
life-giving waters gushed forth to all, free and unlimited. Mrs.
POPE writes of a visit to Hynson's Springs, Texas, situated in
the heart of East Texas woods, six miles west from the pretty
town of Marshall; crowning an elevation 900 feet, is the old-time
popular resort, Hynson Springs. The waters, iron, sulphur and
magnesia, are palatable as well as health-giving. The writer can
recall the earliest days at Hynson's, when, as yet a school girl,
she danced until the wee sma hours "and the merrie party all rode
home over moonlit roads." It is difficult after lapse of years
to realize how swiftly falls the foot of time. Ah! little feet
that danced so lightly, then, where do ye wander now?

Sitting once again on the south veranda, with the soft evening air like a caress, listening to the insect-breathing world
about, the distant note of mocking bird or whip-poor-will calling
his sweetheart home. The dreamy lull of evening hour--once again
we hear the cheery voice of Col. HYNSON with old time Southern
hospitality welcoming the evening guests. We see the beautiful
faces clustering under spreading oak, elm and maple; see the
firefly glow of lighted cigar; catch the mellow, rippling, happy,
carefree laughter, and recall Col. INGERSOLL's beautiful lines:

"Strike with hand of fire, oh weird musician, your harp
string with Apollo's golden hair; fill the vast cathedral aisles

157

with symphonies sweet and dim, deft toucher of the organ keys. Blow, bugler, blow, until your silvery notes do reach the skies and charm the lovers wandering on the vine-clad hills, but know your sweetest notes are discords all, compared to childhood's happy laughter. Where do ye wander now?"

Col. HYNSON's daughters live, one at Baltimore, one at the quaint old city of New Orleans. Many, many miles from this the young men have taken their places among the ranks of men. Some have climbed ambition's heights. Some bear weary loads of care. The sweet girl faces are now the inspiration of homes where young sons recall the father years agone. The daughter--my eyes grow dim--I look again and see "A later and loftier Annie Lee."

Bettie Brownrigg Pope

CHAPTER 13

SCHOOLS

SCHOOLS IN THE AMERICAN COLONIES

Neglect of education was one of the charges of adventure a-
gainst the Plymouth Rock colony in 1624. The colonists were forced to plead that the children depended for it on their parents.
They had no common schools. They must have had some kind of
schools ten years later, for in 1635 the widow of Dr. FULLER was
allowed to have an apprentice, on consideration of keeping him in
school for two years; but common schools were not established in
Plymouth until 1677. In that year it was ordered that in every
town of fifty families and more there should be a "grammar school,"
for which the town was to pay a rate of twelve pounds, the balance
to be paid by those whose children attended it. The idea of having a school in every town had been mooted in 1662, and a year
later it became a proviso in settling new plantations, that they
should have a schoolmaster. In 1673, it was proposed that the
charges of a free school, calculated at thirty-five pounds a
year, should be paid out of the profits of the Cape Cod fisheries; and, after the act of 1667, these profits were divided among
the towns with schools, not more than five pounds being granted
any one. A town with no school of its own had to pay five pounds
a year to the next town that had one.

THOMAS JEFFERSON had the most scientific and far-reaching
scheme of state education that thus far had been elaborated in
America; the capstone of the structure was to be the university.
He enlarged the Albemarle Academy into Central college in 1816,
and it became the University of Virginia, 1819; but he had been
dead for forty years before the state of Virginia established a
common school system. It is true, as above stated, there had
been common schools in the country, but the central idea was in
higher institutions.

The first absolutely non-sectatrian college endowed in America was Girard college, Philadelphia. STEPHEN GIRARD died in
1831 and in his will he set apart two million dollars for the
erection and endowment of a college for the education of poor
white orphans. He specifically requires that the orphans be instructed in the purest principles of morality, love of truth,
sobriety and industry. As for religious beliefs they are left to
adopt such tenets as their matured reason may lead them to prefer; and to assure this he interdicts the employment, and even
the admission into the grounds of any eclesiastic whatever.

ENDOWMENTS FOR SCHOOLS AND COLLEGES IN TEXAS

The Republic of Texas, by act in 1839, set apart fifty leagues of land for two universities in Texas and three leagues in
every county for the purpose of establishing in each a primary
school or academy, and this was increased, by the act of 1840, to
four leagues appropriated in each county to school purposes.
These were protected from settlement by act of 1856, which pre-

cluded settlers upon school lands from the benefits of the statute of limitations. The constitution of 1845 required one-tenth of the annual revenues of the state to be set aside for educational purposes; and the act of 1854 appropriated to this fund two million dollars of United States five per cent bonds, which was to be a special school fund with the interest accruing to school purposes. The act of 1858 established the university of Texas and appropriated one hundred thousand of United States bonds for its maintenance in addition to the fifty leagues set apart for university purposes by the republic, and to this was added one-tenth of the lands which had been surveyed and reserved and set apart for the encouragement of the construction of railroads. A large portion of these funds and the proceeds of sales of the school lands were appropriated and loaned to railroads, that were permitted to replace them with treasury notes and coupons of confederate states and were entirely lost to the school fund.

The constitution of 1866 created a perpetual school fund, consisting of all former dedications and appropriations made for that purpose, and alternate sections of all lands granted to railroads, with the provision that if any portion of the public domain should at any time be sold to the United States, one-half of the proceeds should accru to the public schools. It further provided for the levy of a special school tax.

The constitution of 1875, in addition to all former appropriations, set apart one-half of all the public domain of the state, and all sums arising from any portion of it, to consititute a perpetual fund for school purposes; also one-fourth of all the revenues and a capitation tax of one dollar on every male citizen between the ages of twenty-one and sixty years are to be set apart annually for the benefit of free schools.

The amended constitution of 1883 gave one-fourth of the revenue derived from the state occupation taxes, and added to this the levy of an annual ad valorem state tax of such an amount, not to exceed twenty cents on every one hundred dollars valuation, which, with the available school fund arising from all other sources, will be sufficient to maintain the public free schools of Texas for a period of not less than six months each year. The legislature was authorized to form school districts within all or any of the counties of the state, and authorized an additional ad valorem tax to be levied and collected in these several districts for the further maintenance of public free schools in these districts; provided, that two-thirds of the qualified voters in each district shall vote such tax, which is not to exceed twenty cents per annum on every one hundred dollars worth of property subject to taxation in the district. But this limitation of taxes does not apply to cities and towns constituting independent school districts.

The act of February 23, 1900, appropriated all of the public domain to the public free school fund. The reason for this act was that the constitution of 1876 gave the public schools half of the public domain then remaining. In 1899 it was discovered that more than one-half of the public domain in existence in 1876 had been appropriated for purposes other than free schools. To adjust the account all the public domain then remaining, and $17,000, in money was appropriated to the permanent school fund. Under the grants of four leagues of land to each county for public free school purposes Van Zandt county was exceptionally fortunate in that it received seventeen thousand seven hundred and twelve acres of land, all in one body, principally on Paradise prairie in Wise county, being reckoned among the richest black lands in Texas.

THE FIRST SCHOOLS IN TEXAS

I am indebted to NOAH SMITHWICK for the following story, which I am fully persuaded is literally true, in his pen picture of SAN FELIPE de AUSTIN:

SAN FELIPE de AUSTIN! The shiboleth that flings the door of memory wide; the spell that bids the tide of years roll back, and from the ashes where it has lain these sixty years or more, conjures up the old town which formed the nucleus of the movement that eventuated in extension of the great American Union in an unbroken plain from the Atlantic to the Pacific.

Here in pursuance of the scheme which cost MOSES AUSTIN his life, his indomitable son, STEPHEN FULLER, established his headquarters, from thence distributing the colonist who followed him into the wilderness seventy-six years ago.

SAN FELIPE de AUSTIN itself but a phantom; what a host of phantoms the name summons back to re-people it.

Though not one of the "Three Hundred," the writer was but a few years behind them, and knew them all by repute, many of them personally. The town was then in its swadling clothes when the writer made his advent therein in 1827. Twenty-five or perhaps thirty log cabins, strung along the west bank of the Brazos River, was all there was of it; while the whole human population of all ages and colors could not have exceeded two hundred. Men were largely in the majority, coming from every state in the Union, and every walk in life.

The first preacher to venture in this stronghold of Satan, was THOMAS J. PILGRIM, a Baptist; but, as the colonists were supposed to be Catholic, Colonel AUSTIN did not deam it advisable to establish a Protestant church, so the preacher, willing to make himself useful, turned dominic; teaching the first English school in Texas in 1829. Comparatively few families lived in town--most of them going out to the farm.

JOHN HENRY BROWN, in his History of Texas, Vol. 2, page 515, says: "In 1829, Rev. THOMAS J. PILGRIM, of the Baptist church, conducted a Sabbath school at San Felipe. A similar school the same year was established at Matagorda, and few months later, on "Old Caney," both by members of the Baptist church.

THE OLD LOG SCHOOL HOUSE

The old log schoolhouse served its purpose and served it

SOME HISTORY OF VAN ZANDT COUNTY

well. For a quarter of a century after Van Zandt county was organized, the log schoolhouse was in evidence in this county. It
varied somewhat in size. At first those houses were small, being
about twelve by fourteen feet, and at last they were built of extra large logs hewed thin and the house would be twenty by twenty-
four feet, and the cracks daubed with carefully prepared mud for
that purpose. The foundations were of huge stones, and the sills
were about fourteen by sixteen inches, solid hewed logs. The
walls were, when first put up, twelve feet high, with plates
twelve by fourteen inches solid hewed logs; gables weather-board-
ed up, a good board roof put on shingle fasion; good pine lumber
floor; windows with glazed sash and a hugh rock chimney and large
fireplace.

Education always will be a leading theme among civilized
people, even in a wilderness, and Van Zandt county was no exception to this rule during its struggle for a place on the Texas
map.

Metal pen points came into use about 1830, but in the early
days in Van Zandt county, it was the prevailing custom for the
pupils to furnish the teacher with goose quills, out of which he
carved pens for school purposes. Copy books were made of fools-
cap paper sewed together in small quantities and the teachers
would "set the copies" at the head. A child might enter school
when three years old; by seven he was studying grammar; then he
would write and go into arithmetic. The first book the child had
was the primer. From the primer he progressed to the most universally used book that has ever been written by an American--
NOAH WEBSTER's spelling book.

The first school taught in Van Zandt county was by JAMES J.
KUYKENDALL, in the winter of 1849-50, just twenty years after the
first was taught in Texas. Professor KUYKENDALL was the son of
PETER and PRUDENCE KUYKENDALL. I was well acquainted with all
the older families of KUYKENDALL's; they came to Van Zandt county
in the spring of 1848. JAMES J. was born in Tennessee, and reached New Orleans to hear cannon booming at the joy meeting in
honor of peace between the United States and Mexico. On the organization of the county, his father PETER KUYKENDALL, was elected county treasurer, and PETER S. BENTON was elected sheriff,
"high sheriff," Uncle PETER S. BENTON always put it, and he appointed young JAMES J. KUYKENDALL his deputy, on May 26, 1858.
JAMES J. KUYKENDALL was married to Miss M. J. HATTON. The HAT-
TONS were from Virginia. THOMAS W., the father of Miss. M. J.,
came to South Carolina and married there, in 1834, to Miss ANN
ELIZA LAKE. They were farmers and were the parents of twelve
children. In 1849 they moved to Texas and settled in Rusk county,
Texas. In 1856 they moved and after some detention, came to Van
Zandt county and settled at Creaglevill. Professor KUYKENDALL
and wife had born to them two children; Dr. WOOD KUYKENDALL, now
of Fort Worth was the eldest and OLIVER the youngest.

The school was taught on Saline Creek, about five miles
south of Grand Saline, and Webster's spelling book was the fountain from which that class drank deep during the eventful school.

SOME HISTORY OF VAN ZANDT COUNTY

After the Civil war JAMES J. KUYKENDALL died on his farm in Smith county, east of Garden Valley.

Many, ah, many days have rolled into the dreamy past since we trudged to the old log schoolhouse and occupied a place on a split log bench.

How can we forget this old schoolhouse, and how we used to punch the daubing from the cracks beneath the logs so that we might peep from the narrow sphere upon the passerby, the birds, the trees and the great blue sky that tenderly draped the fleecy clouds that wafted in the horizon? Can we forget the times when we saw the teacher's back was turned, how we tried our marksmanship in flipping paper balls against the ceiling which we had chewed from leaves torn from the blue-back speller, over in the neighborhood of such words as "incomprehensibility" and "immateriality?" Can we forget how we used to puncture the cosmos of some little fellow with the point of a pin, who leaned over the top of the rude desk to whisper to some one in front of him?

Can we ever forget what we learned in the old blue-back speller, or how we lined up in recitation to spell "baker," "shady," "lady," "tidy," or how we read in a declamatory voice such sentences as 'Ann can spin flax," or the thrilling story of Old Dog Tray and the bad boy in the farmer's apple tree? Can we forget the lizards that ran along the logs of the building or the snakes that peeped at us through the cracks of the puncheon floor. During the session the schoolroom buzzed like bees in a hive as we whispered in tongues and spoke in gibberage, and sometimes the teacher caught onto some of the antics, got 'riled' and then it was the dogwood sprout hissed and crackled as it met its counterpart in a thick jeans coat lined with a plaid of lindsey yellow, green and red. As a rule the teacher boarded around at the homes of the different scholars, yet he was held in such reverence that a frown from him was more feared than a daddy's threat. We notched the benches with our knives and cut our sweetheart's name in big capital letters on our desk tops, and pulled the rubbers from our galluses to flip at lazy flies and thus while away the tedious hours.

We were always ready to jump when the dinner hour was announced, and with a flopped wool hat in one hand and a hunk of bread and butter or pie in the other, we sallied forth to the playground to play ball. The bat we usually used was a paddle, and the ball was made from yarn obtained from a ravelled out stocking leg which our grandmother had knit and was covered with leather from the top of a boot whose lower half had seen better days. Soem of the little shavers, not big enough to play ball games would play "frog in the millpond," or "mumble-the-peg," while the girls swung in the grapevine swing, or played "William may trim a toe." Mirth and laughter went hand in hand, and when the stern master ended our frolics with his solemn summons "To Books," it was a lusty bunch of youngsters and dancing eyes that resumed the afternoon studies. Those glorious days are over, and those boys and girls are men and women. Few of them are with us any more, but somewhere out beyond the evening star in the blessed isles of we know not where they rest in that sweet harmonious eternity which is promised to the pure in heart.

SOME FINANCIAL FORECASTS

By what was known as the compromise of 1850 the congress of the United States agreed to give Texas $10,000,000.00 in five per cent interest bearing government bonds, for Texas' interest in a strip of territory extending from the present north boundary of Texas north to the south boundary of Wyoming. Governor PETER H. BELL called the legislature in extra session and by that body an act was passed accepting this offer which was promptly approved by the governor.

The constitution of Texas, 1845, required one-tenth of the annual revenue of the State to be set aside for educational purposes, the act of the legislature, 1854, appropriated to this fund two millions of United States five per cent bonds which was to be a special school fund with the interest accruing to school purposes.

THE SCHOOL BONDS BECOME A TEMPTING PRIZE

"Confederate States of America
War Department"

Richmond, 2d December, 1861
"Sir: The ordnance bureau of this department has employed Mr. G. H. GIDDINGS of your State, as its agent for the purchase of arms. Mr. GIDDINGS has made arrangements for such purchases in Mattamoros, payment to be made in United States bonds now held by your State which he thinks can be used for that purpose, if you consent.

"The object of this letter is to inform you that if you will make use of the United States bonds in your possession in the purchase of arms to be approved by Mr. GIDDINGS, at prices satisfactory to him, this government will receive the arms from you at cost and charges, and pay for them in its own eight per cent bonds.

"By this arrangement you will succeed in exchanging your United States bonds now useless and bearing only 6 per cent, for the bonds of the Confederate States bearing interest at 8 per cent, and receive the interest regularly and punctually.

"I hope your excellency may deem it consistent with your sense of public duty to make an arrangement which seems to be recommended by so many advantages.

I am y'r ob't serv't.
"J. P. BENJAMIN,
"Secretary of War

"His Excellency France Lubbock,
"Governor of Texas."

Other high officials made the following statements commending the above proposition:

General LEWIS T. WIGFALL, December 9th, 1861: "I have no hesitation in advising that you accept the proposition. The United States bonds must, of course, at the end of the war be recognized by the United States government; but will that government ever be able to pay them? I think not. It will come out of this war utterly and hopelessly bankrupt, whereas the bonds of the Confederate States are amply secured, and must be at all times at par, if not above."

Confederate States Senator Hon. JOHN HEMPHILL: "I cordially recommend you to accept the proposition. The State, so far from making any sacrifice, will exchange bonds which are now, and will probably always be worthless to her for stock now at par, and whose value will be, commensurate and co-existent with the government itself."

Confederate Congressman, T. N. WAUL, December 14th, 1861: "Mr. BENJAMIN's letter meets with my cordial approval, and I hope it will meet your approbation. The investment is a good one under any circumstances."

Postmaster General JOHN H. REAGAN, December 14th, 1861: "It is understood that arms can be purchased with United States bonds as cash. Our State cannot at this time realize either principal or interest on the United States bonds. And their payment may be repudiated by that government if they remain the property of the State; and I recommend to your favorable consideration the proposition to exchange them for Confederate bonds."

CONFEDERATE STATES CURRENCY

Simultaneously with the opening of the confederate government at Richmond, dies were cast and presses set to work turning out Confederate States notes of various denominations. For a time this paper circulated fairly well, then it depreciated until its circulation well nigh stopped.

Then new dies were cut, new paper and different colored ink was used and a series of notes brought out called "the new issue." This served to revive the circulation again. Prior to the ending of the civil war schools were taught in Texas on the subscription plan.

In those early days the boy who had passed the ten mile post on life's highway concentrated his mind and fixed his optical nerves on two objects. One was to save up money enough to pay his way through all the circus shows that billed his town from the first gleam of the street parade until the last tent went down. The other was when he entered the portals of the school room, the terms of which lasted for three or four months, to commence laying his plans for feast he was to have about the close of his school when they "turned the teacher out." This consisted in making a demand on the teacher for a treat. Generally speaking, this was a mild affair and the teacher willingly entered in with the whole school and had a pleasant repast together at the teachers' expense. However, if the teacher was obdurate and did not come across he was seized and carried by force to the most convenient lake or pool and given an unceremonious baptising. This auxiliary to school life passed in Van Zandt county with the closing of the civil war. About the last I recall of importance was at old Cedar Grove at the closing of the session of 64-5. When the new issue was in its prime. At that time Cedar Grove was a thriving little village, surrounded by beautiful farms and reckoned for the time, a school center. At that session Professor MAGEE was the whole faculty. It seems that the students and teacher never mixed to any great extent. Since the opening of hostilities the Texas ports had been blockaded and business of all kinds had practically suspended. Occasionally a hogshead of sugar from Louisiana, which was coarse and unrefined, would reach here and out of this some home made candy had been made without starch or paint and put on sale at Cedar Grove in five pound packages at $12.00 per pound "new issue." The term of school was approaching its end.

Professor MAGEE was the proud possessor of a pony he rode and he had surmised something of importance would likely happen. So one morning the boys who were bare footed and all dressed in two-piece suits of homespun goods (that is to say a shirt and pants) had drawn a plan of battle, posted pickets and awaited the arrival of Professor MAGEE, who rode inside the lines when the captain of the squad gave the order "Close in" and the Professor made a dash and broke through the lines. Then the battle was on fast and furious. The boys could clear the old rail fences with a hand-spring and light on their feet a running and by crossing fields could head the professor and turn him about so as to keep him in range of the school house, but they could not get hold of either teacher or pony. The race lasted for about three hours, but the boys had read Commodore LAURENCE's order "Don't give up the ship" so they kept up the race until a passing farmer dismounted and turned his pony over to the captain of the squad when the professor was made a prisoner of war and taken to the school house where the boys told him if he would pay a ransom of five packages of candy he could have his liberty. This the professor grudgingly agreed to do so they went to the village store and the professor flaked out $300.00 "new issue" and the table was spread on a carpenter's bench and the feast was mutually enjoyed.

WILLIAM MANNING

WILLIAM MANNING was born of English parents at Boston, Massauchetts; served three years and nine months in the Revolutionary war; was in the battle of Bunker Hill; afterwards was honorably discharged, but never asked for nor received a pension. After that war was over he served for a time as sheriff in the state of Connecticut. He was the father of two children, ELISHA and WILLIAM. The last named lived to be ninety years old. ELISHA MANNING was born during the Revolutionary war and was a volunteer in the War of 1812, for five years, but after serving three years and nine months, he was honorably discharged, but never applied for nor received a pension. His home was in North Parish, New London, Connecticut, where he married an INGERSOLL and moved to western New York, where he lived for some years, and then moved to Pennsylvania. He was the father of seven children, one of which was MILO MANNING, who was born in Pennsylvania; near the line of New York, December 2, 1805; grew up and was for many years captain of a militia company, but was never called into service. He was married to Miss MARTHA HARVEY, at Falmouth, Kentucky, January 20, 1828. Her father's name was GRESHAM HARVEY, and his daughter, MARTHA, was born at Montpiellier, Vermont, March 20, 1811. Of this union eleven children were born, the fifth of which was HENRY CLAY MANNING, who was born March 14, 1837, in Bracken county, Kentucky. When he was a boy, they had no free schools in the "Blue Grass" regions; all schools were taught under the subscription plan, tuition and books both being high and wages low, and all of HENRY's inheritance was rather a delicate constitution; he had to struggle for an education, and not being able to pay for both tuition and books, he attended school very little, but bought books and by making a large wick out of slack twisted cotton yarn, which was placed in a small tin pan or granite saucer, and, filling the vessel three-fourths full of common lard, it furnished him a lamp by which to study of nights, and in this way when he reached the age of nineteen years he went before Judge SAM T. HOUSER, of Falmouth, Kentucky, a lawyer of good repute, and stood an examination and was given a permit to teach a common country school. Armed with this precious, hard earned paper, he set out on foot among the hills of Penalton county, Kentucky, looking for employment as "professor." So, in the summer of 1856, he opened a subscription school in a log cabin. After the school was out he engaged for a time in cutting cord wood ,which he sold to the Kentucky railroad. On the third day of April, 1857 ,he left his "Old Kentucky Home" for Texas, and reached Red River county on the third day of May, having been on the road just one calendar month, by the mode of fast traveling then in vogue. The remainder of that year and most of 1858 was spent in teaching in that county and going to school at Clarksville. In the spring of 1859 he came to Van Zandt county, and taught a school in the Morehead community. Then he went to Burlison county and engaged in teaching for a time, and from there he went to Austin and secured employment in one of the departments until Civil war spread its sable mantle over this fair land of ours. Being uncompromisingly opposed to war, he went on the frontier of Texas and joined a company of rangers, and did not serve in either army during that war. Peace once more having been restored he returned to Van Zandt county. Provisional Governor A. J. HAMILTON in August, 1865, appointed him sheriff of Van Zandt county. He held this position until the inauguration of Governor THROCKMORTON. He then accepted a position as deputy internal revenue collector, with headquarters at Tyler. He held this position until 1870, then became district clerk of Smith county Texas, which office he held for four years. During this time he became managing editor of the National Index, a weekly newspaper published at Tyler. During the time he edited the paper United States Senator HORACE CHILTON and Governor JAMES S. HOGG both learned the art of printing in the Index office; VAN HAMILTON was foreman in charge of the mechanical department. After his term of office expired as clerk he accepted a position as deputy collector of internal revenue, with headquarters at Sherman, Texas. He was married to MARY MELISSA KIETH, who was born in Penalton county, Kentucky, June 10, 1851, at Falmouth, Kentucky, August 6, 1874. He gave up the office of deputy collector and established a home in Canton and opened a mercantile establishment, which he conducted for five years. Being proficient in mathematics he bought a compass and much of these five years was given over to surveying. He also became an expert draughtsman and made many maps. The commissioners' court directed Capt. JAMES E. MOORE, then county surveyor, to block 17,700 acres of Van Zandt county school lands in Wise county into small blocks and map the same. In this H. C. MANNING was employed in making the survey and did all the mapping. Then the commissioners' court employed him in connection with the county surveyors of Hunt and Kaufman counties, to demark the north and western boundaries of Van Zandt county. The lineal running to accomplish this work was about half the distance of that actually run by the joint commissioners of the United States and the republic of Texas in demarking the western boundary of the Louisiana Purchase. Because this work had to be proven and monuments set up at given distances it was somewhat tedious. The northwest and southwest corners of the county were definitely established.

An accident occurred in connection with the blocking up of the Van Zandt county school lands that deserves recording here. OLIVER PEARCE and J. T. McWILLIAMS, then of Canton, engaged to go out to Wise county and assist in the work. They started from Canton in a two-horse wagon, with supplies and camp equippage to be used during the time the work was being done. At or near Mesquite a gun was accidently discharged and McWILLIAMS lost an arm thereby. He was taken to Dallas and left there in care of Dr. LEEK. When he recovered he returned to Van Zandt county, where he made his home for many years; then moved to Athens, where he died several years since. About 1880 H. C. MANNING built him a home near Wills Point, where he owned a couple of sections of land, which he fenced and used as a hay meadow until his death, which occurred May 12, 1912. He was given a Masonic burial, having been for many years a member of that order. His wife, M. M. MANNING, having preceded him in death; she died July 28, 1906. They both found a last resting place in White Rose cemetery at Wills Point. They had five children who yet survive them, towit, Miss. NORA E. MANNING, TYKE MANNING, DIDE MANNING, ALLIE GIBBARD and EVALYN MANNING TUCKER.

NEWSPAPERS IN THE UNITED STATES

The first newspaper was, supposedly, the Englis Mercurie, published in Elizabeth's time and bearing the date of 1583. In the early settlement of the United States newspapers were the exception to the rule. The first American newspaper was the Boston Newsletter published in 1704. In 1740 there were eleven, all told, in the American colonies; three published in Pennsylvania, two in English and one in German; one in New York; one in Virginia; one in South Carolina and five in Boston. This was thirty-six years after the establishment of the Boston News Letter, practically the first American newspaper. An attempt was made by RICHARD PIERCE, of Boston, to publish a periodical containing the news of the day, which was called Public Occurences--both Foreign and Domestic. But PIERCE announced an intention of printing a list of those who circulated many false rumors about the town, and so the authorities suppressed his paper. One hundred years ago, at the beginning of the nineteenth century, the newspaper was just beginning in this country. In 1784, the first daily newspapers were being issued in only four or five of the larger cities of the country. At that time there were two hundred newspapers published in the country; that meant a newspaper for each 26,450 population. There are now more than 23,000 newspapers published in the country regularly, or one for every 350 of the population.

The Mexican war, however, stimulated the public demand for news and gave to the newspapers their first great stimulus. Circulations increased until it was a mechanical impossibility to supply and circulate papers in sufficient numbers to meet the demand.

NEWSPAPERS IN TEXAS

The first newspaper printed in Texas, so far as I-have been ablt to ascertain, was at Nacogdoches in 1819. LONG's expedition into Texas brought with it a press and HORATIO BIGELOW commenced publishing a paper, but it survived only a short time, because LONG's stay there was of short duration.

NOAH SMITHWICK has this to say about a paper published at San Filipe de Austin, which I reckon among the first newspapers published in Texas; "GODWIN B. COTTON, the pioneer newspaper man in Texas, launched the Cotton Plant, as he facetiously characterized his paper, at San Filipe in 1829. He was a genial old bachelor of fifty or thereabouts, of aldermanic proportions, making him a conspicuous figure. His signature, "G. B. COTTON," prompted an inquiring individual to ask the significance of the initials. "Why, d--n it, can't you see   Great Big Cotton, of course, replied the owner of the name."

The Northern Standard was ushered in the newspaper kingdom in 1842 by CHARLES DeMORSE at Clarksville. This paper was a weekly, eight-page paper and published regularly until after the Civil war, when the editor went to the front, but, before leaving home he had been commissioned a colonel in the confederate army.

In 1848 he was awarded the contract to print and bind the laws of the legislature of Texas. To do this he hauled his supplies, as he did the manuscript, from Austin to Clarksville, Red

River county, in ox wagons, where the printing was done on a Washington hand press. To aid him in this he employed G. A. HILL of Van Zandt county an experienced printer and book-binder. So Van Zandt county helped to print the laws by which it was created. Mr. HILL had the satisfaction of living in five counties while occupying his colony grant on the north bank of the Sabine River, near Emory, towit: Nacogdoches, Henderson, Van Zandt, Wood and Rains counties. The work of getting the laws of that session of the legislature in book form was necessarily slow, under those adverse circumstances, but hwen a copy reached old Buffalo on the banks of the Trinity River, it was learned by the Henderson county people that Kaufman and Van Zandt counties had been divorced from Henderson county, and, on leaving the parent county, they had taken about 1,788 square miles of her territory, leaving her 940 square miles of territory; and all of the indebtedness of the county was left on the parent county. The Henderson county people thought the small debt should have been pro-rated equally as per square miles of territory. Now politicians must have something to talk about, so, in the district elections, the Henderson county politicians would brand Kaufman and Van Zandt counties as "free territory." This was kept up in a jocular manner until 1860. During that year Capt. SID S. JOHNSON came to Canton with a small press and commenced the publication of a small four page newspaper in the old log courthouse on the west side of the public square, being the first newspaper published in the county, and, as I remember it, survived Volume One.

CAPTAIN SIDNEY SMITH JOHNSON

Was born in Choctow county, Mississippi, April 19, 1840. He was a son of D. M. JOHNSON and wife, ADELINE SMITH JOHNSON. His grandfather was a patriot soldier in the war of the revolution. The family came to Cherokee county, Texas, in 1849 and to Tyler in 1854. At the age of twenty he came to Canton and commenced the publication of the "Canton Times." The Civil war came on and put a period to his publication, so he moved press to Tyler. He enlisted in D. Y. GAINES' Company K, of the Third Texas cavalry, and was elected third lieutenant of his company. After twelve months' service he was elected captain, a rank he held during the remainder of the war. After peace was restored he returned to Tyler where he studied law and was admitted to the bar and practiced his profession until 1880, when he became connected with the press of that city, and first and last charge of different editorial adventures. He was married to Miss ZELDA SMITH, October 15, 1867, of Tyler, Texas. They raised a large and interesting family, and he died at Tyler some years ago.

THE FREE STATE OF VAN ZANDT

"Tall oaks from little acorns grow;
Large streams from little fountains flow."

SOME HISTORY OF VAN ZANDT COUNTY

As above stated Van Zandt county was created from territory of Henderson county, and had been stigmatized "free territory." When secession was accomplished it was self evident that war would inevitably follow. Slave owners along the borders at once set about looking out places of safety for their property. Many slaves were brought to Texas during that contest. For that purpose the owner of a large number of slaves were brought to Texas during that contest. For that purpose the owner of a large number of slaves sent a slave driver to Texas to look out a place of refuge for his slaves. This man came by steamboat to Jefferson; there he secured a horse and saddle and came out on horseback to Gilmer, Quitman and on to Canton, stopping at the Bivins hotel, the principal hotel in the town. Editor JOHNSON, of the Times, heard that a slave driver had blown in town and so he called on him at his hotel, and in the run of conversation, made bold to ask him if he thought he would bring his slaves to Van Zandt county. "H--l, no," came the reply, "I had as soon think of taking them to a free state, I came all the way from Quitman here and never so much as saw a slave." At that time very few people living in Van Zandt county owned slaves and as misery loves company, the slave driver felt lonesome in Van Zandt county. Editor JOHNSON commenting upon this in a short paragraph said: "Van Zandt county had been free territory since it had been created, and now it had been admitted as a free state." The war came on and this appellation was carried to the training camps and into the army and was over the whole south, and it has grown to be a byword by many who never knew the significance of it.

I must get back to newspapers. That the readers hereof may know how many newspapers there were in Texas when Van Zandt county was created I will give a list as published in the Texas Republican, published at Marshall, in 1849: Aegis of Truth, Henderson; American flag (Spanish and English), Brownsville; Bonham Advertiser, Bonham; Civilian and Galveston Gazette, Galveston (tri-weekly and weekly); Colorado Tribune, Corpus Christi; Corpus Christi Star; Corpus Christi (Spanish and English); De Cordovas Herald and Emigrants Guide, Houston (monthly); Telegraph and Texas Register, Houston; Galveston News, Galveston (tri-weekly and weekly); Galveston Zeitung (German weekly and semi-weekly); Houston Gazette, Houston; Independent Monitor, Jefferson; Mercantile Advertiser, Houston; Morning Star, Houston (tri-weekly); Nacogdoches Times, Nacogdoches; Northern Standard, Clarksville; The Pioneer, Palestine; Texas Ranger, Washington; Texas Republican, Marshall; Star State Patriot, Marshall; Texas Banner, Huntsville; Texas Presbyterian, Houston; State Gazette, Austin; Texas Union, San Augustine; Wesleyan Banner, Houston; Star, Clarksville; Western Texas, San Antonio.

The number of newspapers in Texas today is 851, and the general improvement in style and literary attainments has advanced much more proportionately than has the increase in number. The large presses are a marvel in labor saving, and the rapidity in which papers are now thrown off the press is wonderful.

I have not made any effort to follow the various newspaper

171

enterprises set up and operated in Van Zandt county, but I feel like a generous demand is on me to reproduce, from the Dallas News, a biographical sketch of Mr. TOOMEY, who was a life-long friend of Van Zandt county.

D. PRESCOTT TOOMEY

D. P. TOOMEY, managing editor of The Dallas News, died at 2:45 o'clock yesterday morning at his home at 2808 Routh street. He had been in failing health for the last four years, but had been confined to his home only about ten days. On the morning of September 30, the date of the opening of the fourth Liberty Loan campaign, Mr. TOOMEY attended the meeting of the News-Journal family in observing the hours between 9 and 11 o'clock in aiding the Liberty loan drive in Dallas.

D. PRESCOTT TOOMEY became managing editor of the Dallas News in July, 1902. He was born December 5, 1868, near Homer, Louisiana, and came to Texas with his parents in 1876. They settled on a farm in Van Zandt county, where he remained until 1888. His father had been educator in Louisiana and directed his son's earlier studies. In January, 1889, Mr. TOOMEY began work as a mailing clerk for the Dallas News. His ability as an artist with pen and ink began to attract attention and he desired to develop his talent. In 1893 he went to New York, where he studied illustration, and, on his return, took charge of the News art department. In addition to his art work he also served as reporter and for several years was special correspondent. In 1900 he was made Sunday editor and in July, 1902, managing editor. In that capacity he has given the assignments for many of the notable series of articles which have appeared in the News and has advised with those who wrote them.

While managing editor he wrote more than most men who hold that position. He took a keen interest in national politics and attended many of the national conventions. He was also a close student of world politics, especially as they are connected with the present war. Several years ago , when judicial reform was an issue in Texas, in which both attorneys and the public evinced great interest, he went to Virginia and made a study of the judicial system of that state, writing a series of articles for the News. His last series of articles for the News was written this year. It was illustrated and he drew the illustrations. It dealt with the pink bollworm, which was then recognized as a pest likely to prove more damaging to the cotton crops than the boll-weevil.

His tact and consideration in dealing with men have endeared him to scores of newspapermen, and nowhere will the news of his death cause more grief than among the many young men now in the United States army and navy who are represented by the News service flag. He was regarded by all who worked under his direction both as head of the department and as trusted friend and adviser. It was his constant endeavor to stimulate the development of a public opinion that would recognize the just claims of all who

serve society usefully, and as part of the endeavor he felt a
keen interest in the welfare of the educators of this state from
primary schools to universities. He knew the problems of the
tiller of the soil through many of the years when their economic
status was most uncertain and in viewing the economic questions
of Texas he never lost sight of the standpoint of the man on the
farm. In discussing such matters he often used the remark that
he had ridden the cultivator and binder.

Mr. TOOMEY's health first began to fail in 1913. He has
been under the care of physicians since then, though he did not
relinquish his desk until a few months before his death. Last
summer he spent in the Ozark Mountains, but returned only slightly improved in strength. Through all his illness he has been
confident and cheerful, feeling certain that his strength would
gradually return. He took the same active interest in the progress of events and particularly enjoyed an ancedote about cur-
rent affairs.

In February, 1895, Mr. TOOMEY was married to Miss MARY CAR-
TER, who, at that time, was visiting relatives in Dallas. Her
home was in Columbus, Georgia, where she was born and reared. He
is survived by his wife and five children. They are MARY, ANNE,
ELIZABETH, DOROTHY and JAMES. Another son, PRESCOTT, died in
1910. Misses MARY and ANNE are students of the Southern Methodist university. Mr. TOOMEY was a member of the Catholic church.

Funeral services were held at 4 o'clock yesterday afternoon
at Calvary cemetery, where the body was buried. Pallbearers were
W. H. BENNERS, M. W. FLORER, TOM FINTY, Jr., H. M. CAMPBELL, G.
B. DEALEY and E. B. DORAN. The Catholic burial service was read
by Father B. H. DIAMOND of Sacred Heart cathedral.

The following messages were received by the News last night:

Wills Point, Texas, Oct. 13.--News of the death of PRESCOTT
TOOMEY saddens me beyond expression. His was a peculiarly sweet
character and I loved him for his almost infinite patience which
the rough places of life seemed unable to change.

W. H. Wingo

St. Louis, Mo., Oct. 13.--Advice of PRESCOTT TOOMEY's death
brings me heartfelt grief. His life was exalted by boundless
sympathy for his fellowman and unswerving devotion to principles
of honor and right. A noble character, a master draftsman has
vanished from this earth.

George Waverley Briggs

Galveston, Texas, Oct. 13.--All of us profoundly shocked and
sincerely sorry to hear of Mr. TOOMEY's death. Please express
our sympathy to sorrowing family.

John F. Lubban

CHAPTER 14

WILD HORSES

When Captain HILL settled on Widow's Prairie, near the
southwest corner of Van Zandt county, he said that a fine bunch
of wild horses ranged on that prairie, and gave him quite a good
deal of trouble. He was forced to keep his horses up all the
time to prevent them from taking up with the wild horses, in
which event he could not corral or catch them. At one time he
had a mule to take up with this wild herd, and he had counted
that mule lost, but a continued drouth prevailed for a time, and
he observed that his mule watered at a hole, to reach which, he
had to descend a deep bank of the creek, by a narrow path, and he
placed a lariat with a noose at the end of it so as to snare the
mule when it came for water, as he usually did about ten o'clock
each morning. Making the other end of the rope secure to a tree,
he climbed another tree near by to await developments. He had
not long to wait before he had the mule securely tied, but it was
some time before it would quiet down so that he could lead it
home and once more place it in captivity.

He said that the leader of this herd was a fine, fleet-foot-
ed stallion, that seemed to have his herd under complete military
control, and he could maneuver and march them around as well as a
captain could a company of men at drill. He said that he had frequently seen that horse, at the approach of a man on horseback,
circle around the herd and they would form a line and maneuver,
stepping up and back until the line was as straight as he had
ever seen men on a parade ground, and the captain was an old soldier. At a given whistle by this leading horse, he would set off
and the herd would follow as long as he would lead.

WILD CATTLE

The Cherokee Indians located in east Texas about 1820.
Their principal village was just south of the present city of
Rusk, in Cherokee county. As will be seen elsewhere, they were
driven out in a two days' fight, in which their Chief BOWLES was
killed, in Van Zandt county. Up to this time, from the beginning
of the fight, the squaws drove their herds in advance of the
fighting, but when their chief was killed, their herds of cattle
were abandoned in the Neches bottom, and they remained in the
eastern portion of Van Zandt county and western portion of Smith
county; and from that beginning quite a number of wild cattle
emanated and were killed by the early settlers to the county. So
far as I have been able to ascertain, the last remnant of this
herd was a fine heifer that was killed by MONROE UPTON, on what
is known as Heifer's Creek, near Martin's mill, in Van Zandt
county. From this incident the creek takes its name. Mr. UPTON
moved to Weatherford back in the fifties.

BUFFALO

Mr. BENJAMIN BRUTON was among the first settlers in Van

Zandt county. He was in Texas at the time of the declaration of independence, and received a league and labor of land therefor. This was located about half in timber and half on the prairie, on the Canton and Wills Point road; his house was a little south of that road and I found him there when I came to this county. He floated one-third of his land certificate and located it in Kaufman county, only two-thirds being patented to him in Van Zandt county. When he settled upon his calim, his mill and postoffice were at Nacogdoches, where he went once a year with pack mules to sell his peltry, get his mail and supplies, including meal and ammunition. He said that when he came to build his cabin here, he could go out on the prairie near his home and count as many as a hundred buffalo in a herd, grazing quietly on the rich grass. These herds would frequent what was known as the salt marsh below what is now known as Hayden's springs. These buffalo had licked the salt there until there was quite a depression covering several acres of land.

Mr. H. M. TEEL, still living in the southwestern portion of the county, has this to say: "I have lived in Van Zandt county since the fall of 1849, except what time I was in the army. The buffaloes had fallen back across the Brazos River, but Four Mile prairie was strewn with buffalo horns, heads and bones, from one end to the other. There could have been a carload of bones picked up on Four Mile prairie." Mr. TEEL also said that there were several herds of wild ponies here when he came. "There were no roads here when I came," he said. "I packed ponies with hides and took them through the woods to Canton to sell them."

By 1860 the buffaloes had been driven west of Fort Worth, but most any time you visited Fort Worth, you could buy a sack of dried buffalo meat for a trifle. Whatever may be said disparagingly of the American Indians, they never would kill more animals or birds, or take more fish than their sustenance demanded, unless it happened to be that they killed an animal too large for consumption. On the contrary, white people will shoot at anything living as long as their ammunition holds out, regardless of the loss. During the seventies the slaughter of buffaloes began in earnest, for their hides and tallow. From the Straits of Juan de Fuka to the Rio Grande the merciless slaughter went on without regard to age or sex of these favorite animals; and in four years' time they had almost been demolished. But few herds of them now live to tell a sad story of what young Americans will do when an opportunity offers. The mode of slaughtering them on the plains of Texas was to have a man well versed in buffalo hunting take hi his long-ranged buffalo rifle and a supply of ammunition, and ride out on the range where he could find a herd of these animals, tether his horse out and creep cautiously up to shooting distance, and select the animal he wanted to bring down, level his gun, take aim and pull trigger and soon the animal would begin to circle around and down it would drop, and this was repeated until as many as were wanted were brought down. Then the gunman was joined by one or more, who would open the animal, take out the tallow and rip the hide from the under jaws and skin the animal's head and slit the hide on all the legs and along the belly to the root of the tail, then a man with a heavy pair of mules, with what is known as a stiff tongue wagon, with rather long chains, reaching from the breast chains to the end of the wagon tongue, so as to allow the mules to spread, would drive up with his wagon that had a large hook attached to the rear axle by means of swivel. The mules were driven up to the head of the animal, the hook was inserted in a hole in the hide that had covered the animal's nose made for the purpose; the word was given and the hide was off the animal in much less time that it takes to tell it. The team was moved to the next animal and the same process was gone through with until all the hides were taken from the slaughtered animals. Other wagons would follow and take up the hides and tallow, and sometimes the hindquarters were saved and dried, and sent to market.

During the slaughter in Texas, one might visit Fort Worth and they would see daily, long teams of oxen coming in with one teamster and one team with two wagons, one trailing behind the other, loaded with buffalo meat, hides and tallow. Thus the noble animals have passed out, with few exceptions. About one-half of the 904 buffaloes reported in June 1900 were "cattloes" a cross between the domestic cow and buffalo bull. Both cattloes and buffaloes are raised on farms as a business.

RED PRONG HORNED DEER

Of these animals only the male had horns, and they were shed annually and each succeeding new set would develop another prong on each of its horns. Thus the first horns were put on when the animal was one year old, and had no prong to it, and was denominated a spike, and the next had two prongs, etc. The female or "doe" would produce from one to three fawns at a time, most frequently two, and sometimes one and three. These animals developed a keen sense of smell and a successful hunter would maneuver to get the deer between him and the wind, so as to avoid being scented by his prey before he could approach near enough to it to bring it down with his rifle. These animals were rather plentiful in the early settlement of the county and were a source of me meat supply, being mostly lean meat, the meat was easily saved even without salt, which was quite an item in those days. By the time of the Civil war they had materially diminished, but during the war men and guns with ammunition were so depleted, these animals increased very materially, and were somewhat abundant for a time following the war. Anterior to the war they seldom injured farm interest; there being an abundance of forage for them on the range. However, after peace was restored and the county began to settle up, and the range gave way, these animals were frequent visitors of farms in quest of food. Then only rail fences prevailed and these animals, if not disturbed, would only visit a field at night, and although they jumped the fence clear light, would go in and out at the same place for a whole season. They were most destructive to pea fields, but if corn produced large

ears, as was most always the case at that time, they would select
an ear that protruded out of the shuck and shell off and eat the
grains without tearing the shucks but little. When farmers would
find that a deer was feasting on his produce he would frequently
walk around inside his fence until he located the animal's place
of ingress and egress, and take some hard stick, most frequently
a heart rail and by means of a hand-ax and drawing knife, sharpen
one end of it and blacken it with lamp black and set it so as
when the deer jumped into his field it would pierce him so that
the next morning the deer would be found on this stob.

In those early days in Van Zandt county people who had occasion to visit the "piny woods," would generally drive out from
the road and gather a supply of pine knots, or heart pine logs
that had fallen in the forest and the sap burned off, leaving the
heart rich with resin and turpentine, and bring that home with
them to make lights, instead of modern lamps now in use. A mode
of hunting deer by night was to construct a fire-pan, so called,
out of hoop iron modeled much after the fashion of the horse muz-
zle of today, only larger. This was attached to one end of a
long handle, at the other end a small fork was set in the handle
with the prongs up, so that the hunter could lay the barrel of
his gun in the fork to shoot. In the fire-pan he would place a
lot of chips or bits of pine knots and invade the deer range, set
the pine knots on fire and place the long handle on his shoulder
and lead out with some one following him leading a pony packed
with pine knots, and carrying a gun loaded with buck and ball,
and when the man with the lamp discovered a deer's eyes, at a
given signal, the gun was passed to him and placed in the fork
and against the hunter's shoulder, and the deer was brought down
by a shot. The animal's entrails were taken out and it was lashed on the pony and the procession moved on after more game until
the pony was packed, and then fro camps or home, as suited the
occasion.

The fawns of this species of deer were somewhat given over
to sleep and the mother would take them usually to some elevated
open place, with a shrub to shade them, where varmints that would
be liable to destroy them, seldom went and leave them napping
while she was feeding and drinking.

The first suit of clothes that these fawns were blessed with
were red and white spotted, a little more red than white, and
were beautiful to behold. The following winter, when they were
from six to eight months old, this suit was shed off, then came a
light slate colored suit, which in the coming spring was exchang-
ed so long as the animal lived, at periods of about six months.

No nicer pet was ever possessed than these young deer and
they were easily brought into close friendship. The writer on
many occasions found these fawns quietly dozing and by slipping
up and grabbing one of them and holding until its fright was over,
would lay it across his saddle before him and take it to his home
and give it some sweet milk, and it would remain his companion
ever afterwards without confinement.

SOME HISTORY OF VAN ZANDT COUNTY

PASSENGER PIGEONS

The wild, or passenger pigeon, is about the size of a common turtle dove, but with long, wedge-shaped tail. The male is of dark slate color on its back, and purplish gray on its breast, the sides of the neck being enlivened by gleaming violet, green and gold. The female is drab colored above and dull white beneath, with only a slight trace of the brilliant markings. On a clear shunshiny day their feathers look fascinatingly beautiful during their rapid flight.

Some four or five miles southeast of Grand Saline, near Jones' schoolhouse, there is a small opening surrounded by a forest of medium large postoaks with evidence of the large limbs having disappeared. Perhaps those seeing the trees minus of their former limbs would be impressed with the idea that the boughs had been carried away by a tornado. Such, however, is not the case. In the early settlement of Van Zandt county, for a mile or so in every direction from this opening in the woods, pigeons by the millions made their home there about three months in the year, say from December to March. Then they winged their flight to other fields until the falling of the sweet mast came around once again. During their stay at this roosting place, it was dangerous to visit their home during the night time, as anything that disturbed their rest would cause so many of them to attempt to fly at one and the same time, that they would break most any limb they roosted upon. Because of so many pigeons roosting thereabouts, the opening was called "Pigeon Roost prairie," a name it bears today. At that early day the grass was prolific and when the woods burned off the fallen limbs were consumed by the forest fires.

Were it not for the fabulous stories told by such ornithologists as AUDUBON and WILLSON, I would feel ashamed to tell of the stupendous volume of wild pigeons that roosted at one and the same time in the vicinity of Pigeon Roost prairie. In one account WILLSON said that he saw a flock of these birds that contained 2,330 million wild pigeons. Now, I used to pride myself as A-1, on estimating the number of cattle in a herd, but when it comes to estimating the number of pigeons in a flock, I pass it up. However, I will say, the wild pigeon is among the swiftest birds that I ever saw on the wing; and, of mornings going or evenings returning to their roost, I have seen flocks of these migratory birds that in passing a given point they were so thick they would almost obscure the sun for half or three-quarters of an hour.

I have witnessed more than one tornado's procedure and heard the tempest's roar from its angry violence; I have stood in Yosemite valley, in California, and have seen the Merced River plunge 2,000 feet over its granite walls to the bottom of the valley beneath and heard the sound thereof; and these sounds remind me and compare favorably with the coming and going of the stupendous flocks of passenger pigeons in their flight.

When these birds made their temporary abode in and around

178

Pigeon Roost prairie, it was said of them, that they would visit
the cross-timber sections on the Paluxy River in Erath county and
Jim Ned Creek in Coleman county, and feed among the shinnery
there during the day and return to their roosting place the same
day. About 1875-76 they paid Pigeon Roost prairie their last
visit. Since then the place that knew them then has not known
them more. I can not give any satisfactory reason for their sudden demise.

THE CAROLINA PARAKEET

Another bird that was rather plentiful in the early settlement of Van Zandt county, which has years since disappeared, is
the parakeet. These birds went in flocks of from twenty to sixty. Their habitation was amid the forest, yet they would visit
farmhouses and oftentimes light on the dwelling and barn roofs.
They would sometimes visit and feed in pea fields, but not exten-
sively; and I never knew them to take up anything planted by farmers. They were about the size of a sparrowhawk; were of the
variety of parrots, but not of the talking species, although they
somewhat resembled them in manners and dress. I cannot remember
of ever seeing one of them in captivity, yet they were of a tame
nature, and, as sportsmen seldom molested them, they appeared of
a domestic nature. They were rather gaudy in dress and prolific
in colors; the feathers on the same bird variagated with red,
blue and green, so that, when a flock was on the wing, they looked as prepossessing as a squad of Mexican lancers on dress parade.
They have much longer tails than the domesticated talking parrot,
and I would infer they were much swifter on the wing. I never
knew any one to use them for food, and yet they were, strictly
speaking, herbiniverous in their diet, except as to small insects.
They did not appear migratory in the habitat, but must have migrated to some other part of the globe when they disappeared from
here.

TURKEYS

In the early settlement of the county, turkeys added much to
the meat supply. They were quite plentiful especially in the
timber belt along the streams. They had a large range, and were
incessant foragers. They would build their nests on high knolls
and barren places so that snakes and varmints would not destroy
their eggs or molest their young, and in this way the young could
soon learn to fly up to roost and thus they would multiply very
fast. As soon as the mast began to fall they would take to it
and soon get fat. At first they were killed only by shooting
them. However, after farms began to open, they would enter the
fields and a farmer noticing this would scatter corn at some
point until they got to visiting it daily, then he would build a
pen and dig a trench deep enough for the turkeys to go in the pen
throught it and cover the top over with boards for a few feet so
the turkeys would come up out in the pen and when they did they

would run around next to the walls with heads up and by stringing corn in the ditch and scattering some about the outside end they would get interested picking up the corn and rush along in the trench until quite a number would enter the pen and in this way could be killed without tearing the flesh like it would be if shot.

BEES

In primitive days grass and herbage grew prolific. And if the foliage burned off in autumn or winter, in early spring innumerable flowers would put forth and as variegated blooms burst forth they looked as beautiful as the reported gardens of Hesperides, and these with the blooms of forest trees furnished rich harvests for honey bees that built their homes in hollow trees, where they stored their food in great quantities. This was easily taken by cutting the trees and with smoke driving the bees away and taking their rich stores.

A SNAKE STORY

Since the publication of the Bible, which contains several snake stories, several fish stories, and a she-bear story, no book worth while can be offered the public with any degree of expectation of meeting the demand, without it contains some semblance of stories along these lines. It is not expected that Van Zandt county could match those old stories, but I feel like I ought to pull off something along that line.

The best that I can offer is by T. J. CATES of Ben Wheeler. Mr. CATES was born in Smith county, Texas, April 15, 1845, three years before Van Zandt county was ushered in. He joined the Methodist church when twenty-one years old; lived an upright, honest life, and at the age of seventy-one years in good health and well supplied with the natural demands of life, and with few cares before him, he says:

I remember riding through the woods one day and saw a large rattle snake stretched out by an old log. I shot the snake and dismounted from my horse to get the rattles, which numbered fourteen. I kicked part of the old log off and found twelve more rattlesnakes about two feet long and killed them. I kicked open the rest of the log, and to my surprise found twelve more rattlesnakes about twelve inches long, making all told, twenty-five rattlesnakes in one log, the largest being four feet seven inches long. Who can beat this for a snake story? I was less than an hour killing them.

Now, this story goes in volume one and the writer will hold all other snake stories for volume two.

BLACK BEAR

Were common, but not plentiful during the early settlement of Van Zandt county. This specie is not the honey-bear, but they eat honey when they can get it. They live on mixed diet of fruit, acrons and small animals. They were disastrous to hogs, catching shoats by the back of the neck, they hold them in their forearms and eat a bait out of the back of their necks, which would result in the animal's death; and when again hungry, they would pounce upon another shoat, or sometimes kill a whole litter of pigs, if they were not protected by a bunch of large hogs. This species of bear was especially fond of roasting ears, and sometimes they destroyed large quantities of corn before it ripened to such an extent as to be too hard for them. They were especially fond of sweet mast, and on the head of Mill Creek is what is known as Chinquepin branch, and these trees were low, and bears would climb them and pull the limbs in and feed upon the acorns. This species of bear were especially adapted to furbearing, which was long and of a silky texture, which made their hides valuable.

During the war they were not hunted and multiplied to some extent, but after peace was declared and restored they were soon killed out. As I remember it, the last one killed in the county was near where White Rose cemetery now is just east of Wills Point. He came up Cedar and Wolf Creeks, and was crossing over to the Sabine River, when he was intercepted and by aid of some dogs was brought to bay and killed.

These animals were much hunted when the people depended largely on wild meat for their supply, because of their fat and oil, which when mixed with dried buffalo, beef and venison, it would soften that kind of meat, making it much more palatable and digestible.

BEAVER

Beavers were never sought after for food, but their fur made them profitable to early settlers who needed money with which to buy supplies, especially ammunition, which they depended upon largely for their meat supply. The largest colony of these animals known to have existed in this county was on Slater's Creek, near the line of Henderson county. Here they put in a dam which created a pond covering several acres of land and made quite an extensive home. They were completely killed out before the Civil war, but, after peace was restored, I think in the winter of 1865, some trappers drove into Edom and asked how far it was to the beaver run; on being told, they said they were going out to catch the beaver. They were told that the beaver had been killed out years ago. The trappers replied that "there were four beavers out there, and they would get them," and passed on. After being gone two nights they passed back through Edom on their way to the east with four fresh beaver skins, which broke up the colony.

These animals are peculiar, in that lone beavers, "bachelors," as they are called, take up an abode to themselves and dam up a swift running branch, which will produce fish enough for his sustenance and live a lonely life all to himself.

On the head of Mill Creek is what is known as Beaver Dam

branch, where one of these animals made his home until killed out.

THE OTTER

This is a fine fur-producing animal; it has an elongated head, low body, short limbs, short broad feet, short strong compressed curve-pointed claws; head small and flat; lives in clear running streams, on a fish diet. The head and body is long, and the tail is about half the length of the head and body, and is flat, which makes it a good swimmer. The otter inhabited most, if not quite all, the running streams in the county, until they were taken by trappers. A few of them were shot, but they seldom came forth in daylight, except when they were hungry, and brought a fish ashore to ear, hence they were seldom killed by a gun. They remained here until about 1870.

CATS

Of these we have four district varieties. The largest, though fewest in number, were the Mexican lion or cougar. They were in make-up very much like lions, only much less in size. In hunting they could take down large animals and usually would remain in the vicinity of anything they killed until it was consumed, before killing another animal, so they were conservators of their food supply in this way.

The second variety was the most beautiful in the kingdom of animals. I have never seen but few of them, and never knew of one being taken without dogs. They were called leopard-cats, and were as regularly spotted as a coach dog with soft fur, small ears and well proportioned all over with strong claws, which was their defense and armament in taking food. If a dog came near enough so one of them could spring upon him, fastening the claws of its forefeet in him, it would dispatch him by tearing him into shreads with its hind claws. No prettier hide was ever dressed than that of a leopard-cat, when shot in the head so as not to leave a hole in its hide. The only way to kill them was by shooting while the dog held them at bay.

SQUIRRELS

Of these we had plenty in early days when big game furnished meat in abundance. There were three kinds of these animals: The large red fox squirrel was the one most sought for eating purposes. The large black squirrel was nearly as large as the red fox, but never was so numerous. Squirrels furnished a considerable amounty of food as the large game began to give out.

MIRGRATION OF SQUIRRELS

In 1858 came the greatest migration of squirrels that was ever known in this country; from whence they came or whither they

SOME HISTORY OF VAN ZANDT COUNTY

went, I know not. They traveled west of southwest; were poor and emaciated. All day long they might be seen like army worms moving on. When they reached the Trinity River they would get a small short stick and hold in their mouths and plunge in and swim across, if their strength would permit. A man could stand on either bank with a club in hand, if he was cruel enough, and kill until he sickened, but they were too poor to eat.

SECOND MIGRATION

In 1872, I believe it was, we had another migration of squirrels, but these animals were not nearly so numerous as before. While there were not nearly so many of them, they were in much better condition than their kind were before. They seemed a determined lot of little creatures, and marched as did those of former years.

The Union--the first Baptist Association organized in Texas-was instituted at Austin, Travis county, October 8, 1840.

The first legislature of the state of Coahuila and Texas was convened at Saltillo, and organized on the 15th of August, 1824. The office of Chief of the Department of Texas was created and DON JOSE ANTONIO SANCEDO was appointed as first incumbent.

The first reunion of the old settlers held in Van Zandt county was in the southeastern portion of the county on Battle creek, where Chief BOWLES was killed, on the 17th day of July, 1857, and was addressed by EVERETT E. LOTT, GEORGE W. CHILTON and R. B. HUBBARD. JOHN WALLING, Sr., was present and pointed out the spot where Chief BOWLES fell after receiving his death wound, which place was marked with a drawing knife in shaving off the bark of a red oak tree. The tree is now living.

CHAPTER 15

THE RIVER AND LAKE SABINE

When Van Zandt county was organized it contained all of its present territory as well as all the territory now allotted to Wood county, and nearly all of the present county of Rains, and the Sabine River approximately divided the county into two moieties. At present it forms the eastern boundary of the state from the thirty-second parallel of latitude to the Gulf of Mexico, and is navigable for 300 miles. It has its source in Hunt county, and drains about 17,000 square miles of Texas, emptying into Sabine Lake near the Gulf of Mexico.

The history of this river is, in a measure, a part of the history of Van Zandt county. I am always, under all circumstances, ready and willing to give everyone a square deal. Give them full measure, heaped up and running over, for every good act done, every good word spoken, which adds to the sum total of human advancement or human happiness. But to my mind there has been entirely too much ink wasted in telling about THOMAS JEFFERSON making the Louisiana purchase. Now, after more than one hundred years have rolled into the misty past, let us tell the truth about it. Let us say THOMAS JEFFERSON sent ROBERT R. LIVINGSTON and JAMES MONROE to offer $2,000,000 which had been appropriated by the congress for that purpose, for the purchase of the Island of New Orleans on the east side of the Mississippi river. That seems to be all that THOMAS JEFFERSON had to do with the purchase of Louisiana until the congress ratified the pruchase made by LIVINGSTON and MONROE, for the sum of $15,000,000, which had been done on the 30th day of April, 1803 ,and Mr. JEFFERSON knew nothing about it until the 14th day of July following. The congress ratified the treaty by and with the approval of President JEFFERSON. By a treaty with Spain, 1819, the river Sabine became the southwest boundary of the Louisiana purchase. So that brought the Sabine River into prominence as an international boundary. Then the pot began to boil. A whole volume could be written about the different faces of the propositions and counter-propositions, as to whether the Neches River or the Sabine was the true boundary line; first with Spain, then with Mexico. Diplomats of the United States and these two other governments played battledoor and shuttlecock for twenty years trying to settle the heavyweight question as to which of these two rivers was the true boundary of the Louisiana purchase. Many were the commissions appointed by the different governments to demark this boundary, but on meeting they "blew up" so to speak, and could not agree as to the demarcation of the line until August 7, 1839, just one week before the battle of the Cherokees and Texans began in East Texas.

The joint commissioners on the part of the Texas republic and the United States met in New Orleans for the purpose of organizing and proceeding with the demarcation of the boundary line but because of prevalence of yellow fever in New Orleans, the commission adjourned to reassemble at the mouth of the Sabine on October 15.

Further dallying and delays deferred the commissioners from meeting until the 15th of May, 1840, the joint commissioners met at Greens bluff on the west side of the Sabine. On the 21st, they proceeded to the shore of the Gulf and erected a circular mound of earth fifty feet in diameter and a bottle was buried containing the following memorandum:

"Be it remembered that on the 21st day of May, 1840, the demarcation of the boundary between the United States and the Republic of Texas was begun at this point, being conformity with the provisions of the convention for the demarcation of the boundary, concluded and signed by the respective plenipotentlaries of said countries at Washington, the 25th day of April, 1838. Witness our signatures this 21st day of May, 1840. JOHN H. OVERTON, commissioner of United States; JOHN R. CONWAY, United States surveyor. Witness J. D. GRAHAM, major United States engineers; MEMUCAN HUNT, commissioner on the part of Texas. By the commissioner, GEO. W. SMYTH, surveyor of Texas; JOHN HENRY YOUNG, clerk United States commissioner."

On the 4th day of June, the thirty-second parallel was reached and marked. When the commission adjourned, and met again February 14, 1841. Many more delays were encountered and finally, on the 24th day of June, 1841, the Red River was reached, the line being found to be 106 miles, 2,083 feet in length from the thirty-second parallel. With the completion of this survey, the history of the western boundary of the Louisiana purchase as an international line abruptly ends.

In early days in Texas the freebooters, who plied the African slave trade, made Sabine Lake a port of entry, for the reason they could land in Texas or Louisiana, as best suited their convenience to dispose of their cargoes of human freight. From 1822 to 1839 the Sabine River was the eastern boundary line of the Cherokee Nation, so-called because that tribe possessed the lands west of that stream; the Prairie Indians holding the Trinity, and the Caddoes occupying Red River from Texarkana to Shreveport. During the war between the states four engagements were fought on Sabine Lake.

On the morning of September 23, 1862, two sail vessels of the federal blockading fleet entered Sabine Pass and opened fire on the confederate fort at that place, which was promptly replied to. The cannonading continued all day, but the confederate guns, being of inferior calibre, their shots fell short, while the enemy's long range guns threw their shot into and around the fort. When night came on Major IRVINE spiked his four cannon and retreated to Beaumont.

On the night of October 29, 1862, a small body of Lieut. Col. A. W. SPAITS' battalion, under Captain MARSH, secreted themselves below the town of Sabine, and as the United States steamer Dan, with a schooner in tow approached going up the channel, poured a heavy fire into the crowded decks not more than a hundred yards distance, killing and wounding about thirty of the enemy. The next morning the enemy took revenge by shelling the town and burning Wingate's sawmill and dwelling and Stamp's dwelling. On January 31, 1863, two confederate cotton-clad gun-boats, JOSIAH BELL and Uncle BEN, passed out of Sabine Pass and attacked a Union warship of nine guns and a schooner of two guns, and compelled their surrender. On the 8th of September, 1863 , a spirited affair took place at Sabine Pass in which two federal gunboats, the Sachem and Clifton, were surrendered to the confederates.

Because of the heavy long leaf yellow pine forest on the lower Sabine River for thirty years Sabine Pass has been a busy theater of lumber exporting trade to all Europe. Then the Beaumont oil fields gushed forth a million dollars' worth of oil for export.

EVOLUTION OF ENVELOPE

There are many persons now living who can remember the days when letters went through the mails in the form of a folded sheet of paper sealed at one edge, for envelopes were not in common use until about 1855. In that year a machine was patented for producing these now indispensable covers for epistolary correspondence--a machine which, as compared with hand labor, did the work of five girls. A better machine was produced in 1862, which performed the work of seven girls. Three years later came the machine with a device for gumming the flap of the envelope, which did the work of ten girls. Next came another machine of American device, which did the work of twnety girls, and is still largely used. This has a rival in an invention which gums, prints, folds and counts the envelopes and binds them with a paper band in packets of twenty-five. This machine supplants the labor of thirty girls.

The first steamboat to ply between New Orleans and Galveston was the Columbia. This service was inaugurated in 1839.

The first law against dueling was passed by congress during the session of 1838-39. The author of the law was JAMES KERR, for many years surveyor of De Witt's colony. Col. KERR was the uncle of the historian, the late JOHN HENRY BROWN. Kerr county is named for him.

CHAPTER 16

THE NECHES RIVER

This beautiful and historic inland river has its source in
Van Zandt county, about Tunnell's chapel or Colfax, where never
failing springs of clear, freestone water gushes forth, forming
a stream of considerable size from the time they reach the surface. The river runs in a southeasterly direction, parallel with
the Trinity River, emptying into Sabine Lake, which is about
eighteen miles long by nien miles wide, lying between Texas and
Louisiana. This lake is fed by both the Sabine and Neches Rivers,
and discharges into the Gulf of Mexico.

The first historic event that claims our attention regarding
this stream occurred on the 20th of March, 1687, when DUHAUT, one
of SIEUR de la SALLE's companions fired a shot into his brain,
and he fell dead on the banks of the Neches river. LA SALLE was
a French explorer of considerable note; a man of wealth, genius,
fortitude and courage.

In 1819 the United States and Spain made a treaty, in which
it was agreed that the Sabine River should be the dividing line
between these two countries for a stipulated distance, and for
twenty years the commissions appointed by these governments
first, and later Mexico and the United States, wrangled over
which river was meant in the treaty--the Neches or the Sabine.
For nearly twenty years the Neches River was the western line of
the Cherokee Nation, and the eastern line of Texas. When the
Cherokee's were driven out, two important battles were fought,
both on the west, or Texas side of the Neches river. A portion
of that river now is the dividing line between Smith and Van
Zandt counties.

Since the first settlement on the Neches River, this magnificent waterway has played a prominent part in Texas' development.
Its first commercial use on an extensive scale came with the inception of the lumber business; and for three score years and
ten, its waters have contributed to the success of that business
in east Texas, both in the floating of logs to the mill and moving the finished product to market. As the lumber business developed and communities sprang up, a general commerce ensued,
which continued until the coming of railroads. In the southeast
corner of Van Zandt county, on the Neches River, is what are
known as the piny woods of Van Zandt county. In early days this
territory was almost exclusively covered with gigantic pine forest. Magnificent specimens of the yellow pine well-nigh covered
that small area of land.

JAMES W. THOMAS

Judge JAMES W. THOMAS, probably numbered among the oldest
lawyers in Texas, died at Abilene, January 15, 1916, at the age
of eighty-eight years.

In 1846 he went to Dallas from Georgia, and, not being able
to secure any employment there, he walked 200 miles east to Rusk
county. He was a clerk at the first election held under the con-

stitution of Texas.

Judge THOMAS was admitted to the bar following his services in the war of the confederacy, having served in Company D, Twenty-second Texas infantry volunteers, WALKER's division.

JAMES W. THOMAS was an early settler in Van Zandt county; came to this county in 1848 and settled in the Edom country. On his return from the war he became a partner in the mercantile business as a member of the firm of RIDGELL, MALONE & THOMAS, at Edom for a few years. He then moved to Comanche, where he engaged in the newspaper business for several years, during which he studied law, and was admitted to the bar, then moved to Ailene and practiced his profession until his death.

It was from Judge THOMAS that this writer learned that Judge JOHN C. McCOY hauled lumber from Colthorp's mill, in Van Zandt county, to build the first framehouse ever built in Dallas; also that the first courthouses, both in Dallas and Kaufman, were built out of lumber cut by JAMES COLTHORP in the piny woods of Van Zandt county.

The first white child born in Van Zandt county was JOSEPH HUFFER, a son of SAM HUFFER, a prominent surveyor in early days, and a grandson of NEAL MARTIN, a pioneer who settled and died in Van Zandt county about three miles north of Wills Point. Mr. MARTIN was on the island of Galveston on the day that JACKSON fought the battle of New Orleans

The first printer to settle in Van Zandt county was GEORGE A. HILL, who settled on the north bank of the Sabine river about 10 miles northeast of Wills Point. His home is now in Rains county.

The first cotton sent out of Texas by water was shipped from Velasco to Matamoros in 1831, and brought 62½¢ a pound.

The first synod of the Presbyterian church in Texas was organized at Austin in 1851 and consisted of three presbyteries. The first presbytery was that of the Brazos, instituted April 3, 1840.

The first Cecil Rhodes scholarship awarded to a Texan was given to STANLEY ROYAL ASHBY, of Alvin, in 1904.

CHAPTER 17

GOOSE LAKE

Nine Miles East of North From Wills Point Deserves a Place in the
History of Van Zandt County, Because of the Fact That a Cavalry
Company Regiment Was Drilled and Mustered in There During 1861.

Just at this time much interest is being manifested in the
league of nations now before the United States senate, for ratification or rejection. Those advocating its ratification do so
believing it will prevent future wars. If the Civil war in the
United States is any criterion to go by, a war may be started
without any parliamentary ceremony.

JAMES BUCHANAN was elected president of the United States,
because he had advised the seizure of Cuba, a province of Spain,
if Spain would not sell it to the United States, on terms dictated by the republic.

During President BUCHANAN's administration, the Knights of
the Golden Circle, a secret organization, was organized in this
republic with a view to obtaining Cuba and perpetuating slavery.
The national democratic convention met at Charleston, South Carolina. The Knight's of the Golden Circle attempted to control the
convention. Failing to do this, the convention failed to make
any nomination, and another effort was made to nominate candidates at Baltimore, Maryland, which resulted in the nomination of
two candidates for president and two for vice-president. The result of this was the constitutional election of ABRAHAM LINCOLN,
as president and HANIBAL HAMLIN, as vice president. I should
think by the time the new administration came in on the fourth of
March, there were fully fifty thousand men under muster in the
south, by reason of the activities of the Knights of the Golden
Circle.

The secession convention met at Austin, January 28, 1861.
The ordinance of secession was adopted February 1st, and submitted to the people to be voted upon February 23d, the convention
recessing until March 2d, on which day the vote was to be counted. At that time there were very few newspapers in Texas, and,
the fact of the business was, many people never knew there was
any election on that date. The vote reported for Van Zandt county was: For secession, 181; against secession, 127.

The convention, during its first sitting, appointed a committee of safety, of which JOHN C. ROBERTSON, of Smith county,
was chairman. This committee was given plenary powers and furnished rosters of the officers and men in Texas, organized and
officered by the Knights of the Golden Circle; with power to recruit by volunteers, as many as possible. Under the direction of
the committee of safety, a substantial force under Col. BEN Mc-
CULLOUGH, during the night of February 16, 1861, invested the
federal barracks at San Antonio, and by noon, February 17th, General TWIGGS, United States Army, had signed all the articles of
surrender of all federal troops in Texas. If space would permit,
I could give the number of all troops at a line of post twelve
hundred miles long in Texas, that were surrendered on that occa-

sion.

When the convention met, as per adjournment, JOHN C. ROBERT-SON, chairman committee of safety reported: "The committee are confident of having obtained federal property amounting to near $3,000,000, at a cost of less than $75,000 all told.

Remember this was all done before President LINCOLN was inaugurated; we were being told there would be no war.

The history of Goose Lake in Van Zandt county, worth perpetuating, was brought about in this way: During the summer of 1861, Goose Lake became the place of rendezvous for recruiting a cavalry troop of one regiment, afterwards known as the Tenth Texas cavalry, Confederate States of America, Col. M. F. LOCK, commanding. This regiment was organized about the first of October, 1861, as follows:

Co. A--C. D. McKNIGHT, Captain, from Wood county.
Co. B--J. WILLSON, Captain, from Wood county.
Co. C--J. H. TUCKER, Captain, from Upshur county.
Co. D--ELLIE A. ARP, Captain, from Upshur county.
Co. E--RAS REDWINE, Captain, from Rusk county.
Co. F--W. D. L. F. CRAIG, Captain, from Panola county.
Co. G--MAT BARTON, Captain, from Rusk county.
Co. H--ANDERSON WHETSTONE, Captain from Van Zandt county.
Co. I--R. H. MARTIN, Captain, from Cherokee county.
Co. K--J. H. TODD, Captain, from Smith county.

Of all the men that went out in ANDERSON WHETSTONE's company from Goose Lake, in 1861, I can only call among the living today, Dr. W. A. ALLEN, of Silver Lake, Van Zandt county.

CANTON

The county seat of Van Zandt county was laid out in 1850. The first term of the district court was opened in the new log cabin on the 7th day of September, 1850. Judge ORIN MILO ROBERTS presided, in exchange with BENNET H. MARTIN, judge of the ninth district; A. J. FOWLER, district attorney; B. W. ANDERSON, sheriff, and ALLEN BLAIR, clerk of said court.

It was said that Judge ROBERTS was at that time living at San Augustine, that it was then customary for all the lawyers to fall in with the judge and as they expressed it, "ride the circuit" with him. That when they reached the Neches river they threw heads and tails with a Mexican dollar to see who should swim across the river for a boat to cross over the stream on and Judge ROBERTS lost in the game and swam over and secured the boat.

The town is located near the geographical center of the county. On Mill creek, a tributary of the Sabine river, which creek is fed by numerous springs of pure freestone water. A brick courthouse stands near the center of the court plaza. Long rows of brick buildings encircle court square. A brick schoolhouse is located about half a mile to the south, a brick jail two blocks to the north of the courthouse. Two church buildings are located in the town, which has two strong banks. Numerous department stores and other business houses go to make up the quota and fill the demand for a well-developed country round about. Double daily car mail service is had from Edgewood, ten miles distance on the Texas and Pacific railroad, which is also the shipping point for the town, which has local and long distance telephone service, a modern hotel, two brick kilns, one lumber yard, one cotton gin, two corn mills, lodge halls for each, the Masons and Odd Fellows, and a weekly newspaper and a mayor, town council and marshal.

WILLS POINT

Was laid out in the winter of 1873, by General GRENVILLE M. DODGE, of Iowa, then construction engineer for the California Construction Company, and was named "Iola" by Major W. H. ABRAMS, land commissioner of the Texas and Pacific railroad. It wore this name for a time and the people hereabouts received their mail at Canton, which was supplied at that place by Bradfiels stage line from Marshall via Tyler, Canton, Prairieville and Kaufman to Dallas, three trips per week. But it dawned upon the "Iolans" that as the Texas and Pacific railroad trains then operated between Shreveport and Dallas, the fuel which was used to generate steam was wood and no time schedule was then observed by the hands operating on those trains, and Iola had several business houses in which the counters had top and bottom rails and the operating hands would nearly always stop the trains and look at those counters, that Uncle Sam might be induced to supply Iola with mail. To this end a petition was drawn up asking the postmaster general to appoint T. H. WHITE, one of Iola's citizens, postmaster. Uncle Sam agreed to this but wrote back that the name would have to be changed, as one postoffice in Texas already wore the sobriquet of Iola. Then the name of Wills Point was sent in and T. H. WHITE was appointed postmaster and the office was opened, with THOMAS McKAIN as assistant postmaster of Wills Point.

The city is located exactly on the summit between the Sabine and Trinity rivers, being 537 feet above sea level, and is the highest point of said road east of Fort Worth, in Texas. It has a mayor and city council and city marshal. It has a commodious brick schoolhouse, five church buildings, lodge halls for the Masonic order, the Odd Fellows and Knight of Pythias. The city has a splendid water works and sewage system, tem miles of cement walks. Three strong banks are located here, one wholesale hay and grain dealer, one wholesale grocer, several department stores, together with hardware and furniture stores, grovery and dry goods stores and wagon and farm implement dealers. One 50-barrel-a-day flour mill, one cotton oil mill, two cotton gins, two corn mills. An express office and electric light plant and an undertaking establishment, also a newspaper. There is a splendid opening for a cotton compress, a modern hotel, an ice plant, a potato curing plant, a bacon curing plant, a fruit canning plant and a steam laundry. A Carnegie library and hot-house floriculture garden is much needed.

EDGEWOOD

"Oh, vot ish all dis earthly pliss?
Oh, vot ish man's socksess?
Oh, vot ish various kinds of dings?
Und vot ish habbiness?"

The bustling little city of Edgewood, ten miles west of north from Canton, was born in the early part of 1888, under peculiar circumstances. There had been a siding about one mile east of where this little city now stands called Stevenson, and the T. & P. had a section house there. But Wills Point and Canton pulled off a frightful war, in fact the fright was all there was to it. Anterior to that, Canton had done all its shipping at Wills Point, but Canton decided to cut the acquaintance of W. P. and to that end wanted another shipping point. Col. JOHN C. ROBERTSON and Judge JOHN L. HENRY were attorneys for TOWLES ETALS in the contest about the county seat and Colonel ROBERTSON and his law partner, Col. W. S. HERNDON, owned a league of land upon which this thriving little city, just at the edge of the woods, is now located. So they told Canton if they would ship to that point, they would have a siding put in there and a depot put up at that point. This was all agreed to and Colonel HERNDON, who by the way was something of a railroad man, went to work and had the depot put up and Canton employed JOHN P. GROOME to run a line from Canton through the woods to the depot. ROBERTSON and HERNDON employed HENRY C. MANNING to survey and map their land and they divided the same between themselves and Edgewood was put on the map and has been Canton's shipping point ever since. This is a hustling little city of live merchants, with two banks, a large brick schoolhouse, two cotton gins, two commodious church buildings, a spicy little newspaper, long rows of brick buildings, good clean stocks of merchandise, hardware and implements, and a general variety of all that the surrounding country wants are on display at competing prices; an express office, a local and long distance telephone system, a lumber yard, and up-to-now hotel. Edgewood is an original dry town, nothing stronger than soda pop was ever vended there.

BEN WHEELER

Situated in central southeast Van Zandt county, is a promising little burg. Situated in a rich farming country, where can be produced a greater variety of stuff than any other part of the county. It is on Dixie Highway, has a daily mail from Chandler on the Cotton Belt Railroad, has a well-kept little bank in a substantial brick building, other bricks are going up, right along. A large school building, two churches, two cotton gins, one corn mill, a telephone system, good substantial, well-kept

stocks of merchandise are offered to the public. A newspaper.
The town derived its name from a pioneer mail carrier, BEN-JAMIN WHEELER. It is surrounded by gushing springs of pure limp-id water. Well-to-do farmers make up the citizenship in that im-mediate locality. An annual fair is held there and the collec-tions are taken from there to Tyler and Dallas Fairs and the BEN WHEELERITES carry off many prizes.

MYRTLE SPRINGS

Is located on the Dixie Highway between Canton and Wills Point. It is surrounded by a good farming and fruit-growing country. Has a commodious brick schoolhouse, two churches; has a concrete lodge hall; several good, substantial business blocks; well-kept stocks and nursery of well-selected varieties of trees and shrubs.

MARTIN'S MILL

Ten miles east of south from Canton is a village worthy of note. Has a commodious school building, two church buildings, a cotton gin and corn mill, several substantial business houses, has a daily mail; is located on the road from Canton to Athens, on Heifer's creek, in the oldest settled part of the county.

CHAPTER 18

SOME CRIMES IN VAN ZANDT COUNTY

Just now we hear considerable talk about preventing a future war. In my opinion, the master stroke to prevent such an occurrence would be for all civilized countries to enter into an agreement that all future wars shall be fought, if fought at all, with voluntary forces only.

After secession was accomplished, the confederate congress passed a conscript law, under which, all men were ordered to enroll for military service, who were between the ages of eighteen and fifty years. Enrolling officers were appointed for each county and they were authorized to appoint others for each subdivision of the county to see to it that all names of men subject to service was properly enrolled therefor. Then a bill was passed exempting all men who owned twenty slaves from military service in the confederate states. All who evaded service, or failed or refused to enroll for service, were to be treated as deserters, and hunted down, put in irons and taken to some camp and turned over to the commanding officer for court-martial.

The first blood spilled by reason of these strictures in Van Zandt county, was a man by the name of JACKSON, who lived in an humble cabin at Lawrence Springs. His foreparents had fought in the War of 1812, and he said he would never fight against the flag of his fathers.

Gen. HENRY E. McCOLLOUGH was stationed at Bonham, and COURTS B. SUTTON, a son of "BLACKSTONE," who would rather hunt others down and manacle them for refusing to enroll for service, than scrap with the yankees, and whose home was at Clarksville, in Red River county, came to this county at the head of a bunch of "rough riders," to hunt down those evading service, and visited Mr. JACKSON's cabin early in the spring of 1863, shot him down and dragged him out of his cabin and left him for dead; but he lived several days before the death angel relieved him. Many other horrible atrocities were enacted under these laws, but I only recount this one to show the depravity of war.

THE FIRST DEATH PENALTY

THE STATE OF TEXAS,
      Murder.
No. 351 Va.   To-Day,
FRANK WILEY DINK,
      Negro Boy   Spring Term, 1866.

On this day came the prosecuting attorney, who prosecuted in behalf of the state, and the defendant, FRANK WILEY DINK, in his own proper person; JOSEPH RUSHING, Esq., was appointed by the court attorney for the defendant. The parties announced themselves ready for trial; the defendant plead not guilty of the allegation as set forth in the bill of indictment.

Whereupon came a jury of good and lawful men, to wit, M. MANNING and eleven others, who elected, tried and sworn to try this cause according to law and evidence and essess the punishment. Who, after hearing the evidence and argument of counsels, retired under the charge of the court to consider of a verdict, and, after due deliberation therein had, returned into court the following verdict, towit: "We, the jury, find the defendant guilty of murder in the first degree as charged in the indictment, and over the age of seventeen years at the time the offense was committed."

"M. MANNING, Foreman"

It is therefore, ordered, adjudged and decreed by the court, that the defendant, FRANK WILEY DINK be kept in close confinement in the jail of Van Zandt county, until Friday, the 6th day of July, 1866, when the said defendant will be taken by the sheriff of Van Zandt county from said jail to a gallows near the town of Canton, to be prepared for that purpose; then and there between the hours of ten o'clock a. m. and two o'clock p. m. of that day, the said defendant, F. WILEY DINK, will be hanged by the neck until he is dead, dead, dead.

On the 19th day of June, 1865, Governor ANDREW J. HAMILTON, of Texas, reached Galveston by steamship, and issued a proclamation, putting in force the laws of the United States, and declaring that the emancipation proclamation was then and thereafter to be in full force and effect in Texas.

Some time during the latter part of 1865, a Mr. HOUSTON, living south of Canton, went to Wood county with a wagon and team, and was on his way home, somewhere south of the Sabine River, when he camped for the night. While he was preparing his supper a young negro boy came to his camp and Mr. HOUSTON gave him his supper. Later Mr. HOUSTON laid down and went to sleep, and the next morning he was found dead; having been killed, as I remember it, with an ax. The neighborhood was aroused, and a man by the name of WOMAC struck the trail of the negro boy, followed him up and brought him back. My recollection is that the boy confessed the crime. He was lodged in jail and later tried, convicted and hanged for the crime. He being the first person hanged by law for crime in Van Zandt county; and the only negro so hanged in this county up to this time.

MURDER AND ARSON

In the spring of 1860 Mrs. McCLANAHAN and her only son by a former marriage, JAMES C. WHEELER, of kin to Associate Justice ROYAL T. WHEELER, of the supreme court of Texas, came out from Indiana, and for that season rented land of Dr. J. D. WRIGHT, on the Canton and Saline road where it crosses the old Cherokee boundary line. The following fall she bought, as I remember it, 520 acres of land of the JOHN C. PAYNE grants on Saline Creek, near the long bridge and built them a home thereon. In the winter of 1866 Mr. WHEELER, the son, went to take cotton to the gin and it was far in the night when he reached home to find his

house burned and his mother a charred crisp in the smouldering
ruins. He gave the alarm and the neighbors responded and he buried the charred remains of Mrs. McCLANAHAN by the side of J. M.
IRISH, her father, who had moved out here and preceded her in
death. In a day or so, AUGUSTUS MIDDLETON, a young man of twenty
or more years of age, was seen on the Saline selling and exhibit-
ing things that people knew belonged to Mrs. McCLANAHAN. He was
arrested and given a preliminary trial before a justice of the
peace who refused him bail. A habeas corpus writ was applied for
and granted by Associate Justice of the Supreme Court STOCKTON P.
DONNELLY, at Tyler in August, 1867. On this hearing MIDDLETON
was granted and made bond for his appearance at the fall term of
the district court of Van Zandt county. At the fall term of the
court the defendant failed to appear and a forfeiture was taken
on his bond. His father appeared before the court, and, after
being duly sworn, testified that his son, AUGUSTUS MIDDLETON, was
dead. In this way the forfeiture was set aside and Mr. MIDDLETON
decamped; but several times after that AUGUSTUS MIDDLETON was
heard of, "all alive and kicking," but was never apprehended for
the crime.

AN OUTRAGEOUS MURDER WITHOUT APPARENT CAUSE

During the summer of 1868 a number of lawless characters
banded themselves together round about the Saline, with sympath-
izers in other portions of the county and organized a Ku-K   -
Klan, so called; the cause, if any there was for this organization, was best known to its participants. Dr. PAGE, a modest,
unassuming gentleman, of which I never heard anything approaching
bad, or immoral act, was taken out, maliciously murdered and his
head severed from his body and hung to a limb in a conspicuous
place, with a warning card attached thereto stating that others
would be summarily dealt with. A little later a mob of these
culprits visited Canton, took possession of the courthouse, and
for several days drank and caroused around there. At that time
the state was under military rule, with J. J. REYNOLDS, whose
headquarters was at Austin, in command. Governor ELISH M. PEASE
was civil governor of the state. Capt. CHARLES STEELHAMMER, United States Army, was at that time stationed at Cotton Gin, on the
line of Limestone and Freestone counties, and he was ordered to
Canton to aid the civil authorities in maintaining law and order;
several arrests were made but the prisoners all escaped and none
were ever brought to trial.

THREE KILLINGS IN ONE DAY AT CANTON

In the spring of 1870 a circus was billed for a show at Canton. Most people were armed, and a feud ensued between some men
named MOORE, on the one side, and BOTTOMS, on the other. As I
understood, they were entire strangers to each other, but little
said on either side, a shooting scrape ensued, and the toll was
one of the MOORE's and two of the BOTTOMS were killed, in less

time than it takes to tell it. I never knew of anyone being put
upon trial for this outbreak.

BILL OF INDICTMENT AGAINST D. C. WHITE

THE STATE OF TEXAS

County of Van Zandt

In The District Court:
May Term, 1877

In the Name and by the Authority of the State of Texas: The
grand jurors, good and lawful men of the state of Texas and county of Van Zandt, duly sworn on their oaths by the judge of the
district court of Van Zandt county, touching their qualifications
as grand jurors, elected, empaneled, sworn and charged to diligently inquire into and true presentment make of all offenses
against the public laws of the state of Texas committed in the
borders of Van Zandt county, do, upon their oaths, present to and
in the district court of Van Zandt county, that D. C. WHITE, a
transient person, did, in said state of Texas and county of Van
Zandt, on or about the 20th day of February, A. D. 1877, with
force and arms, did then and there, in and upon the person of
GEORGE CONQUEST, reasonable creature in the peace of God and the
said state then and there being, wilfully, feloniously and of
malice aforethought, did make an assault, and that the said D. C.
WHITE with a certain shotgun then and there charged with gunpow-
der and leaden bullets, which the said D. C. WHITE in his hand
then and there held, the said gun being then and there a deadly
weapon, then and there wilfully, feloniously and his malice aforethought, did strike, penetrate and wound him, the said GEORGE
CONQUEST, in and upon the back of the head of the said CONQUEST
giving to him, the said CONQUEST, then and there with leaden bullets aforesaid discharged and shot out of the gun aforesaid by
the said D. C. WHITE and inflicting in and upon the back of said
CONQUEST's head aforesaid one mortal wound, of which one mortal
wound, he, the said CONQUEST, did instantly die, and so the jurors
aforesaid upon their oaths aforesaid do say that he, said D. C.
WHITE, the said GEORGE CONQUEST in the manner and by the means a-
foresaid, did kill and murder him, the said GEORGE CONQUEST, contrary to the statute made and provided, and against the peace and
dignity of the state.

JNO. F. BLANCHARD,
Foreman of the Grand Jury.

Filed May 11, 1877.
    R. H. Allen, Special Clerk D. C. V. Z. Co.
State Witnesses: R. C. McKENZIE,
                  J. W. BARNETT,
                  J. W. CLOWER,
                  JOHN PRESCOTT,
                  J. E. BRAGG

The facts about the GEORGE CONQUEST murder case, as I remember them, are about as follows:

SOME HISTORY OF VAN ZANDT COUNTY

Mr. CONQUEST was an Englishman. He had lived in Missouri but had moved to Shreveport, Louisiana. He was suffering from tuberculosis and wanted to travel for his health; he therefore bought a few goods, a wagon and two mules and hired WHITE to drive the wagon for him and started out peddling. He had reached the Owlet Green neighborhood, in Van Zandt county, and struck camp for the night. He was later found dead at his camping place. D. C. WHITE was indicted for the crime. The matter had lain dormant for sometime, when Mr. A. D. TANNER (now of Oklahoma), who was then deputy sheriff of Van Zandt county, came to me and talked the matter over with me. I remembered that PHILIP KOONCE, a tenant of mine, had brought DAN WHITE to me some years before for me to pay him for cotton picking. I told Mr. TANNER that I thought that we might get a line upon WHITE. So the next Sunday morning I drove out to Mr. KOONCE's and we walked out over the fields looking at the crops, when I asked Mr. KOONCE what had become of WHITE. He told me that WHITE was at, or near Minden, Louisiana; that he, himself, came from Minden to Texas, and had known WHITE there many years. With this information Mr. TANNER secured a requisition from the governor of Texas on the governor of Louisiana, and had it honored by the governor of Louisiana. With these papers, he asked me to go to Minden with him and I consented to do so. We went to Shreveport, where I had a friend, who gave us a letter to a trusted friend of his in Minden. With this we boarded a Concord Stage and was driven through the Red Shoot country, over terrible bad roads, and the stage lurched quite a good deal, so by the time we reached Minden, Mr. TANNER was very sick and nervous. I secured for him a good room in a hotel, and requested the landlord to attend to all of his wants and went out to see what could be done regarding Mr. WHITE. I was only a private citizen and the officer who was authorized to execute the writ was physically unable to do so. The letter that I had enabled me to secure the services of a deputy sheriff there, and Mr. TANNER turned over the papers to me and the deputy and myself went some eight miles north of Minden; and, as we were traveling along, met Mr. WHITE in a narrow bridle path, in a great pine forest, and made him a prisoner. At his request we went with him to his sister's home nearby, where he changed his clothes and gave some instructions about his business affairs. We then started with him and reached Minden just as the sun was setting. To my delight we found Mr. TANNER very much improved and ready for his return trip. We secured a stage and reached Shreveport just at daylight next morning and placed our prisoner in jail. We rested up there until the next morning when we caught an early train out for Texas. We got off the train at Wills Point and started for Canton, reaching there by the middle of the evening, where the prisoner was delivered to the sheriff of Van Zandt county for safe keeping.

JUDGMENT OF CONVICTION

THE STATE OF TEXAS

No. 1465 Vs.   6th May, 1881
D. C. WHITE

This cause being called for trial May the 6th, A. D. 1881, and the plaintiff being represented by her counsel, J. H. HOGG, and the defendant appearing in open court in person as well as by attorney, both parties announced ready for trial; whereupon the defendant was arraigned in open court and plead "not guilty" to the allegations of the indectment; whereupon a jury of good and lawful men, towit: J. F. BARFIEDL and eleven others were selected, empanelled and sworn according to law.

May 7th, A. D. 1881. This day the evidence in this case being submitted to the jury after receiving the charge of the court retired in charge of an officer to consider of their verdict, and after due deliberation returned into open court the following verdict: "We, the jury, find the defendant guilty of murder in the first degree and assess his punishment at death."
                                        "J. F. BARFIEDL, Foreman,"

It is therefore ordered, adjudged and decreed by the court that defendant, D. C. WHITE be punished as it has been determined by the jury in this case, and that he be remanded to the county jail to await the further action of this court.

SENTENCE OF DEATH PRONOUNCED

THE STATE OF TEXAS
                        District Court, November Term, A. D. 1881
County of Van Zandt   November 26th, 1881

                        The State of Texas
                           Vs. No. 1465
                           D. C. WHITE

This day came the district attorney, J. S. HOGG, prosecuting the pleas of the state, and the sheriff by order of the court brought the defendant, D. C. WHITE, into open court, who on a former term of the district court of Van Zandt county, towit:

May term, A. D. one thousand eight hundred and eighty-one, had been tried and convicted of murder of the first degree, and his punishment fixed at death, by a jury of Van Zandt county, Texas, on a bill of indictment presented in the district court of Van Zandt county, Texas, and an appeal having been taken by the defendant to the court of appeals of the state of Texas, on the judgment of this court, which said appeal being heard by the said court of appeals, and the mandate of said court of appeals having been received; and it appearing that it was the opinion of the said appelate court that there was no error in the judgment of the court below;

It was therefore ordered, adjudged and decreed by the court of appeals that the judgment be in all things affirmed;

It is therefore the order and sentence of this, the district court, that the defendant, D. C. WHITE, be, on Friday the 3rd day of February, A. D. 1882, by the sheriff of Van Zandt county, Texas, hanged by the neck until he is dead, dead, dead; and that the same be done according to law in such cases. And it is further ordered by the court that he be remanded to the custody of the sheriff of Van Zandt county, Texas, until the day and date last aforesaid, then to be executed as aforesaid, and the clerk of this court issue to said sheriff this order of execution as required by law.

This is the only white man hanged after a fair and impartial trial before a judge and jury in Van Zandt county.

JUDGE JOHN C. ROBERTSON

The subject of this sketch was born March 10, 1824, in Hancock county, Georgia, and moved to Chambers county, Alabama, in 1837. He was educated in Oakhowery college, and graduated in 1845 from the Harvard university in Massachusetts. He was married to Miss SARAH GOODMAN in September, 1845, and moved to Texas in 1851, locating at Tyler. He was a member of the secession convention held at Austin in 1861, and was chairman of the committee of safety, appointed by that convention. In 1866 he and the late W. S. HERNDON formed a co-partnership in the practice of law at Tyler. In 1877 he with the late Associate Judge JOHN L. HENRY was employed by Capt. T. J. TOWLES and others as attorneys in the contested election case from Van Zandt county, which resulted in the records of Van Zandt county being returned from Wills Point to Canton. In 1878 he was elected to the office of district judge, and re-elected in 1880. During his term of office as district judge D. C. WHITE, a transient person, was tried before him in Van Zandt county, for the murder of GEORGE CONQUEST, and was convicted. Judge ROBERTSON pronounced the sentence that "he be hanged by the neck until dead, dead, dead."
In 1884, Judge ROBERTSON resigned the judgeship and died in Tyler, in 1895.

GOVERNOR JAMES STEPHEN HOGG

Was born March 24th, 1851, in Cherokee county, Texas. He was of Scotch-Irish extraction. His parents were JOSEPH LEWIS and LUCINDA McMATH HOGG, who came to Nacogdoches in 1839 and, after the expulsion of the Cherokee Indians, they settled in Cherokee county.
JAMES STEPHEN was left an orphan at the age of twelve, and he set about fighting the battles of life in an honorable, manly way. At the age of seventeen, a strange freak on life's highway caused him to enter the office of the National Index, a weekly newspaper published at Tyler, Texas; H. C. MANNING, managing editor, and VAN HAMILTON foreman of the presswork. Here, as I remember it, he worked as typesetter until he attained his majority, when he secured a small press and a few fonts of type and

established a paper of his own at Longview. Subsequently he moved it to Quitman, in Wood county, where the "Quitman News" was edited and published by Mr. HOGG for several years. He was elected justice of the peace of the Quitman precinct in 1873, when he retired from the newspaper business. He commenced the study of law while meting out justice to the transgressors of the law in Quitman precinct. In 1874 he was married to Miss SALLIE STINSON, daughter of JAMES A. STINSON of Wood county, Texas. He joined the church and was baptized by the Rev. AMBROSE FITZGERALD, who was the first county clerk of Van Zandt, Wood and Rains counties. Mr. HOGG was admitted to the bar in 1875; he entered upon the practice of his profession and was elected county attorney of Wood county in 1878. In 1880 he was elected district attorney of the Seventh judicial district. While discharging the duties of the office of district attorney, he prosecuted some hard characters in Van Zandt county, and frequently, when a venire was summoned in a felony case, he would bring the list to the writer hereof, and would go over it, asking about the character and standing of the jurors, and make notations thereof to aid him in selecting a jury to try the case. He prosecuted DAN WHITE, the only white man ever hanged by law in Van Zandt county. WHITE was charged by bill of indictment with the murder of GEORGE CONQUEST a peddler, who was killed in the OWLET GREEN settlement and his body found in a lonely place on a dim road some days after his death. The evidence was all circumstantial and WHITE was not apprehended for some years after the murder was committed, but he received a sentence of death and was executed for the crime.

At the expiration of four years' service as district attorney Mr. HOGG voluntarily retired to private life. He was a conspicuous figure at all state democratic conventions, as member from his county, and, in this way, in early life, became personally acquainted with the politicians of the state. In 1884 he moved to Tyler and devoted his time to the practice of law. At that time Tyler held the keys to the political situation in Texas; and from that headquarters, state and district officers were made and unmade to order. In 1886 Mr. HOGG's name was entered as an aspirant for attorney general of the state. When the state democratic convention met he was nominated by acclamation for attorney general on the democratic ticket. He was elected along with the balance of the state ticket. He was nominated a second time in Dallas on August 15, 1888, by acclamation, to succeed himself and was elected. In 1890 he was a candidate on the democratic ticket for governor of Texas. The state convention met at San Antonio, August 13th, and, at the close of the first ballot, he was nominated for governor, by acclamation. He received at the polls, the following November, a majority of 197,000 votes--the largest ever polled for a candidate for that office in Texas. The inauguration occurred in the hall of the house of representatives in the new state capitol, January 20, 1891. The inaugural address was worthy of the occasion.

When the state democratic convention met at Houston, in 1892, he was opposed by GEORGE CLARK, who had quite a following.

However, the state organization was with HOGG. The CLARK faction, on account of the irreconcilable differences with the main body, withdrew from it and effected a separate organization. So, when the roll of delegates was called, Governor HOGG was nominated by acclamation and subsequently elected. After his term of office expired Governor HOGG retired to private life. He formed a co-partnership, in the practice of law, with JAMES H. ROBERTSON of Austin, which lasted some years. In 1895 Mrs. HOGG died in Colorado; her remains were brought to Austin and laid to rest in the city cemetery. They had a large and interesting family, most of whom live in Texas. Governor HOGG died March 7, 1906, and his remains found a last resting place in Austin by the side of his life companion.

CHAPTER 19

HENRY F. GOODNIGHT, WILLS POINT, TEXAS

The GOODNIGHTS came from Kentucky, and the father of our subject was named HENRY also. He was a farmer and, later in life, moved to Missouri and died there. He was the father of JAMES GOODNIGHT who was born and reared in Tennessee and was also a farmer, and came to Texas in 1849. He married ELIZABETH HELM in 1838. She was born and reared in Kentucky. They had seven children. Neither of the parents are now living. He died in 1854, she in 1873, in Henderson county, Texas. Mr. GOODNIGHT himself was born in Marshall county, Kentucky, November 11, 1844. He was educated in the common schools of Henderson county. He has been engaged in several varieties of commercial life, being at the date of his death president of the Van Zandt National bank. He began to be a banker January 2, 1902. He served his city as alderman for five years. In 1872 he married Miss B. H. NALL, of Howard county, Arkansas, but who was a native of Alabama. They had two daughter, one of whom is the wife of Dr. H. T. FRY. Mr. GOODNIGHT lived in the county for twenty-six years, and came from Goshen, Henderson county. He came with his father to Texas from Kentucky in 1849 ,and may well be denominated an old Texan. He was a member of the Christian church and a Mason. He served in the civil war, first as a private, then as corporal. He was in the Thirty-fourth Texas cavalry, and engaged in the battles of Mansfield, Pleasant Hill and Yellow Bayou. He was murdered in his home at Wills Point, Texas, on June 7, 1916.

TWO OUTRAGEOUS MURDERS AND ONE DESPERATE ASSAULT TO MURDER

Among the modern homes in Wills Point, the GOODNIGHT residence, in east Wills Point, ranks first. At this palatial home, on or about the seventh day of June, A. D. 1916, Captain HENRY F. GOODNIGHT and his wife, Mrs. B. H. GOODNIGHT, were foully murdered, and their daughter, Mrs. ALICE MOREAU, wife of ROBERT J. MOREAU, was beaten into insesibility. The deed was done in the nighttime, and the evidence adduced on the trial of the case showed that Dr. HARRY T. FRY and his wife, who is a daughter of Captain and Mrs. GOODNIGHT, called at the GOODNIGHT home in the early evening and took Mrs. MOREAU and little daughter, JOSEPHINE, and Captain GOODNIGHT for an automobile ride, returning about nine o'clock p. m. R. J. MOREAU, his little son and daughter and Mrs. GOODNIGHT were left at home. About 3:25 o'clock next morning R. J. MOREAU called City Marshall J. H. HARRIS and told him his wife had been injured. He also called Mrs. A. W. MEREDITH and told her of his wife's condition. This alarming news caused the people of the city of Wills Point to collect in numbers and make some investigation. Captain GOODNIGHT was found in his room mortally wounded and the lifeless body of Mrs. GOODNIGHT was found in the cellar underneath the residence. Captain GOODNIGHT died the next day about 2 o'clock p. m.

R. J. MOREAU was arrested and charged by a bills of indictment with these crimes. On Monday, April 2, 1917, R. J. MOREAU was arraigned before District Judge J. P. WARREN on the indictment charging him with the murder of Capt. H. F. GOODNIGHT, alleged to have been committed in Van Zandt county, on or about the seventh day of June, A. D. 1916. The state was represented by District Attorney D. M. MAYNOR, ANGUS WYNNE, County Attorney EARL M. GREER, CLARENCE E. GILMORE and W. B. WYNNE. The defendant was represented by J. G. KEARBY, R. M. LIVELY and J. C. MUSE. On the following Monday, at 5 o'clock p. m., the judge submitted his charge to the jury and they retired to consider their verdict.

AN INTERESTING TRIAL IN THE DISTRICT COURT OF VAN ZANDT COUNTY

R. J. MOREAU GIVEN LIFE TERM SENTENCE

Defendant Accepts Sentence After Being Convicted of the Murder of Captain H. F. GOODNIGHT

We, the jury, find that the defendant is now sane.

L. WALTERS, Foreman

We, the jury, find the defendant, R. J. MOREAU, guilty of murder as charged in the indictment and assess his punishment at ninety-nine years in the penitentiary.

L. WALTERS, Foreman

These were the verdicts rendered Tuesday morning, April 17, 1917, about 8 o'clock by the jury in the case of state vs. R. J. MOREAU, charged by indictment with the murder of Capt. H. F. GOODNIGHT at the GOODNIGHT home in Wills Point, on the night of June 6, 1916. It is stated that on the first ballot eight of the jurors stood for hanging, two for either life term or hanging and two for life term. Most of the jurors were farmers and it is stated that but for the fact that they were badly needed on their farms the death penalty would have been more strongly insisted upon before the final verdict was rendered.

The following citizens constituted the jury:

J. O. MARTIN, farmer, residing in the Willow Springs community.
KIRG WALTERS, farmer, five miles south of Canton.
L. H. PETTIGREW, farmer, near Edgewood.
W. J. MARTIN, farmer, Canton.
R. R. MOORE, merchant, Edom.
N. B. HENNEGAR, farmer, near Edgewood.
S. A. NEELY, farmer, Willow Springs.
R. F. LEE, farmer, Small.
W. J. McCAFITY, farmer, Stone Point.
W. T. PIERCE, farmer, Willow Springs.
J. W. VINES, farmer, near Small.
W. X. HALBROOK, farmer, three miles east of Canton.

After a consultation of the attorneys with the defendant and his relatives, he appeared in open court Tuesday evening about 8 o'clock and accepted sentence. The final scene was quite a contrast to scenes on the days of the trial when the crowds filled all available space in the courtroom, not more than a half dozen people outside of the attorneys and court officials being present when the defendant accepted the sentence. It will be remembered that MOREAU still has two cases on the docket against him in connection with the GOODNIGHT tragedy, one a charge of murder in connection with the death of Mrs. GOODNIGHT and one for assault with attempt to murder his wife. These cases will remain on the docket subject to call but they will not be called for trial so long as the defendant remains in the penitentiary serving the present sentence. Should he be pardoned, then these cases will be tried.

BIOGRAPHICAL SKETCH

ROBERT J. MOREAU is about forty-two years of age, born and reared near Cottonport, Louisiana, on a farm. Educated in the public and private schools of his parish, and at the age of about eighteen years began teaching school. He taught for seven or eight years, after which he studied law for two years at Marksville, Louisiana, where he was admitted to the bar and practiced some two years before marrying Miss ALICE GOODNIGHT of Wills Point. He is of French nationality and spoke both the English and French language, the parish in which he lived having mostly people of French descent. He stood the bar examination in Texas after coming to Wills Point.

CHAPTER 20

WHITE ROSE CEMETERY. RELIGIOUS AND FRATERNAL
ORGANIZATIONS. RED CROSS ORGANIZATIONS.
WHITE ROSE CEMETERY, WILLS POINT

No history of Van Zandt county will ever be complete without
a word of commendation of the White Rose cemetery association of
Wills Point. This association has been chartered by the state of
Texas. It purchased a plat of ground which it had laid out in
lots and blocks, with appropriate drives and walks through it.

The association will sell a family lot for ten dollars, and
the purchaser is inhibited from ever selling the lot for more
than that amount. If, after one has bought a lot and chooses to
do so, such purchaser can enter into a contract for the care and
upkeep of said lot for all time to come, by placing with the association a sum of money or securities to be held in trust, using
only the interest accruing therefrom, for the care and upkeep of
the lot, and from time to time re-investing the principal so as
to keep it on an earning basis. Those, who have no permanent endowment fund and have friends or relatives buried in White Rose
cemetery, are annually requested to donate something for the care
and upkeep of the lot in said cemetery owned by those buried there.

The association employs a sexton annually, whose duty it is
to constantly attend to the cemetery day by day the year round.
Kindly disposed people have by will and otherwise made handsome
donations to the White Rose Cemetery association to be by the
same expended in beautifying the drives and walks of the cemetery,
and to pay for the services of the sexton; and in this way the
White Rose cemetery is being kept as neat and tidy as is national
cemetery.

RELIGIOUS AND FRATERNAL ORGANIZATIONS IN THE COUNTY.

There are organized churches in almost every community in
the county; all, however, of the Protestant faith. They are:
The Primitive Baptists; the Methodist Episcopal Church south; the
Missionary Baptists; the Presbyterians; the Christians; the Holi-
ness; the Adventists and the Apostolics. There are two branches
or organizations of the Baptist church; one known as the "board"
and one as the "anti-board or convention." The difference between the two not being a matter of faith, but a matter of control of finances. There are also two branches or organizations
of the Presbyterian church; one known as the Cumberland Presbyterian and the other the Presbyterian church United States of
America. There are also two branches or organizations of the
Christian church; one known as the "progressives" and the other
as the "non-progressives."

Each of the foregoing churches have their Sunday schools and
other auxiliary institutions.

Another organization in the county that is very worthy of
mention is the Red Cross, which did so much good work in the
world war. There was a Red Cross organization in almost every
community in the county, and one Red Cross chapter, which was

located at Wills Point.

FRATERNAL ORDERS

The following is a list of the fraternal organizations in Van Zandt county, so far as the writer has been able to ascertain. There may be others in the county, and, if such is the case, they are not intentionally left out. There are also fraternal-mutual insurance organizations in the county that we are unable to give the names and locations of.

MASONIC LODGES

The following is a list of the Sub-Ordinate or Blue Lodges of the Masonic Order in Van Zandt county, showing their number and location: Castillian Lodge No. 141, Canton; Pine Lodge No. 303, Ben Wheeler; Wills Point Lodge No. 422, Wills Point; Grand Saline Lodge No. 864, Grand Saline; Edgewood Lodge No. 870, Edge- wood; Colfax Lodge No. 904, Colfax.

The following is a list of other Masonic orders in the coun- ty. Royal Arch Chapter No. 108, Council No. 76, Commandery No. 44, all located at Wills Point.

ODD FELLOW LODGES

There are nine Odd Fellows lodges located in the county as follows:

Wills Point, Canton, Grand Saline, Myrtle Springs, Pruitt, Martins Mill, Colfax, Edgewood and Ben Wheeler.

The Odd Fellows of the county also have an organization known as the Van Zandt County Odd Fellows association, which meets semi-annually, at or near the full of the moon in February and August of each year. There are also Rebekah lodges in the county.

OTHER ORGANIZATIONS

Other organizations in the county are: One lodge Knights of Pythias at Wills Point, The Woodmen of the World, the Modern Woodmen, the M. B. A.'s, the Woodmen Circle, the Maccabees and perhaps others that we are unable to get the names of.

ABBERNATHY, Jack   82
ABRAMS, Maj. W. H. 191
ADAMS, H. C. 98
        Mrs.   88
AIKEN, Wm.   54
AKIN, Wm.   56
ALEXANDER, Sam   142
ALLEN, -----   114
        Dr. W. A. 190
        James   107
        Jas. M. 107
        John R. 108
        John R. 108
        John R. 109
        R. H. 197
        Sim   114
ALMONTE, Col. Juan   86
ANDERSON, B. W. 107
        B. W. 190
        Berry   109
        Ike   125
        Isaac   107
        Isaac   107
        Mrs. W. R. 134
ANGLIN, Adrian   70
        Adrian   78
ANN, Tecks   82
ANTHONY, Susan B. 135
APR, Ellie A. 190
ARBUCKLE, A.   52
ARNOLD, L. V. 109
        L. V. 109
        Maj. Ripley A. 113
ARRINGTON, C. C. 98
ARTHUR, Mrs. Dora Fowler 103
ASBARRY, I. A. 109
ASBERRY, I. A. 109
ASHBY, Stanley Royal 188
ASHLEY, Robert   22
        Robert   23
ASSBURY, Jesse A. 126
ATKINSON, Gen.   57
AUDUBON, -----   178
AUSTIN, -----   86
        J. L. 108
        Moses   161
        O. F. 12
        San Felipe de 161
        Stephen F. 40
AVANT, Wm.   89
BAKER, Jno.   89
BALDWIN, John   98
BALENTYNE, Lieut.   72
BALL, Flemming   89
        James   89
BALLARD, Barkley M. 89
BARBER, Samuel R. 108

BARBO, Gil Y. 86
BARBON, Jos   23
BARFIEDL, J. F. 199
BARKER, Julius   89
BARNETT, J. W. 197
BARON, Jules   114
BARR, William   22
BARRY, James   73
BARTON, Mat   190
BASS, -----   103
BATEMAN, John   108
        John   109
BATES, James   108
        Silas   70
BAUGHMAN, L. H. 98
        Lilburn H. 104
BAUTITA, Juan   23
        Robert   23
BAXTER, Mrs. Mary W. 98
BAYLOR, Gen. John R. 65
        John R. 66
BEALL, Dr.   81
BEAN, -----   24
        -----   25
        -----   26
        Ellis P. 21
        Ellis P. 22
        Ellis P. 23
        Ellis P. 27
        J. M. 27
        Peter E. 21
        Peter E. 27
BEAR, Yellow   81
BEARID, H. P. 148
BECK, William   108
        William   108
BECKETT, C.   105
        Calams   107
        Columbus   107
BEEMAN, John   112
        John   112
BEESON, B. S. 109
BELL, -----   143
        Fred   143
        Gov. Peter H. 164
        Josiah   186
        Sam   88
        Sam   142
BENGE, Samuel   39
        Samuel   40
BENJAMIN, -----   165
        J. P. 164
BENNERS, W. H. 173
BENTON, P. S. 99
        P. S. 108
        P. S. 109
        Peter S. 98

BENTON, Peter S. 105
        Peter S. 106
        Peter S. 107
        Peter S. 107
        Peter S. 150
        Peter S. 162
BENTY, John   107
        John   107
BEXAR, San Antonio   21
BILLIE, -----   144
        -----   145
BINGHAM, Mathias A. 40
BIRD, Capt. John   111
BIVINS, A.   108
BIXIR, Allen   104
BLACKBURN, Ephraim   24
BLACKNURN, Ephraim   23
BLAIR, Allen   98
        Allen   106
        Allen   107
        Allen   109
        Allen   150
        Allen   190
BLANCHARD, Jno. F. 197
BLUE, Miles D. 89
        Miles D. 89
BOBO, Wm. C. 89
BOGGS, James   90
BOLES, Henry   89
        Wm.   89
BOND, Frank   12
BONNER, F. W. 140
        Judge   141
        Micajah Hubbard 140
        Rev. William   140
BOON, James W. 89
BOTTOMS, -----   196
BOWER, Col.   129
        Col. E. G. 137
        E. G. 138
        Lieut.Col. E. G. 136
BOWL, John   40
BOWLES, Cheif   174
        Cheif   183
        Chief   35
        Chief   46
        Chief   47
        Chief   48
        Chief   49
        Chief   50
        Chief   51
        Chief   52
        Chief   62
        Chief   116
        Chief   157
        Chief   183
        Col.   40

BOWLES, John   49
BOX, Thomas   89
BRAGG, Capt.   67
        J. E. 197
BRATCHER, N. S. 109
        N. S. 109
        Nancy Ann 150
        Nathahiel   89
BREAGLE, Henry   109
BREWER, Wm. T. 89
BRIGGS, George Waverley 173
        Wm. W. 89
BRINGHURST, John   114
BROTHER, Nolen   138
BROWN, -----   31
        Capt.   85
        John   106
        John   107
        John Henry 53
        John Henry 161
        John Henry 186
        John Red 98
        Jonathan   98
        Leonard   98
        Leonard   105
        Leonard   106
        Lieut.   72
        Mahala   97
        Mr.   53
        Wm. A. 89
BROWNING, Joseph   66
BRUN, -----   15
BRUTON, Benjamin   174
        E. R. M. 108
BRUTONS, -----   150
BRYAN, Co. John Nuff 112
        John Neeley 111
        Mr.   148
        Mrs. A.   148
BUCHANAN, James   189
        Pres.   136
BUNDY, David T. 126
        James   100
        James   105
        James   126
        W. H. 109
BURDETTE, Robert J. 155
BURFORD, Judge Nat   102
        Judge Nat M. 101
BURK, R. E. 135
        Samuel   98
BURLISON, A. B. 73
        Capt. Ed.   71
        Capt. Ed.   73
        Col.   41
        Col.   49
        Col.   50

BURLISON, Gen.   46
            Gen.   142
BURNET, David G. 18
            David G. 45
BURNETT, -----   49
            David G. 53
            David G. 56
            David G. 139
            Pres.   124
BURTON, Joab   108
BUSTAMANTE, Don J. R. 24
BUSTAMENTS, Jose Diaz 24
CAIN, Fannie Fowler 121
            Rev. D. L. 122
CALHOUN, John C. 60
            John C. 87
CAMERON, Dr. John   37
            John   37
CAMP, John L. 121
CAMPBELL, H. M. 173
            John   54
            John   56
CAREY, -----   4
            Emerson 146
CARRINGTON, -----   149
            B. W. 147
            W. B. 146
CARTER, Col. Jim   49
            John   107
            Margan   109
            Mary   173
            Morgan   107
            Morgan   108
            Morgan   109
            Wm.   89
CASE, George W. 40
CASEN, Green   145
            Mrs. Mary J. 145
CASTILLO, Mr.   42
CATES, T. J. 82
            T. J. 180
CHILTON, George W. 116
            George W. 183
            Horace   168
            William P. 138
CHOAT, C.   89
CHRESTMAN, J. W. 98
            John   104
            John   106
            John   150
            Johnnie   118
CLARDY, William   108
            Wm. B. 109
CLARK, -----   202
            Amos   88
            Capt.   16
            George   201

CLARK, Isham   99
            Isom   98
            M. M. 89
            M. M. Sr. 89
CLEVELAND, Gen.   60
                Pres.   136
CLOWER, J. W. 197
COCHRAN, Lieut.   72
COHEA, John   105
            John   106
COHEE, John   98
COKE, Gov.   140
COLLIER, W. R. 145
COLONDELET, Baron de 21
COLTHARP, James   101
COLTHORP, James   157
COLTHROP, James   188
            Wm.   107
COMPTON, Jessee   98
CONNER, Capt. John H. 71
            Henry   51
CONQUEST, George   197
            George   200
            George   201
            Mr.   198
CONWAY, John R. 185
COOK, Abediah   98
            Capt. William G. 111
            Obediah   106
            Obediah   107
COOLY, Solomon   23
            Solomon   24
COOPER, -----   134
CORDRA, -----   46
            -----   48
COTHERAN, John   105
            John   106
COTHERN, Clabe   150
            John   150
COTTON, Godwin B. 169
COWAN, Lieut.   72
            Mary Jane 134
COX, Dr. M. L. 104
            Francis   87
            John G. 98
            Jos.   150
            Joseph   98
            Joseph   105
            Joseph   106
            Joseph   107
            Joseph   109
            Joseph   109
            Mr. John   87
            Thomas   104
            Thomas   106
            Thomas   109
            Thomas L. 108

MOORE, J. P. 90
     James 108
     James 108
     John 98
     John 107
     John 108
     John 109
     John 109
     Law 109
     Levi 109
     Mcdonald 109
     Michael 23
     R. R. 204
     Sallie 134
MOREAU, Josephine 203
     R. J. 204
     Robert J. 203
     Robert J. 205
MORELOS, ----- 26
MORGAN, Martin 109
MORRIS, Littleton 121
MOUGHON, Clota 121
     Dr. W. C. 121
     Mrs. W. C. 121
MUNOZ, Don Manuel 21
MUSE, J. C. 135
     J. C. 204
MUSH, Big 40
     Big 48
MUSQUIZ, Lieut. 22
NALL, B. H. 203
NAPOLEON, ----- 16
NAVARRO, Galindo de 24
NEAL, Hugh 106
     Hugh 107
     Joseph 109
     Wesley 107
NECOROCO, Chief 22
NEELY, S. A. 204
NEIGHBORS, Maj. R. S. 66
NELSON, A. A. 54
     Aslac 98
     Helena 27
     Lieut. 72
NEY, Elizabeth 59
NIBLACK, S. C. 148
NO-KO-NIC, ----- 80
NOBLE, Col. George 138
     Judge 46
     Judge 53
NOLAN, ----- 22
     ----- 24
     N. A. 133
     Philip 21
     Philip 23
NORMAN, Jennie 145
     John 108

NORMAN, John 127
     M. R. 145
NORTON, D. O. 98
     David O. 78
O'HAIR, Lieut. 72
O'HARA, Jack 145
     Martha 145
O'KELLEY, Mary Ann 96
O'KELLY, Francis D. 105
     Francis D. 106
O'QUINN, Ruff 82
OCHILTREE, ----- 88
     J. W. 89
     Judge William B. 101
     Wm. B. 89
OHELLY, C. C. 98
     F. D. 98
OLSON, E. 98
     Ola 98
OSOOTA, ----- 40
OVERTON, John H. 185
OWENS, David 108
     David 108
     David 109
     Obey W. 125
PACE, M. C. 109
     M. E. 108
PADILLO, Don 28
PAGE, Dr. 196
PAMPHILO, ----- 4
PARHAM, Anthony 109
     Anthony 109
     Wyatt 89
     Wyatt 107
     Wyatt 108
PARKER, Benjamin F. 78
     Benjamin F. 79
     Bynthia Ann 65
     C. P. 98
     C. P. 108
     C. P. 108
     C. P. 109
     Chief Quanah 69
     Col. 77
     Cynthia Ann 70
     Cynthia Ann 74
     Cynthia Ann 76
     Cynthia Ann 77
     Cynthia Ann 78
     Cynthia Ann 79
     Cynthia Ann 80
     Cynthia Ann 82
     Isaac 78
     Isaac 78
     John W. 70
     Quanah 79
     Quanah 80

THOMAS, Gen. George H. 68
      Gen. George H. 68
      Judge James W. 188
      Judge James W. 187
      Maj. George H. 67
THOMPSON, E. J. 90
      W. D. 154
THROCKMORTON, Gov. 131
      Gov. 167
TINNEN, E. C. 126
      Enoch C. 125
TINNIN, Enoch C. 127
TODD, J. H. 190
      Mrs. Eva 133
TOLLETT, John 98
TOMLINSON, Capt. Peter 72
      David 108
TOOMEY, Anne 173
      D. Prescott 172
      Dorothy 173
      Elizabeth 173
      James 173
      Mary 173
      Mr. 173
      Prescott 173
TOWLES, Alice 133
      Capt. T. J. 136
      Capt. T. J. 200
      Capt. Thomas Jefferson 132
      T. J. 129
      T. J. 130
      T. J. 132
      T. J. 133
      T. J. 140
TOWNLY, Timothy 109
TRESPALACIOS, Felix 35
TROUTMAN, Joanna 59
      Joanna 60
      Joanna 61
TROUTMANN, ----- 85
TRUETT, ----- 30
TUCKER, Evalyn Manning 168
      J. H. 190
TULINSON, James 107
TULL, Allie 134
      G. W. Jr. 134
      George W. Sr. 133
      George Washington 133
      Mary 133
      Stephen 133
      W. N. 134
TUMLINSON, David 105
      David 106
      David 107
      David 109
      James 98
      Jas. 107

TUNLINSON, David 107
TUNLISON, David 107
TUNNELL, O. A. 148
TWIGGS, Gen. 189
TYLER, George B. 66
      John B. 66
UPTON, Monroe 174
VAN DORN, ----- 75
      Maj. 74
VAN HOSER, Isaac 89
VAN ZANDT, C. J. 126
      Isaac 87
      Isaac 93
      Isaac 95
      Isaac 96
      Isaac 99
      Jacob 93
      Mary 93
VANSICKLE, Ben A. 51
VARNER, Mrs. R. R. 98
VEASY, John P. 116
VERA, Don P. R. 24
VINES, J. W. 204
WADDLE, Judge 135
WADKINS, John V. 89
WAGES, Sarah Jane 134
WALDRIP, Wm. 89
WALKER, ----- 71
      ----- 188
WALLING, John 183
WALTERS, Jonah 24
      Joseph 23
      Kirg 204
      L. 204
WAPER, Joel 98
WARD, Capt. William 59
      Morris 89
      Wm. 89
WARREN, Judge J. P. 204
WASHINGTON, ----- 83
      George 123
WATKINS, Lieut. 72
WAUL, T. N. 165
WAYNE, Maj. 114
WEATHERFORD, Jefferson 78
WEBSTER, Noah 162
WELCH, Capt. O. G. 134
      Col. 135
WELKINS, Jonathan 106
WHEELER, Ben 82
      Ben 101
      Ben 192
      Benjamin 109
      Benjamin 193
      Benjamin F. 100
      James C. 195
      Royal T. 195